Retirement Policy in an Aging Society

Retirement Policy in an Aging Society

Edited by Robert L. Clark

Duke University Press Durham, N.C. 1980

Library of Congress Cataloging in Publication Data
Main entry under title:

Retirement policy in an aging society.

  Includes bibliographies and index.
    1. Retirement—United States—Addresses, essays,
lectures. 2. Retirement—Economic aspects—United
States—Addresses, essays, lectures. 3. Pensions—
United States—Addresses, essays, lectures. 4. Aged
policy—United States. I. Clark, Robert Louis,
1949–
HQ1062.R444   305.2′6   79–56502
ISBN 0–8223–0441–4

Contributors

Kathryn Anderson, Postdoctoral Fellow, Yale University

Richard V. Burkhauser, Institute for Research on Poverty, University of Wisconsin, Madison.

John J. Carroll, Director, Office of Research and Statistics, Social Security Administration, Washington, D.C.

Robert L. Clark, Associate Professor, Department of Economics, North Carolina State University.

William C. Greenough, Chairman, Teachers Insurance and Annuity Association and College Retirement Equities Fund.

Peter Henle, Deputy Assistant Secretary for Policy Evaluation and Research, U.S. Department of Labor.

Thomas Johnson, Professor, Department of Economics, North Carolina State University.

Juanita M. Kreps, Economist, Duke University.

H. Gregg Lewis, Professor of Economics, Duke University.

John A. Menefee, Postdoctorate Fellow, Duke Center for Aging and Human Development.

Alicia H. Munnell, Assistant Vice President and Economist, Federal Reserve Bank of Boston.

Solomon W. Polachek, Associate Professor, Department of Economics, and Fellow, Carolina Population Center, University of North Carolina at Chapel Hill.

Joseph F. Quinn, Department of Economics, Boston College.

Cordelia W. Reimers, Assistant Professor of Economics and Public Affairs, Princeton University.

Joseph Spengler, Professor Emeritus, Department of Economics, Duke University

John A. Turner, Office of Research and Statistics, Social Security Administration, Washington, D.C.

Contents

Introduction

Developing a National Retirement Policy   *Juanita M. Kreps*

It is unfortunate that approaches to complex social issues tend to draw on generalities—on appearances that frequently are undocumented or are even in violation of research findings. Whereas the gap between research and social policy is broadly applicable, it is especially pervasive in the field of aging.

The special difficulty here is understandable. Aging research draws on many disciplines, each with its major emphasis directed toward other questions, and since each of us brings a particular methodology to bear on this field, consensus is elusive even on the formulation of the questions. Going from research results, to their dissemination, to effective lobbying for action is consequently a long process calling for many different players.

When we ask ourselves how public policy pertaining to the elderly comes to be so confused, we must remember that many impediments are strewn along the way. In addition, it is my clear impression that since social scientists are, for the most part, research oriented, they have (with certain notable exceptions) lacked the resources—time or money—to publicize what they know and to draw sufficient attention to its importance.

One may legitimately argue that scientific research should be separated from the promotion of policy goals—goals that ought, instead, to reflect the views of the electorate. There is, of course, a vast literature on this subject, so I shall tread lightly. Moreover, I am aware that social science research has already influenced the thinking of the United States Congress and has also helped to turn public attention toward the pressing needs of older people. I shall argue here only that this job is unfinished, that public policy needs an even greater gift of knowledge from social scientists, that expertise in a field confers certain rights, and that one should not be reluctant to insist on exercising those rights.

There is some pain involved in the process of promoting policy goals, as all of us have learned. My own efforts in public life have left their scars, for in public life one can say very little that is not subject to extreme interpretation. To go public with one's views is a bit like voting without a secret ballot. Yet in looking back to my years of study of the subject, I wonder what alternative there is. Does one pretend that such study does not matter—that there is no rational basis for public policy? Suddenly, when the careful research results are hanging out there subject to the slings and arrows of public opinion, the tendency is to try to avoid taking a position. Yet in a way, a heated response is reassuring; it tells you at the very least that the subject is important to a great many people.

How can we do a better job of bringing expertise to bear on public policy in the field of aging? The problem can be illustrated by drawing on the area of aging study most familiar to me—that nexus of research that deals with the interrelationships of age, work, and income. I shall use the analyses in this field to show some of the contradictions between study findings and policy, and to raise the question of whether, under the aegis of retirement policy, we are in fact headed in the best direction.

Let us start with the findings. Age-related decrements in work capacity seem to play a very small part in the determination of retirement age. Across a wide age span and within most occupations that have been studied, abilities appear to lie well above those required by the job and do not seem to diminish with age in any consistent pattern. Now introduce the retirement practice. Retirement practice moves workers out of their jobs at or before age 65, regardless of personal abilities or preferences. Rationalizations for such policy are quickly forthcoming, one being that the higher costs usually associated with retaining older persons are conducive to fixed and early retirement. Unless persons of usual retirement age are known to be extremely productive (in the case of senior professors, who are perhaps twice as productive as new Ph.D.s), the higher pay expected for the former provides a strong incentive to replace senior with junior employees.

What happens? Retirement policy, reflecting labor market conditions rather than adequacy of performance, and reflecting further an excess of job applicants at going rates of pay, has the expected effect: the pay declines, or unemployment results. Given the institutional arrangements that maintain the job of the senior worker and specify not only that wages and salaries not be cut, but that they increase with length of service, unemployment falls mainly on the younger worker. The only significant route by which unemployment can be shared with older workers is that of lowered retirement age, negotiated individually or collectively.

What is the usual public response? Depending on who responds, several answers emerge. There is the facile answer that the economy ought to generate enough jobs for all persons, young and old, so it will not be necessary to force the older to retire to make a place for the younger. Any economist, however, would quickly point out that the only way the economy can accommodate this need is to allow real annual incomes of both groups to fall by reallocating work between the age groups. To attempt to stimulate growth and create more jobs in an inflated economy is to penalize all persons, especially the elderly.

When real growth cannot provide fulltime jobs to all workers, is there a policy that would extend worklife for those who choose it and yet support those who cannot work or choose not to work in later life? What incentives and/or penalities ought to be built into such a policy? Again, observe the facts. Worklife is not likely to be lengthened in the short run (except possibly for a few occupations) unless an increase in the growth rate lifts the demand for labor above its present sluggish rate, or wages become more flexible, or working time per person declines through workweek or workyear decreases. In a longer time frame, the numbers of youth coming into the workforce will decline during the last two decades of this century. Some offset to this decrease will be provided by a continued although slower rate of growth in women's market work, but the labor force will nevertheless shrink relative to the total population. A reversal of the downward trend in retirement age would then be likely, all the more because after the turn of the century the costs of retirement per worker will be higher and offsets will be sought.

Observe further that the per-worker cost of retirement (that is, the cost to each current worker of supporting the retired population) will increase substantially after the turn of the century because of a rise in the dependency ratio. Assuming no change in retirement age or in the replacement ratio, the taxes needed to support social security benefits are even now rising faster than the public seems willing to pay.

Given all this, where do the members of the profession stand with respect to retirement policy in the immediate future and in the longer run? And how do we articulate our views, however diverse, in such a way as to influence the outcome of events?

There are many levels of discussion, and many fora in which to hold these discussions, but let us start with a recognition of what today's events tell us. Recognize first, that the higher social security taxes we now face focus attention on the obvious truth that the cost of retirement, even at levels of living lower than those enjoyed by persons still at work, is extremely high. As labor market forces have squeezed more and more persons out of the work force, the proportion of total income allocated to retirees via public and private pensions has grown dramatically. Public awareness of the costs of this new lifestage has lagged behind its actual appearance. As a result, the rate of saving necessary to support families through two decades of retirement is inadequate, and resistance to taxes of the required magnitude has stiffened. Eventual resolution of this dilemma calls for greatly improved understanding of the costs involved; a careful consideration of alternatives that would tend to extend worklife (increased wage flexibility; expanded opportunities for parttime work); and a reexamination of the financial arrangements under which old age presently is managed.

Note further that age was central to the initial appearance of these issues, and it continues to be the variable on which policy considerations turn. The availability of a job, and consequently earnings, depends to a significant degree on chronological age, often without regard for productivity. Similarly, income transfers are automatic after a certain age and one is expected to accept transfers in lieu of earnings. The net effect of these institutional responses to labor market imbalance is to impute to age the equilibrating role although other, more satisfactory ways of balancing the size of the labor force with the number of jobs clearly are needed.

In broader perspective, the allocation of work and earnings through the life course, along with provision of income in nonworking stages of life, are not new issues. The questions have been resolved by different arrangements at different stages of history; as Hareven [1, p. 21] notes, collective economic strategies become necessary for workers "as an intensifying industrial system was gradually ousting them from their jobs." The issue gains importance with the aging of the nation's population and work force.

Today's question of retirement policy is the question of whether the institutional arrangements that have evolved are those best suited to perform the temporal allocation function, or whether given our understanding of the society and its multiple goals, we can devise better strategies and get them adopted.

All this discussion presently occurs at the level of research and reflection; before expanding the retirement issue to a broader audience we need to take several preliminary steps.

Clearly, to achieve something resembling an acceptable retirement policy, students in the field must lay out the many variables that affect retirement decisions and call attention to the need for coordination across a wide range of social decisions. We must make explicit the relationships between the retirement income available and labor force participation; pension regulation and the cost of pension benefits; predicted rates of inflation and withdrawal from work.

From the policymaker's point of view, an understanding of the way in which a change in any variable influences the individual to retire or not retire is fundamental. But an even more difficult set of issues pervades the policy process. To develop a national policy, one must identify the goals of that policy. Precisely what is the policy designed to achieve? Is it expected to minimize cost to the taxpayer or the employer with a private pension plan? If so, what standard of at least minimum retirement income is to be set? How much redistribution of income do we seek, and how much do we demand that pensions be earnings-related? Or do we look upon retirement policy in a broader perspective as a mechanism for providing a better fit between earnings and income needs over the life span?

I recognize that none of these are new questions; but neither have they been resolved with any clarity. It is the lack of consensus on what we want to achieve through retirement policy that makes its formulation so difficult. Ambivalence and conflicting signals have underscored our inability to come to agreement in the past, although there has been one fairly consistent theme: public policy often has provided some incentive to leave the work force at or before age 65 in order to provide job access for younger workers.

Actions recently taken to restrict employers from requiring retirement at any age weaken this policy and most of us would applaud such moves. But we should remember that pension arrangements have not yet been altered. The availability of full social security benefits at age 65 is not in question, and seems unlikely to be affected any time soon.

Where then does this leave us in our attempts to direct the nation's attention to the need for a consistent set of rules that would make up an overall policy on retirement from work?

First, there is a need to respond to the national debate on retirement policy by clarifying the reasons for this debate, i.e., the aging of the American population and the maturing of our pension systems. The significance of these long-run demographic movements and their financial implications cannot be overstated. Second, we can, as students of the field, set out some reasonable objectives of retirement policy—objectives that can then be discussed in research seminars and the halls of Congress with many stops along the way. Ultimately, some tradeoffs have to be agreed to and the terms, however flexible, established.

But there is a third step on which we here can perhaps be especially useful. Along with a broad understanding of the reasons, we have to develop a better strategy for coping with an aging population and for identification of the social ends we hope to achieve—ends which will be refined by public debate. The policymaker needs a clear statement as to the ways in which each component of such a policy complements or contradicts another, and as to what the total impact will be on the behavior of work and income in, say, the last third of life.

Examples are easy to cite, difficult to resolve. Suppose one of our objectives is to encourage a phasing in of retirement over several years, as opposed to a sudden departure from work. Can industrial patterns accommodate such a goal? What would be the necessary changes in pension arrangements? What retirement test, if any, is appropriate? The researcher's job is to answer such questions, thereby indicating what is possible, through which policy tools, at what prices in dollars and in foregone alternative directions. Only when these many pieces of the puzzle are clearly identified can we expect a coordinated set of programs that serves any set of retirement goals adopted for the nation.

It is clear that these questions—why do we need some broad formulation of a retirement policy? what should a retirement framework seek to do? and what are the specific components that would add up to a reasonable policy?—are not questions being addressed adequately in any forum other than the gerontological research community. The more clearly we can delineate the issues, the better are our chances of helping to coalesce public opinion and the actions of policymakers.

It would be naive to argue that even with such systematic attempts the resulting effect on the policymaker will be altogether satisfactory. In retrospect, it would be gratifying to conclude that past decisions have reflected the best of our research efforts and that the progress made is due in significant measure to improved knowledge of age-related issues. In fact, I would argue that such a relationship exists, although the time lag between the discovery of knowledge and its use in policy formation seems painfully long. Only now do we see a public concern with some gerontological issues that were being discussed in the literature two decades ago.

Impatience with policymakers now runs high, according to all public polls, strong opposition to growth in governmental activities being the most frequent expression of discontent. In contrast to the decade of the sixties when federal programs were expected to expand as needs grew, there now is public sentiment for reduced spending and taxes, and for a greater reliance on private sector initiatives.

Such shifts in public opinion can temporarily overshadow the work of researchers who must, to some extent, isolate their efforts from the popular view of the moment. It would be a mistake to look to such swings in view for solutions to social problems, in aging or any other area, since they seldom offer demonstrably better alternatives than the policies being rejected. However, one cannot ignore the obvious signals that are being sent to public officials, who must respond.

Responses must somehow reconcile any popular wave of opinion with social needs and the attendant costs. In voting to raise social security taxes, despite the inflationary impact and fiscal burden, the Congress was motivated by the need to collect enough revenues to balance total benefits and health care costs for the elderly. In extending to persons aged 65 and 70 some guarantee against age discrimination, Congress confirmed the view long held by gerontologists that chronological age alone is an inadequate basis on which to compel retirement.

Neither of these actions was without serious challenge. In the debates on the two proposals, estimates of their impact came from studies familiar to all of you, some of them made long ago. What was it that finally produced this year's action? In the case of the social security tax increase, surely it was the need for additional revenues and a continued belief that payroll taxes were the best source of such revenues. In the decision prohibiting age discrimination, again the evidence for action was overwhelming. In both cases, however, the striking thing to note was the extent of the opposition—stronger opposition than ever before in the case of the tax increase, in part because of the current antitax fever; in the case of age discrimination, equally vocal proponents of maintaining jobs for younger persons were heard, as were those who feared the loss of upward mobility on the job.

For both actions, however, the literature was richly supportive. The long lag between the appearance of research and congressional action can surely be shortened, but the connection is unmistakable. A catalyst for policy change— an approaching crisis in funding, the leadership of a particular political figure— also is necessary. More attention might well be directed toward key persons and issues that could serve this role, although age-related issues will always have to compete in the political arena with the threat of carcinogens, the promise of tax reform, and the preservation of bowhead whales, or their future counterparts.

I have argued here that the first forum—scientific inquiry—is fundamental to sound public policy, a position that is not exactly revolutionary. To the extent that we can sharpen our reports on what the research tells us and what its implications are for the society, we shall speed the utilization of our findings by the policymaker. Those fora that lie in between (such as associations that promote action programs to serve the elderly directly) can be excellent disseminators of information and technique. Better still, such organizations help to test researchers' conclusions and to send the dubious ones back to the drawing boards. In influencing public opinion, moreover, these groups play a central role.

I confess, after almost two years of observing the policy-making process at close range, that it is considerably less tidy than the textbooks say. And although no one has ever argued that democracy was efficient—merely that it was better than any of its alternatives—the multiplicity of goals now being pursued by the federal government helps to explain why each goal seems to be ill defined and poorly attended. In competing for the attention of the nation, however, no segment of society has a more critical story to tell.

Reference

[1] Hareven, Tamara K., "Historical Adulthood and Old Age," *Daedalus,* 105 (Fall 1976), 21.

Impending Age Structure Changes   *Robert L. Clark*

Retirement has become a distinct period in the life of most Americans only during the last half century. Today, however, the retirement behavior of older workers is one of the most important individual life-cycle decisions and has significant implications for the national economy. Decisions to withdraw from the labor force are influenced by the availability of social security benefits, private pension benefits, wages, health, family responsibilities, and other socioeconomic variables. Retirement has an obvious and important influence on expenditures for government support programs and the tax revenues that are collected. The various chapters in this volume examine the labor force participation decisions of older workers and the nation's retirement policy within the framework of continuing population aging. They contribute to our understanding of the future role of retirement policy and its growing importance if the current low fertility rates are maintained.

What is Retirement?

Despite considerable public debate concerning its causes and effects, the term *retirement* does not have a clear and unambiguous connotation. Many people consider retirement to be the termination of a long career, but it can also be viewed as a significant reduction in hours of work below some minimum. The term *retirement* is frequently used to mean the acceptance of pension benefits, and the age of eligibility for these benefits is called the retirement age. The "retirement" or earnings test that determines the amount of social security benefits is dependent upon an individual's earnings during a month or year. Empirical studies of the retirement process have employed other variables such as an individual's perception of retirement status, his labor force participation, annual work rates, and expectations of retiring as indications or proxies for retirement.

Clearly, it is possible for a person to be counted as retired by some of these measures, but not by others. For example, military personnel can retire from the service (termination of a career) and begin receiving pension benefits, yet still work 40 hours a week for another employer. The diversity of retirement indicators increases the difficulty of explaining the labor market activities of older persons. Although the writers represented in this volume differ in the specific questions they raise concerning the interaction of retirement policy and individual labor supply behavior, each chapter represents an important contribution to a comprehensive view of retirement policy. Future population age structure must be considered in any assessment of the long-run implications of alternative retirement policies. The primary objective of this paper is to outline impending age structure changes that follow from continued low fertility rates.

Determinants of Age Structure Changes

Shifts in the age structure of a population are the result of fluctuations in fertility, mortality, and immigration. Recently, changing demographic conditions have produced shifts in the population age distribution that can best be described as population aging, a phenomenon characterized by an increase in the proportion of a population in the older age groups and reflected by an increase in the population's median age. Most current projections indicate that further population aging is likely in the United States and other developed countries. This has economic significance because of its impact on the public and private pension systems of these nations. Such changes in age structure of the U.S. population and their resultant effect on the nation's retirement policy are the main concerns of this book. Determinants of age structure changes and projections of further aging are discussed in this chapter.

The age composition of a population is determined primarily by national fertility behavior, particularly in countries with the relatively low mortality characteristics of the industrialized countries [3,5]. Within a stable population, a high fertility rate and hence a high rate of natural increase results in a relatively high proportion of the population being in the lower age categories. Conversely, low rates of fertility imply a population with relatively more older persons. Projected low fertility rates over the next half century will generate further population aging.

Variations in fertility from year to year give rise to fluctuations in the annual number of births, thus producing short-term age structure changes. If age-specific mortality and fertility rates were to remain constant, the graph of the population age structure would be smoothed, and a stable population would result. Most population projections assume that a specified fertility rate is attained and then maintained over the forecasting period. A more likely occurrence, however, is that fertility will tend to oscillate around a particular rate, perhaps in response to changing economic conditions [4,9]. These variations may generate bulges in the age structure creating a pseudo-stable population [11].

Age-specific mortality rates influence the age structure by determining the proportion of each cohort surviving to older ages. Mortality declines do not necessarily imply population aging because a fall in the mortality of the very young affects the age composition in a way similar to an increase in fertility. However, an increase in longevity only at higher ages increases the relative number of older persons in a stable population. Population projections by the

Census Bureau in 1977 estimate that life expectancy at birth in 2050 will be 71.8 for males and 81.0 for females compared to the current estimates of 68.7 years for males and 76.5 years for females.[1]

Immigration can temporarily modify the age composition of an immigrant-receiving country if the age structure of the immigrants differs from that of the native population. Nonsustained in-migration will have only a transitory effect on the age distribution of a population if the migration does not affect the prevailing patterns of fertility and mortality. Immigration will, of course, affect the size of the population but should have only limited influence on its age structure. High rates of illegal immigration create the prospect of significant underestimating of the future population in the official projections.

During the first half of this century, interaction of these factors resulted in an aging of the U.S. population that is illustrated by the increase in the proportion of the population aged 65 and over from 4 percent in 1900, to 8 percent in 1950, to 10.7 percent in 1976. Three projections summarized in Table 1 illustrate how age structure changes when fertility approaches and settles around or below the replacement level [8].[2] Series II is based upon the assumption that fertility quickly settles at the replacement level, but net immigration continues at 400,000 per year. Series IIX is based upon the same fertility assumption but with immigration at the zero level; it generates a stationary population. Series III is based upon the assumption that fertility settles at 1.7, 0.4 below the replacement level, but with net immigration continuing at 400,000 annually, a number that is insufficient to offset the lowness of fertility.

Examination of these projections indicates that the proportion of the population aged 65 and over rises significantly from 10.7 percent to 17.6 percent with replacement-level fertility, and the median age is increased by almost nine years during the period 1976 to 2050. The proportion of persons in the principal working ages, 18–64, however, remains around 0.6 and actually increases prior to the year 2000. The maintenance of a high proportion of the population of working age is due to the relative decline in the youth population. If fertility were to remain near 1.7 births per woman, even greater population aging would occur. In this case, the proportion of the population aged 65 and over would rise to 22.6 percent and the median age would increase to 43.7 years.

1. The continued decline in mortality, combined with recent medical research, has led some researchers to anticipate further significant gains in life expectancy. Sheppard and Rix [7, chap. 4] review this literature and conclude that a biomedical revolution extending life may be less than a generation away.

2. The difficulty in projecting future population size and age structure is illustrated in a comparison of the 1975 and 1977 census estimates employing similar fertility assumptions. The estimated population size in 2025 has been reduced by four million in the new projections with replacement-level fertility; however, the predicted number over age 65 has been increased by 2.8 million. These modifications produce a shift in the proportion of the population aged 65 and over in 2025 from 16.1 in the 1975 report to 17.2 in the 1977 projections [8, p. 4].

Table 1. *Population projections for the United States (millions),*
1976–2050

Age	1976	1985	2000	2025	2050
Series II					
Total	215.1	232.9	260.4	295.7	315.6
0–17	65.2	62.3	69.0	72.5	76.5
18–64	127.0	143.3	159.6	172.3	183.6
65 and over	22.9	27.3	31.8	50.9	55.5
18–64/total	.590	.615	.613	.583	.582
65 and over/total	.107	.117	.122	.172	.176
Median age	29.0	31.5	35.5	37.6	37.8
Series IIX					
Total	215.1	228.9	248.4	267.4	269.4
0–17	65.2	60.8	64.9	64.3	64.2
18–64	127.0	140.8	152.1	154.5	155.5
65 and over	22.9	27.2	31.5	48.6	49.8
18–64/total	.590	.615	.612	.578	.577
65 and over/total	.107	.119	.127	.182	.185
Median age	29.0	31.7	36.0	38.4	38.6
Series III					
Total	215.1	228.9	245.9	251.9	231.0
0–17	65.2	58.3	56.9	49.4	43.8
18–64	127.0	143.3	157.2	151.6	134.9
65 and over	22.9	27.3	31.8	50.9	52.3
18–64/total	.590	.626	.639	.602	.584
65 and over/total	.107	.119	.129	.202	.226
Median age	29.0	32.0	37.3	42.4	43.7

Note: Series II assumes fertility at 2.1 and immigration at 400,000 per year. Series
IIX assumes fertility at 2.1 and no immigration. Series III assumes fertility at 1.7
and annual immigration of 400,000.
Source: [8, Tables 8–12, D-2].

Economically Important Age Structure Variables

The economic reaction of a nation to population aging is determined by
the response of individuals to aging and the reaction of a population to the
collective impact of changes in the relative size of certain age cohorts. Shifts
in behavior patterns with age are a result of reactions to the physical and psychological effects of aging and to changes in economic behavior over the life cycle
as the remaining preretirement years diminish and prospects for economic opportunities decline. The response of an individual to the aging process is governed
by changes in the social institutions that affect economic behavior and by social
expectations concerning the capacities of older people. Macroeconomic responses
to population aging may vary from cohort to cohort when the life histories of
cohorts differ significantly.

Aggregate economic responses to aging may occur through a variety of

Table 2. *Age structure ratios with economic implications, 1976–2050, with replacement-level fertility*

Age	1976	1985	2000	2010	2015	2025	2050
0–17/18–64	.5133	.4348	.4324	.3920	.3980	.4206	.4168
18–64/total	.5903	.6153	.6129	.6275	.6155	.5827	.5817
65 and over/18–64	.1806	.1906	.2000	.2016	.2268	.2955	.3022
18–24/55–64	1.4038	1.2814	1.0600	.8614	.7546	.7804	.8076
18–24/18–64	.2218	.1944	.1545	.1642	.1565	.1565	.1586
55–64/18–64	.1580	.1517	.1457	.1906	.2074	.2006	.1964
20–39/40–64	1.1590	1.3319	.8968	.8009	.8388	.8835	.8811
75 and over/ 65 and over	.3811	.3941	.4521	.4323	.3888	.3923	.4420

Source: See Table 1.

transition mechanisms;[3] several principal links between age structure and economic variables are examined below.

Low fertility rates will alter the age composition of the labor force as well as influence the proportion of the population in the prime working ages of 18–64. Table 2 illustrates that with replacement-level fertility, the proportion of the population aged 18–64 increases from its present 59 percent until around 2015 and then returns to approximately its 1976 rate. Slow rates of population growth produce a relatively high proportion of the population of working age. Such an age structure may be more conducive to economic growth and greater per capita output.[4]

A macroeconomic impact of aging may be its influence on labor force productivity. Life-cycle patterns of investment in human capital and age-specific health limitations influence the productivity of workers over their worklife. If older workers are less productive,[5] then any rise in the percentage of those of working age (note the change in the ratio 55–64/18–64 in Table 2) may lower the average rate of productivity. This should be counterbalanced by the decline in the number of those with relatively little job experience, i.e., the ratio 18–24/18–64. Aging may not affect productivity as much in the future as it has in the past if conditions associated with productivity decline are reduced or averted.

The level of aggregate unemployment also is influenced by the age composition of the labor force. Large numbers of youths just entering the labor market tend to raise the overall unemployment rate. Table 2 indicates that the ratio

3. Clark, Kreps, and Spengler [1] provide a review of these and other economic responses to age structure changes.
4. This argument may hinge on the relative costs of supporting young as compared to old dependents.
5. Many researchers consider the hypothesized negative relation between age and productivity to be invalid. See Clark and Spengler [2], and Riley and Foner [6] for reviews of this literature.

Table 3. *Dependency ratios, 1977–2050 (percent)*

Year	Youth dependency ratio (0–17/18–64)	Old-age dependency ratio (65+/18–64)	Total
Series II			
1977	51.3	18.2	69.5
1985	43.5	19.1	62.6
2000	43.2	20.0	63.2
2010	39.2	20.2	59.4
2015	39.8	22.7	62.5
2025	42.1	29.6	71.7
2050	41.7	30.2	71.9
Series III			
1977	51.3	18.2	69.5
1985	40.7	19.1	59.8
2000	36.2	20.2	56.4
2010	31.6	21.2	52.8
2015	31.3	24.4	55.7
2025	32.6	33.6	66.2
2050	32.5	38.8	71.3

Source: See Table 1.

of youths 18–24 to those 18–64 declines from its high of 22.2 percent in 1976 to 15.5 percent by 2000 and remains around 16 percent for the next 50 years. Another important indicator is the ratio of new entrants to those leaving the labor force. If this ratio exceeds unity, the total number of jobs in the economy must be increased to maintain a constant unemployment rate. As measured by the ratio of those 18–24 to those 55–64, population aging has a favorable effect on this indicator as it declines from 1.4 in 1976 to .75 in 2015 before rising slightly. Wachter [10] finds that population aging should reduce the "noninflationary rate of unemployment" during the next decade.

One particular aspect of age structure changes that has received considerable attention in recent years is the significant rise in the older age dependency ratio—those aged 65 years and older relative to those 18–64—and the corresponding decrease in the youth dependency ratio—those 0–17 years of age to those 18–64. Using replacement-level fertility, future shifts in these ratios noted in Table 3 indicate that the youth ratio declines by about 10 percentage points, whereas the relative number of older individuals increases by over 11 percentage points. Therefore, the total ratio of the dependent population increases slightly when comparing 1976 to 2050; however, considerable fluctuation occurs throughout this period. The lower fertility of Series III exacerbates both of these changes.

These projected age structure changes indicate the importance of considering demographic variables and their impact on the economy when formulating public policy. The nature of the continuing trend toward population aging is especially important in an examination of future retirement policy. The significant rise in the ratio of persons aged 65 and over to those aged 18 to 64 indicates the difficulty of financing future retirement benefits. Changes in retirement programs that have only minor short-run impacts may prove to be very important over the next 50 years. It is hoped that this book will illustrate the important relationship between retirement policy and population aging and advance our understanding of these important issues.

References

[1] Clark, Robert, Juanita Kreps, and Joseph Spengler, "Economics of Aging: A Survey," *Journal of Economic Literature* (Sept. 1978).

[2] Clark, Robert, and J. J. Spengler, *Economics of Individual and Population Aging* (Cambridge: Cambridge University Press, 1980).

[3] Coale, A. J., and Paul Demeny, *Regional Model Life Tables and Stable Populations* (Princeton: Princeton University Press, 1966).

[4] Easterlin, R. A., "Population," in Neil W. Chamberlin (Ed.), *Contemporary Economic Issues,* Revised Edition (Homewood, Ill.: Richard D. Irwin, Inc., 1973), pp. 301–352.

[5] Keyfitz, Nathan, *Introduction to the Mathematics of Population* (Reading, Mass.: Addison-Wesley, 1968).

[6] Riley, Matilda, and Anne Foner, *Aging and Society,* Vol. 1 (New York: Russell Sage Foundation, 1968).

[7] Sheppard, Harold, and Sara Rix, *The Graying of Working America* (New York: The Free Press, 1977).

[8] U.S. Bureau of Census, "Projections of the Population of the United States: 1977–2050," *Current Population Reports,* Series P-25, No. 704 (Washington, D.C.: U.S. Government Printing Office, 1977).

[9] Wachter, Michael, "A Time-Series Fertility Equation: The Potential for a Baby Boom in the 1980's," *International Economic Review* (Oct. 1975), 609–623.

[10] Wachter, Michael, "The Demographic Impact on Unemployment," in *Demographic Trends and Full Employment,* National Commission for Manpower Policy, Special Report No. 12 (Washington, D.C.: 1976).

[11] Wander, Hilde, "ZPG Now: The Lessons from Europe," in Thomas Espenshade and William Serow (Eds.), *The Economic Consequences of Slowing Population Growth* (New York: Academic Press, 1978), 41–69.

Individual Retirement Decisions

The Demand for Health and Retirement   *John A. Menefee*

Good health and the ability to maintain it is one of the most important factors for satisfaction in life at any age. Illness exacts economic costs in terms of both lost opportunities for productive work and charges for health services necessary to restore functioning [1, p. 592]. This is especially true for the individual aged 50 to 65 as he enters the period between peak involvement in the labor market and retirement. Health status becomes a significant determinant in the work-related problems found in the older worker and may, in some cases, limit retirement alternatives. As a consequence, retirement has become associated with several paradigms that propose that there are predictable negative effects associated with withdrawal from the labor force, and that such effects are reflected in the decline of a person's health and in increased medical expenditures. The argument states that as individuals retire, the abrupt change of pace and activity precipitates physiological deterioration [10, p. 26]. This is reinforced by an individual's tendency to overestimate the adverse effects of work stoppage upon his health. Support for this paradigm is found in cross-sectional studies that show a disproportionate incidence of poor health among retirees in comparison to those actively employed. In the longitudinal studies of Martin and Doran [5], however, the relationship between health and retirement is found to be equivocal at best. Their findings show that for men over age 55, the incidence of illness requiring medical attention declines 30 to 50 percent after retirement. In a similar longitudinal study conducted by Thompson and Streib, findings suggested only a one-way causality running from poor health to retirement [11, pp. 20, 22].

The contradictions among the findings of these and other studies have been confounded by the ways in which health was defined and measured. The definition and evaluation of health status in later life focuses on the individual in one of two contexts: in terms of the presence or absence of a pathological condition, or alternatively, in terms of the individual's ability to function [1, p. 496]. These two alternative perspectives are based upon either subjective evaluation through self-assessment or objective evaluation by observation, examination, and medical testing. The use of subjective self-assessed health measures has gained increased acceptance due to the belief and supportive evidence that an individual may have relevant and possibly even conflicting information as compared to that gained through objective medical evaluation. Moreover, perceived health status may be a more significant factor in an individual's decision

This research was supported by NIH training grant AG00029 and by the National Science Foundation grant APR76–11164. I am grateful to Carol Swartz, Lew Silver, H. G. Lewis, Robert Clark, and Robert Leech for comments on an earlier draft, discussions, and technical assistance.

process than actual health status. In a fifteen-year study of the aged, Maddox and Douglass [4] found that self-health ratings were a "better predictor of future physicians' ratings than the reverse." However, the reliability of self-assessment has been questioned. Ostfeld [6] and others have found that despite the presence of chronic illness many aged did not identify themselves as limited by their health because they viewed their physical decline merely as a function of the process of normal aging.

With the above in mind, it seems appropriate in this study to analyze the health-retirement relationship in two ways. First, alternative measures of health must be compared to ascertain if they yield comparable results as predictive instruments. Second, the demand for health and medical care must be examined as an individual's employment status changes. This chapter presents one approach for analyzing these two aspects of the health-retirement relationship. A sample group of older adults was evaluated as to how their demand for health varied in relation to alternative definitions of health. Cognizant of differences arising from the specification of the health measure, comparisons were then made to determine if there was any significant change in health needs and demands as employment status changes.

In conjunction with this analysis, effects of aging (such as the deterioration of health) are discussed in terms of functioning ability, restricted activity days, and medical expenditures. The correlation between socioeconomic traits, health, and aging also is discussed.

Methodology

The complementarity of health and retirement among older individuals was analyzed based on Grossman's [3] model of the demand for health and medical care. In conjunction with the model, two indexes of functional status, a mental and physical health scale, were developed to measure health. The rationale for the use of a measure of functional status is based on previous findings that health may best be measured in terms of function [1, pp. 596–597]. The degree of fitness provides an indicator of both individual health and of the degree of medical care an individual might require.[1] In terms of analysis, such functional assessments permit aggregation of information across diagnostic categories, providing some common basis for assessing the status of entire populations.

The study's scope was limited in that it concentrated on the demand for health and medical care in the later worklife and in retirement. This approach was selected in an attempt to delineate some of the different yet correlative relationships presently used to explain the reciprocity between health and retire-

1. See Fillenbaum and Maddox [2], and Reynolds, Rushing, and Miles [8].

ment. Data were taken from the Social Security Retirement History Study for 1969 through 1973 [9]. A group of 6550 males was stratified according to employment status, health, and retirement. This classification provided group-specific information on work history, health status, medical expenditures, and retirement patterns. Admittedly, the interdependence of many of these factors makes the declaration of any definitive statement difficult. Yet the availability of panel data does provide an information source that can be used to formulate and to analyze more thoroughly the apparent anomalous relationship between health status and retirement.

The Model

The theoretical basis for determining the demand for health comes from Michael Grossman's work.[2] The derivation of his investment model is well known and is presented elsewhere, so only the structure and implications of the model will be briefly recapitulated here. In the model, Grossman assumes that each individual inherits an initial stock of health that depreciates over time. An individual may choose, to some extent, his level of health by allocating resources—market goods and time—to augment his initial stock. Health capital, one component of the stock of human capital generated by investment in oneself, is demanded based on its utility as a consumption and investment commodity [3, p. xv]. As a consumption commodity, it helps to eliminate sick days, a source of disutility. As an investment commodity, it determines the total amount of time available for market and nonmarket activities.

An individual tries to produce the optimal quantity of health capital at each stage of the life cycle to maximize his utility and to maintain a preferred state of health. The individual produces health capital according to a set of household production functions. The direct inputs used are the individual's own time, medical care, his stock of human capital, and market goods.[3] The output of this process is a function of the amount of resources employed, the productive efficiency of the individual, and production and resource constraints.

To optimize his use of resources, the individual must try to equate the value of additional health stock with the user cost necessary to produce that stock. The presence of time lost due to illness or injury reduces both the individual's own time and earnings income available for the production of health and for use in market and nonmarket activities. Thus, the individual must adjust his decision calculus to encompass the impact of ill health upon his output of all commodities, including the stock of health.

In accordance with economic laws, the quantity of health demanded by

2. See Appendix A. For a more complete discussion, see Grossman [3].
3. Other inputs also included in the production process would be such things as rich food, alcohol, cigarettes, and exercise.

the individual is negatively correlated with its shadow or imputed price. The imputed price of health depends on the price of medical care as well as other factors such as assets, wage rates, insurance, human capital, and the rate of depreciation of the health stock. Shifts in these variables may alter the optimal amount of health and the derived demand for gross investment in health. For the older adult this may cause an increase in the imputed price of health while simultaneously reducing the quantity of health capital demanded and increasing the quantity of medical care demanded.

It is important to point out that the returns to an investment in health differ from investments in other forms of human capital—such as education—because health is assumed not to be a determinant of the wage rate [3, p. 8]. An investment in health capital determines the amount of total time the individual can spend producing money earnings and commodities. The amount of health capital may be related positively to the wage rate, but its impact is reflected in the alteration of time lost from all activities due to illness or injury [3, p. 8]. In this respect the model is appropriate for use in the analysis of the activities of retirees. Since both nonmarket and market time are relevant, the retiree has an incentive to invest in his health stock to equate the marginal product of his health capital with his user cost, the marginal utility of own time.

The demand for health capital is based upon the relationship between the stock of health and the marginal efficiency of health capital, MEC. The rate of return to the individual is subject to the specification of the production function for healthy days.[4] The upper limit of 365 healthy days suggests that the output produced by health capital is subject to diminishing marginal productivity, increasing from some initial quantity at a decreasing rate as it approaches its upper limit. This diminishing marginal productivity of health capital yields a downward sloping MEC demand schedule, indicating an inverse relationship between health stock and the rate of return on an investment.

In the later worklife, the demand for health also may vary because of depreciation of the health stock. A positive relationship between the depreciation of health capital and age represents the decline in mental and physical functioning associated with aging. A rise in the depreciation rate increases the user cost of health capital. This reduces the amount of health capital demanded as well as the amount of capital supplied by a given amount of gross investment. At some point, the cost of maintaining an adequate level of health capital becomes prohibitive. Therefore, the individual is forced to reject the prospect of a longer life by allowing his health stock to fall to an inadequate level, referred to as the death stock.

The decision to increase gross investment to offset the decline in health

4. The marginal product of health capital is $G_i = BCH^{-C-1}$, or alternatively $\ln G_i = \ln BC - (C + 1) \ln H_i$. The production function used is $h_i = 365 - BH_i^{-C}$, where B and C are positive constants.

stock is subject to the sensitivity of an individual's demand for health stock, the elasticity of the MEC schedule. If the elasticity is less than 1 (i.e., a change in the price of a unit of health leads to a smaller percentage change in the demand for health), as Grossman suggests, an individual would opt to continue to invest in the production of health to offset an increase in the rate of health capital depreciation.[5] This means that gross investment and the depreciation rate would be correlated positively over the life cycle, whereas the stock of health and gross investment would be correlated negatively.

Grossman states that the correlation between the depreciation rate and the utilization of medical services is based on the magnitude of the elasticity of the MEC schedule. With an elasticity less than 1, the correlation between need or illness (measured by the level of the rate of depreciation) and the use of medical services will be positive. As the elasticity value increases, however, the power of need to explain health care decisions is, relative to other factors, substantially reduced. For the older adult, this has important implications. The rise in the depreciation rate along with an increasingly elastic MEC schedule results in a decline in the level of health stock. A lower health stock necessitates increased investment to maintain a preferred state of health. However, if the elasticity and depreciation rate increase with age, then the health capital supplied by a given amount of investment will only offset a declining percentage of the loss in health capital. Coupled with the shorter time horizon for older adults, investments in future health stock become less attractive. Other forms of investments such as health insurance will become of increased importance. Insurance acts as a substitute for health stock by providing additional resources to maintain health. It would also help to compensate for the monetary value of time lost for the worker and retiree from market and nonmarket activities.

In summary, Grossman's model provides a framework that can be used to estimate an older individual's demand for health and medical care. To test the implications of this model in relation to health status and retirement, it is necessary to estimate health demands for specific groups of the population in conjunction with alternative measures of health. Four separate yet related measures of health status were developed to use as proxies for the stock of health capital. The following section describes the empirical formulation of the model for these purposes.

Empirical Formulation

The derivation of the basic estimating equations in Grossman's investment model is based upon a health stock demand function, a depreciation rate equation,

---

5. Based on the production function, the corresponding MEC schedule, $\ln \alpha_i = \ln BC - (C + 1) \ln H_i + \ln W - \ln \pi$. Grossman proposes that the elasticity is less than one. Since $\ln \alpha_i = G_i + \ln W - \ln \pi$, the MEC schedule is obtained from substitution of $\ln G_i$ into the equation for the marginal product of health capital.

and a household gross investment production function [3, p. 18]. These functions are used to generate reduced form demand curves for health and medical care. The estimating equations are:

$$\ln H_i = C_1 \ln Y + C_2 \ln W + C_3 E + C_4 A + C_5 FS + C_6 IS + C_7 R + U_1, \qquad (1)$$

$$\ln M_i = C_{1i} \ln Y + C_{2i} \ln W + C_{3i} E + C_{4i} A + C_{5F} FS + U_2, \qquad (2)$$

where

   $Y =$ full wealth,
   $W =$ wage rate,
   $E =$ stock of human capital,
   $A =$ age of the individual,
   $FS =$ family size,
   $IS =$ insurance,
   $R =$ race,
   $C =$ regression coefficients, and
   $U =$ a disturbance term.

The demand curve for the flow of services yielded by health capital is formulated based upon the production function of healthy days. If the complement of healthy time, time lost due to illness or injury, TL_i, or for our purposes, restricted activity days *(RAD)*, serves as the dependent variable, the production function of healthy days implies

$$-\ln TL = -\ln C_0 + C \ln H_i, \qquad (3)$$

or

$$-\ln RAD = -\ln C_0 + C \ln H_i. \qquad (3')$$

Substituting Equation (3') for health stock in Equation (1) yields the flow-of-services demand curve:

$$-\ln RAD = DC_1 \ln R + DC_2 \ln W + DC_3 E + DC_4 A + DC_5 FS + U_i. \qquad (4)$$

The flow coefficients are estimated by regressing the negative of the natural log of *RAD* on the relevant set of exogenous variables.[6]

The lack of concurrent tabulation over the survey's three rounds of time lost from market and nonmarket activities due to illness or injury prevented the estimation of a demand curve for the flow of services based on work loss days. Therefore, restricted activity days were used as an approximate measure of time lost due to health resources. A restricted activity day, *RAD*, was defined as a day on which the individual had to interrupt his usual activity pattern because of health-related matters. The number of times an individual received

---

6. In comparison to the stock demand curve coefficients, the flow coefficients would be equal, greater or smaller as D equals, exceeds or is less than 1. Ibid., p. 45.

treatment or had contact with a physician in or out of the home, and the total number of times an individual entered the hospital were used to proxy the number of health-restricted activity days.[7]

In relation to the other variables used in the estimating equations, the stock of health, H, was proxied following Grossman's procedures by using the individual's self-assessed health status. The respondents were asked to evaluate their health compared to that of their peers as better, worse, or the same. Since units of health capital are unknown, the three responses were formulated as a measure of health capital in index number form. The responses were indexed using the respondents with the lowest health rating as the base group. The index structure was based on the gross relation between the stock of health and medical expenditures. From the model, a positive correlation between medical outlays and time lost, TL_i, indicated a positive relationship between medical care and the depreciation rate. Based on this proposition, the gross relation between the medical outlays and the stock of health was assumed to be

$$H = bM^{-d}, \qquad b \text{ and } d > 0.$$

M is the mean outlays by individuals whose health is conceived to be the same (s), better (b), or worse (w) than that of their age-cohort, M_s, M_b, or M_w, respectively. The stock of health was then expressed in index number form as

$$H_b/H_s = M_s/M_b$$

which indexed each individual's stock of health in conjunction with the base group's medical expenditures. With such an approach, changes in the magnitudes of the health stock reflect improvements in health status.

The variable used as a measure of human capital, E, was the number of years of formal schooling completed by the respondent. As with health capital, the stock of human capital tends to vary over the life cycle, depreciating during the latter worklife. Thus, the regression coefficient of human capital might reflect forces other than the depreciation rate associated with aging.

The wage rate variable used was the hourly wage rate, W, adjusted for work loss earnings. The use of such a measure may introduce a spurious negative relation between the wage and sick time implying a causality running from sick time to the wage. To deal with such a problem, estimation was done using out-of-pocket expenditures for medical care such as hospitalization, physician fees, medical services, dental, and drugs as proxies for earnings lost due to health. With this format the wage rate was calculated as

$$W = (52/ww)(EA + n),$$

where

7. The possibility of a RAD occurring during a nonworking period may cause this measure to be biased upward for the employed sample.

ww = weeks worked,
EA = actual earnings, and
   n = net earnings lost (gross earnings lost minus health insurance disability
      payments).

For retirees, the wage from their last job was used if they had retired within the last year. If the respondent had been out of the work force for a longer time period, then pension or retirement benefits were used to proxy the value of the respondent's time.

The dependent variable, medical expenditures, M, in the demand equation for medical care is personal medical outlays. This expenditure measure includes outlays for hospital care, doctors, prescribed drugs, dental care, and medical services and supplies such as nursing care, physical therapy, chiropractors, eyeglasses, and hearing aids. Other variables such as family size, FS, were calculated as the number of persons in the household who were partially or completely supported. This included children of both spouses and in some cases, the parents of the respondents and spouse. Family income, Y, was calculated as the total income that the family unit received from all sources in the specified yearly interval. This measure was adjusted to account for the earnings lost by family members due to medical expenditures, similar to the adjustment mechanism concerning the wage rate discussed above. The insurance variable, IS, was calculated as the total amount of private health insurance expenditures.

Three explanatory variables were used in the form of dummy variables. The race variable, R, was defined as two groups, white and nonwhite, with nonwhites being the omitted group. Occupation, OC, was split into white and blue collar professions with blue collar workers being the excluded group. Marital status was defined as married with spouse present with the excluded group being nonmarried and widows.

Functional Status Measures

In Grossman's model the stock of health was proxied by the individual's self-reported health status scaled by health expenditures. As an alternative measure, a functional status health scale was developed based upon the work of Fillenbaum and Maddox [2]. A functional classification of health was employed because it enabled the assessment of an individual's health stock based on multiple indicators of mental as well as physical well being. The evaluation of the stock of health capital in terms of functional ability provides a more broadly based criterion on which to determine the relationship between health and withdrawal from the labor force.

Assessment of the level of functioning was based on a uniform six-point functional rating scale in which the rating points ranged from excellent (1) to total impairment (6).[8] A scale was developed for both mental and physical health. The mental health scale, *MH*, measured a level of well being based on four items in the RHS survey dealing with life satisfaction and retirement. A person who indicated he felt satisfied with life in both absolute and relative terms compared to his peers was considered in excellent mental health (rating of 1). A person at the other extreme, unhappy, dissatisfied with his life, and viewing his way of life as substandard to that of his peers, was considered moderately impaired (rating of 5).

The physical health scale, *PH*, was composed of eight items that dealt with the presence of health conditions that restricted mobility and work activities. For physical health to be considered functionally excellent, physical activity had to be possible subject to no significant impairments or illnesses (rating of 1). At the other extreme, a person confined to the house or to bed due to ill health was considered severely impaired (rating of 6). Two items, the total number of nights in a hospital in the previous year and the number of times medical treatment other than a physical examination was postponed, were used as modifiers in an attempt to clarify further the scaling range.

The scales were indexed as was the self-assessed health status variable in conjunction with medical expenditures. Justification of such a procedure stems from the fact that both are measures of health stock that are subject to depreciation. Based on the assumption of a positive correlation between medical care and the depreciation rate, a positive correlation should exist between medical outlays and the decline in functional ability.

The basic estimating equations were also expanded to include some explanatory measures of previous health status and expenditures. The various measures of health status and medical outlays were used as independent and lagged dependent variables in the appropriate demand equations. In regression analysis if prior status and expenditures were omitted as explicans, they were implicitly assumed to be unrelated. In terms of health status, however, the existing stock of health capital becomes important as an explanatory measure, especially for older adults. As the cost of health capital rises with age, the demand for additional health capital depends upon the previous health stock. Similarly, the demand for medical care may also reflect previous expenditure patterns as individuals continuously combat the disutility of chronic illness in later life.

Empirical Findings

The estimation of the demand for health and medical care was done on a sample of males who reported positive sick time as measured by restricted activity days. Similar analysis was also done on a sample in which persons reported

8. See Appendix C.

Table 1. *Means and coefficients of variation of selected characteristics of males with positive sick time*

Sample group	Age (A)	Years of education (ED)	Family size (FS)	Insurance (IS)	Restricted activity days (RAD)	Medical outlays (M)	Family income (FY)
B1[a]	60.1	10.2	2.5	$153	15	$404	$7,628
	(2.8)[b]	(35)	(52)	(139)	(47)	(281)	(147)
B2	61.9	10.4	2.4	258	5.5	344	11,765
	(3.4)	(36)	(46)	(455)	(172)	(443)	(287)
R2	63.2	9.4	2.3	225	9	390	8,622
	(2.5)	(34)	(53)	(268)	(175)	(351)	(107)
HR2	62.4	8.9	2.3	226	13	856	8,229
	(2.7)	(33)	(55)	(359)	(131)	(268)	(140)
B3	63.6	10.4	2.3	355	7.5	357	13,219
	(2.3)	(36)	(42)	(464)	(329)	(296)	(71)
R3	64.8	9.4	2.3	332	11.5	356	8,069
	(2.3)	(34)	(44)	(417)	(182)	(329)	(86)
HR3	64.1	8.9	2.5	348	22	733	6,972
	(2.5)	(24)	(50)	(176)	(130)	(265)	(72)

[a] B1, B2, and B3 refer to base group of employed workers, R2 and R3 refer to retired workers and HR2 and HR3 refer to health-related retired workers in successive rounds as indicated.

[b] The coefficients of variation are shown in parentheses.

Source: [9].

no sick time, but the findings are not reported here.[9] The sample was stratified into three sample groups based upon employment and health status between consecutive rounds of interviewing the survey participants. An initial sample group of 6550 individuals employed in the survey's first round was followed over the next two rounds and classified based on employment, health, and retirement. The base group was comprised of those respondents who were employed in all three rounds, hereafter referred to as groups B1, B2, and B3. Two separate groups were formed composed of respondents who retired in round two, group R2, or stopped working because of health reasons, group RH2. These retirees also were followed through the third round to look for differences in health status and the demand for health after the initial retirement period. They are identified as R3 and RH3, respectively.

Tables 1, 2, and 3 present some descriptive statistics on the three sample groups. Table 1 presents the means and coefficients of variation for selected characteristics of the three groups. There are shifts in the characteristics for each group and between the three groups over the three rounds. These differences suggest the hypothesis that the variations in the demand for health and medical care are a function of the differentials in characteristic inputs necessary to produce health. Retirees, for example, are older and have lower levels of educational

9. The findings of individuals with no *RAD*s did not differ significantly from the findings reported in this study.

Table 2. *Means and coefficients of variation of health and functional status variables*

Health measure	Round 1	Round 2			Round 3		
	B1[a]	B2	R2	HR2	B3	R3	HR3
Health status, H_i	2.38	1.83	1.82	1.79	1.83	1.77	1.74
Physical, PH	1.86	1.96	2.63	3.09	2.02	2.78	4.15
Mental, MH	2.20	2.12	2.39	2.58	2.15	2.46	2.84
	Coefficients of variation (percent)						
Health status, H_i	25	52	47	40	52	48	34
Physical, PH	42	39	46	37	39	49	32
Mental, MH	33	35	38	37	36	33	28

[a] B1, B2, and B3 refer to base group of employed workers, R2 and R3 refer to retired workers and HR2 and HR3 refer to health-related retired workers in successive rounds as indicated.
Source: [9].

training than the employed groups. This hypothesis is discussed in a subsequent section on group comparisons.

Table 2 presents the means and coefficients of variation of the health and functional status variables for the three sample groups. Initially it is important to notice the downward trend of the health scales among and between the

Table 3. *Means of health, functional status and health capital series*

Health measure	Round 1		Round 2			Round 3		
	Scale[a]	B1[b]	B2	R2	HR2	B3	R3	HR3
H	$\overline{H}$	1.56	1.071	.995	.881	.9898	.8919	.717
PH	$\overline{PH}$	1.111	1.11	1.314	1.07	1.01	1.33	1.296
MH	$\overline{MH}$	2.29	1.68	1.912	1.40	6.72	2.25	1.653
H[c]	1	1	1	1	1	1	1	1
	2	1.56	1.58	1.42	1.65	.48	1.45	.39
	3	1.68	1.27	1.25	1.01	1.08	1.08	1.58
MC[d]	1	.81	1.38	1.68	.86	.88	2.07	2.92
	2	1.18	1.03	1.42	1.07	1.04	1.40	1.32
	3	1.22	1.03	1.42	1.01	.89	.99	1.05
	4	1	1	1	1	1	1	1
	5	.81	.04	—	—	.66	—	—
PH[e]	1	2.69	1.07	4.10	2.26	8.62	3.25	2.27
	2	2.3	2.20	2.70	2.20	7.44	2.43	2.22
	3	1.56	1.07	2.97	1.07	4.16	2.01	1.29
	4	1.36	.71	.49	.66	3.55	1.10	.76
	5	1	1	1	1	1	1	1
	6	.38	.21	—	.36	.65	—	—

[a] $\overline{H}$, $\overline{PH}$, and $\overline{MH}$ represent mean values; numeric values correspond to various scale ranges.
[b] See notes to Table 1.   [d] MH is a descending scale.
[c] H is an ascending scale.   [e] PH is a descending scale.
Source: [9].

groups over the three rounds. Significance tests of means comparisons between the employed groups and the two subgroups of retirees indicated that the variance between the health scales signified a true difference.[10] The calculation of similar statistics for the groups for each separate round also signified a difference of the scale values.

Table 3 presents the health status variables in capital series form. An improvement in the health status is reflected as an increase in the health stock. For example, looking at the physical scale, the level of health stock declines as functional ability declines. This sliding scale supports the gross relation between health stock and medical outlays based on the positive correlation between medical needs and the depreciation rate. The presence of some inconsistencies in the scale indexes reflects the fact that health improvements may be due to increased expenditures caused by a nonmonotonic or rapidly rising depreciation rate in the later years. This would make the amount of health stock supplied by gross investments in health fall, necessitating additional expenditures to maintain a preferred state of health.

Prediction

The demand for health was estimated using five definitions of the dependent variable. To determine if the predicted values based on these alternative definitions were significantly different, a prediction interval was calculated for each measure of health.[11] The intervals were estimated at a .05 percent level of confidence for the three sample groups at each age, 58 to 67. One consistent finding was that the predicted values of the medical care equation were statistically discernible from the other measures for all groups over the age range 58 to 65. For employed individuals, the predicted values of health based on *PH*, *MH*, *H*, and *RAD* were statistically indiscernible over the age range 58 to 65. In the age range 65 to 67, the predicted values of *PH* were found to be statistically discernible from the other predicted values but not from the predicted values based on the medical care equation. This suggests that after age 65 the worker's demand for medical care is closely associated with the decline in his physical functioning. The same pattern was found for health-related retirees over the two age ranges, 58 to 65 and 65 to 67. The predicted values of health capital for retirees, however, were not statistically discernible over the entire age range. Therefore, at a 95 percent confidence level, the various measures of health capital were not found to predict significantly different estimates of health demands

---

10. The significance tests were based on a two-tailed t test at the .05 level.

11. The 95 percent prediction interval for an individual H observation is

$$H = \hat{H} \pm t_{.025} \sqrt{\frac{1}{n} + \frac{x^2}{\Sigma x_i^2} + 1}$$ where $\hat{H}$ is the predicted value for H. See [12, pp. 15–53].

except for random fluctuations over the age range 58 to 65. After age 65, the predicted values of health capital based on physical functioning were statistically discernible except for retirees.

Tables 4, 5, and 6 present the regression coefficients for the estimates of demand for health stock and medical care based on the use of the health status variable, H, the physical and mental functioning variables, PH and MH, the health flow parameter, $-RAD$, and medical expenditures, M. The predicted relationships of the variables will be discussed in terms of the model's assumption as pertaining to the demands of older individuals in later life. The expected relationship among certain variables for older adults will differ from those for younger adults ages 18 to 54 because of differences in human and monetary capital generation. Variance among observed findings also will occur due to age-specific factors. It is important to remember that the sample groups contain only individuals who remained in the survey for the three rounds. Although those included had positive sick time, respondents who died during the survey have been omitted, causing some underestimation of the health demands of these age cohorts. Such a sampling format also raises the issue of selectivity bias, but estimation done on sample groups including the omitted respondents did not produce significantly different estimates.

The age coefficient should be negatively correlated with the health stock and the health flow variables in the regression equations.[12] The inverse relationship reflects the depreciation of health with age and the individual's inability to offset health deterioration completely. This implies that a positive correlation should exist between the age coefficient and medical care in the medical care demand equation. In all three sample groups, the age coefficients indicate a fall in health capital stock and a decline in health status with both the mental and physical functioning measures and the flow measure, RAD. As expected, the demand for medical care rises with age. The coefficients associated with the health measure, H, however, indicate an improvement in health status. One possible interpretation of this apparently anomolous finding parallels Ostfeld's thesis that older individuals perceive functional limitations merely as a normal part of aging. Nevertheless, such a disparity illustrates the need for careful assessment of health variables as to their use in quantitative analysis and prediction.

The regression coefficients for age can be used to determine the continuously compounded rate of change in health capital over the life cycle. The various measures except the health status variable indicate a decline in health capital. Defining health with the physical functioning scale, employed individuals' health capital declined .36 percent per year compared to .9 percent for retirees and 1.3 percent for health-related retired. The decline based on the mental well

12. In looking at the regression results, it is important to remember that the stock measures, PH and MH, are descending scales so that a positive change in a stock indicates a lower level.

Table 4. *Regression coefficients for employed males with positive sick time*

Dependent variable	Sample group	ln Y	ln W	ln FS	R	ln IS	OC	MS	ED1	ED2	Age	ln PH[a]	ln MH[a]	−ln RAD[a]	ln H[a]	ln M[a]	R²[b]
ln PH	B1[c]	.0015 (1.05)	.016 (2.23)	−.015 (−1.26)	.015 (.89)	.0004 (.21)	.031 (2.89)	−.0008 (−.05)	−.005 (.37)	−.031 (2.07)	.003 (.92)						.02
	B2	.001 (.61)	−.011 (−1.84)	−.025 (−1.15)	−.016 (−.56)	−.001 (−.39)	.02 (1.12)	−.002 (−.06)	−.02 (−.87)	−.031 (−1.05)	.005 (.90)	.03 (.54)	.11 (2.39)	.006 (.23)	−.071 (−.98)	.11 (−.106)	.07
	B3	.002 (.72)	−.005 (−.70)	−.016 (−.67)	.10 (3.09)	.003 (.51)	.02 (−.58)	−.004 (−.49)	−.016 (−.58)	−.007 (−.22)	.010 (1.75)	.071 (2.94)	.105 (1.75)	.06 (5.62)	.33 (7.86)	.007 (1.30)	.11
ln H	B1	.0007 (.76)	−.006 (1.29)	.004 (.51)	.0095 (.89)	.0003 (.20)	−.003 (.42)	.0037 (.35)	.0149 (1.96)	.033 (2.99)	.0017 (1.86)						.008
	B2	.0001 (1.00)	.0014 (.50)	−.0040 (−.37)	−.0125 (−.88)	.0003 (−.21)	.008 (.80)	.024 (1.76)	.040 (3.34)	.052 (3.51)	.0015 (.57)	.182 (7.84)	−.018 (−.81)	.011 (.91)	.318 (8.76)	.0035 (−1.81)	.011
	B3	.0008 (.37)	−.0008 (−1.80)	−.0008 (−.50)	−.0213 (.99)	.0006 (.17)	.0001 (.16)	.021 (1.54)	.0161 (.89)	.024 (1.14)	.0064 (1.64)	.037 (2.28)	.099 (2.48)	.029 (4.46)	.267 (9.64)	−.0014 (−.43)	.13
ln MH	B1	.002 (1.31)	−.011 (−1.84)	.004 (.43)	.015 (1.12)	.003 (1.98)	−.007 (−.84)	−.009 (−.70)	−.003 (.28)	−.023 (−1.66)	−.0044 (−1.77)						.011
	B2	.0006 (−.38)	−.0006 (−.27)	−.009 (−.95)	.006 (.53)	.002 (1.38)	.016 (2.08)	.004 (.36)	−.0034 (−.35)	.019 (1.58)	.008 (3.80)	.017 (.88)	−.082 (−4.47)	−.002 (−.22)	.056 (−1.90)	−.002 (−1.06)	.032
	B3	−.0023 (−3.73)	−.002 (−1.01)	.0008 (.13)	.005 (−.54)	.0001 (−.05)	.014 (.67)	−.002 (.46)	.010 (1.37)	−.011 (−.13)	−.0008 (−.47)	.016 (2.43)	−.081 (−.491)	−.005 (−1.68)	−.008 (−.67)	−.004 (−2.81)	.05
−ln RAD	B1	−.0056 (−2.36)	−.0085 (−.73)	.005 (.26)	.015 (.17)	−.005 (−1.61)	.0023 (.13)	−.013 (−.49)	−.033 (−1.45)	−.06 (−2.13)	−.0017 (−.34)						.009
	B2	−.0017 (.28)	−.024 (−1.33)	−.014 (−.19)	.073 (.76)	−.002 (−.16)	−.083 (−1.36)	.113 (1.23)	.019 (.24)	−.002 (−.02)	−.006 (−.38)	.453 (4.43)	.267 (1.86)	.335 (3.13)	.878 (4.17)	−.035 (−2.69)	.095
	B3	−.209 (1.19)	.021 (−.97)	.079 (1.01)	.242 (−2.20)	−.008 (−.48)	−.071 (−1.21)	.212 (1.76)	.132 (1.48)	.195 (1.92)	−.014 (.73)	.114 (1.44)	.039 (.20)	.339 (10.4)	.365 (2.81)	−.036 (−2.07)	.16
M[d]	B1	.343 (2.34)	.117 (1.58)	−.240 (−1.87)	.318 (1.83)	.0725 (3.41)	.269 (2.35)	.404 (2.33)	.400 (2.75)	.932 (5.18)	.024 (.76)						.05
	B2	.024 (2.37)	−.020 (−.62)	−.554 (−4.17)	.219 (1.30)	.040 (2.06)	.432 (3.84)	.562 (3.37)	.022 (.15)	.394 (2.22)	.015 (.47)	−.476 (−1.66)	−.027 (−.10)	−.800 (−5.35)	−.513 (−1.18)	.304 (13.2)	.19
	B3	.320 (1.44)	.019 (.46)	−.122 (−.83)	.804 (4.0)	.013 (.41)	.242 (2.89)	.10 (.20)	−.040 (−.24)	.390 (1.99)	−.005 (−.15)	−.133 (−.88)	−.182 (−.49)	−.219 (−3.60)	−.540 (−2.09)	.280 (8.85)	.134

[a] One-period lagged values.

[b] The stratification of the sample into three groups resulted in approximately a 10 to 15 percent reduction in R^2.

[c] B1, B2, and B3 refer to the sample group and round, *t* values are in parentheses and intercepts are not shown. The sample group sizes are B1 = 6,556, B2 = 2,162, and B3 = 2,162.

[d] Since 7 percent of the sample reported no medical outlays, the value of *M*, and not its natural logarithm, is the dependent variable in Tables 5 and 6. The regression coefficients were converted to elasticities or percentage changes at the mean by multiplying by 1/*M*.

Source: [9].

Table 5. Regression coefficients for retired males with positive sick time

Dependent variable	Sample group	ln Y	ln W	ln FS	R	ln IS	OC	MS	ED1	ED2	Age	ln PH[a]	ln MH[a]	-ln RAD[a]	ln H[a]	ln M[a]	R^2
ln PH	R2[b]	.003 (1.41)	-.011 (-1.39)	-.044 (-1.89)	.05 (1.60)	.0013 (.36)	.071 (3.22)	-.018 (.71)	.089 (4.07)	.17 (5.46)	.027 (5.22)	.208 (7.87)	.226 (8.47)	.098 (4.23)	.308 (8.12)	-.004 (-1.05)	.14
	R3	.007 (3.23)	.046 (3.59)	.048 (2.08)	.004 (1.81)	.056 (.80)	.031 (.67)	-.081 (2.19)	.065 (2.89)	.135 (4.44)	.0014 (.25)	.153 (7.89)	.126 (4.26)	.063 (6.29)	.280 (9.79)	.0084 (2.05)	.20
ln H	R2	.0011 (.92)	.0056 (1.23)	-.0095 (-.69)	-.0156 (-.85)	-.003 (-1.19)	.045 (3.45)	-.022 (-1.43)	.055 (4.30)	.107 (5.91)	.0081 (2.64)	.097 (6.26)	.0901 (5.77)	.071 (5.24)	.387 (17.41)	-.006 (-2.48)	.203
	R3	.004 (2.47)	.004 (.39)	-.010 (.57)	-.031 (-1.32)	-.0010 (.27)	.011 (1.2)	-.189 (2.11)	.076 (4.51)	.060 (2.64)	.016 (3.99)	.09 (6.19)	.083 (3.72)	.040 (5.27)	.304 (14.1)	-.003 (-.91)	.21
ln MH	R2	.0009 (-.79)	-.014 (-3.11)	-.028 (-2.03)	.015 (.85)	.004 (1.96)	-.019 (-1.52)	-.019 (-1.22)	.0212 (1.67)	.068 (3.68)	.0274 (8.98)	.017 (1.09)	.092 (5.91)	.034 (2.50)	-.034 (-1.52)	-.0014 (-.59)	.05
	R3	.0002 (-.23)	-.012 (-2.16)	-.010 (-.95)	.011 (.79)	.0001 (.07)	-.028 (1.1)	-.029 (-1.92)	.022 (2.18)	.056 (4.14)	-.003 (-1.11)	.025 (2.86)	.0204 (1.56)	.015 (3.47)	.067 (5.42)	.0043 (2.36)	.06
-ln RAD	R2	.0006 (.15)	.022 (1.30)	-.029 (-.62)	.013 (.21)	-.0005 (.06)	.068 (1.48)	.028 (.51)	.065 (1.44)	.251 (3.96)	-.0083 (.77)	.234 (9.34)	.175 (3.30)	.426 (4.47)	.73 (9.38)	-.047 (-5.65)	.16
	R3	-.003 (-.54)	.024 (.84)	-.0026 (-.05)	.008 (.12)	-.011 (-.98)	.049 (1.52)	.272 (1.99)	.105 (2.2)	.144 (2.22)	-.008 (-.71)	.124 (2.95)	.084 (1.32)	.32 (14.8)	.294 (4.83)	-.015 (-1.64)	.18
M	R2	.018 (1.88)	.010 (.27)	-.231 (-2.16)	.362 (2.53)	.028 (1.66)	.345 (3.43)	.443 (3.63)	.403 (4.03)	.504 (3.56)	.0164 (.69)	-.055 (-.46)	.056 (-.46)	-.505 (4.79)	-.317 (-1.82)	.312 (17.2)	.15
	R3	.027 (2.65)	-.039 (-.65)	.185 (1.73)	.655 (4.58)	.025 (1.04)	.404 (2.76)	-1.3 (1.99)	.079 (.76)	.475 (3.38)	.005 (.20)	.137 (1.52)	.078 (.57)	-.226 (-4.87)	.298 (-2.26)	.355 (18.6)	.18

a One-period lagged values.
b The sample size of R2 is 3,405.
Source: [9].

Table 6. *Regression coefficients for health-related retired males with positive sick time*

Dependent variable	Sample group	ln Y	ln W	ln FS	R	ln IS	OC	MS	ED1	ED2	Age	ln PH[a]	ln MH[a]	−ln RAD[a]	ln H[a]	ln M[a]	R²
ln PH	RH2[b]	.005 (1.20)	.048 (3.90)	.019 (.51)	.05 (.99)	.0004 (.06)	.070 (1.67)	−.029 (−.77)	.0075 (.19)	.066 (.92)	.0135 (1.40)	.053 (.74)	−.012 (−.18)	.015 (.33)	.264 (3.06)	.010 (1.26)	.08
	RH3	.025 (4.28)	.282 (3.46)	.048 (.91)	.02 (−.27)	.014 (1.07)	.042 (.89)	−1.24 (−1.1)	.075 (1.46)	.078 (.84)	.027 (1.99)	.169 (−2.49)	.064 (.83)	−.004 (−.15)	.179 (2.01)	−.0005 (−.05)	.09
ln H	RH2	−.0005 (−.18)	.036 (4.21)	−.0009 (−.03)	−.031 (−.87)	−.004 (−.83)	.044 (1.42)	.064 (1.90)	−.005 (−.19)	.033 (.66)	.004 (.55)	.065 (1.29)	.062 (1.31)	.019 (.61)	.283 (4.67)	−.004 (−.80)	.123
	RH3	.006 (1.22)	.063 (.92)	.079 (1.79)	−.029 (.51)	.015 (1.42)	.022 (1.32)	.046 (2.21)	.08 (2.06)	.013 (1.7)	.042 (3.67)	.007 (.13)	−.041 (−.64)	.005 (.23)	.241 (3.25)	−.014 (−1.58)	.08
ln MH	RH2	.003 (.90)	.009 (1.04)	.060 (2.09)	.073 (1.99)	−.003 (−.56)	−.0005 (−.02)	−.037 (−.98)	.0503 (1.79)	.139 (2.66)	.0184 (2.62)	.070 (1.32)	−.027 (−.55)	.04 (1.22)	.015 (.23)	.003 (.53)	.06
	RH3	.002 (.55)	−.018 (−.47)	.0009 (.04)	−.026 (−.84)	.005 (.88)	−.0065 (−.04)	−.07 (1.96)	.041 (.172)	.026 (.62)	.001 (.17)	.067 (2.16)	−.006 (−.17)	−.002 (−.16)	.019 (.46)	−.01 (−2.21)	.032
−ln RAD	RH2	.008 (.77)	.097 (3.03)	−.063 (−.62)	−.067 (−.53)	−.016 (−.94)	−.125 (−1.12)	−.025 (−.19)	.010 (.10)	.129 (.70)	−.057 (2.36)	.046 (1.03)	.178 (1.07)	.115 (.25)	.436 (2.05)	−.071 (−3.62)	.010
	RH3	.005 (.48)	.049 (.36)	−.057 (−.65)	−.123 (−1.06)	−.030 (−.36)	−.120 (−1.1)	.26 (1.96)	−.11 (−1.29)	−.19 (−1.28)	−.036 (1.53)	−.337 (−.292)	.023 (.18)	.051 (1.12)	−.002 (−.01)	−.022 (−1.25)	.05
M	RH2	.015 (.64)	−.144 (−.195)	−.180 (−.77)	.719 (2.38)	.046 (1.11)	.437 (1.66)	1.08 (3.60)	.062 (.27)	.069 (.16)	−.059 (−1.03)	.334 (.78)	.061 (.15)	−.272 (−1.01)	−.482 (−.94)	.350 (7.78)	.21
	RH3	.026 (1.14)	−.198 (−.63)	−.107 (−.52)	.426 (1.59)	.091 (1.81)	.325 (1.84)	−1.72 (3.1)	.349 (1.74)	.846 (2.36)	−.113 (2.11)	.399 (1.51)	.794 (2.62)	.042 (.40)	.462 (1.33)	.260 (6.44)	.17

[a] One-period lagged values.
[b] The sample size of RH2 is 636.
Source: [9].

being measure is .05 percent per year for employed individuals, .3 percent for retirees, and .64 percent for health-related retirees. The health status measure, however, indicates an increase in health stock for workers, retirees, and health-related retired of .2, .3, and 1.5 percent per year, respectively.

The education coefficients should be positively correlated with the health stock and flow measures. A positive relationship indicates increased productive efficiency of the individual due to educational training. In the regression analysis, education is set up as two dummy variables. The variable, $ED1$, represents individuals with 7 to 12 years of schooling; the variable $ED2$ represents individuals with more than 12 years of schooling. Individuals with 0 to 7 years of education are the omitted group. For employed individuals, the education coefficients indicate that the stock of health increases with educational attainment. For both groups of retirees, however, increasing levels of educational attainment result in reduced health stocks. Such findings, along with a positive correlation of education with respect to medical care, are contrary to the assumed relationships. Educational attainment might be expected to enable individuals to be more productive and efficient, thereby reducing the costs and amounts of inputs to produce gross investments in health. In fact, however, higher levels of educational training raise the cost of producing health stock in terms of the income foregone by diverting resources from work-related activities. Controlling for income, one finds that medical care outlays rise with income. This shift reflects the fact that the value of own time in market and nonmarket activities has increased to the point where individuals substitute medical care for own time in the production of health. For older adults, the ability to be efficient producers is hampered by rising depreciation rates that reduce the productive abilities enhanced by educational training at an earlier age. Thus, the positive effects of education on productive efficiency and gross investment may have been diminished greatly at this stage in the life cycle.

The wage coefficient should be related positively to health stock based on the assumption that an increase in the wage rate raises the rate of return on an investment in health. With the three stock measures, one finds such a relationship with the exception of health-related retirees. For health-related retirees, the positive correlation between the wage rate proxied by pension benefits, and the decline in the functional status measures suggest that the rate of return on an investment in health may not be sufficient to increase one's health stock that has been diminished by some health limitation earlier in life. The positive wage coefficient for medical expenditures, M, illustrates that an upward shift in the wage rate increases the demand for medical care as an input in the production of health days.

A small positive correlation is found between the health stock measures and income. This finding suggests that an increase in income would raise the demand for health and the demand for inputs, especially on individuals' own time in the production of health stock. An increase in the time input would result in a decline in health stock as measured by functional ability because the marginal productivity of own time relative to market goods would decline as the depreciation rate rose with age. For retired individuals, however, a positive income coefficient indicates that an increase in wealth would raise the ratio of market goods to consumption time.[13] This would make the marginal productivity of consumption time, and hence the monetary rate of return on an investment in health, rise. Stated differently, an increase in wealth would raise the incentive to invest in health because the return, increased healthy days, relative to the input cost of own time would be increased.

The presence of a negative income elasticity in terms of healthy days, $-\ln RAD$, suggests that some inputs into the gross investment production function, such as alcohol and/or smoking, may have negative marginal products [3, p. 64]. If their income elasticity exceeded the income elasticity of beneficial inputs, such as medical care, exercise, and diet, then the shadow price for health would be positively correlated with income. Thus, an individual could simultaneously reduce his demand for health but increase his demand for medical care.

The inclusion of a health insurance variable revealed a negative correlation between insurance and the demand for health stock. For the older worker and retiree, insurance is one form of protection against the uncertainty and disutility of illness. It provides a way to supplement or offset a reduction in one's stock of health capital, suggesting that insurance acts as a substitute for health stock. In terms of the physical and mental functioning stock measures, insurance was found to be associated with individuals with lower levels of functional ability. This is supported by the positive relationship between insurance and medical outlays. The negative correlation between the flow measure, $-RAD$, and insurance also illustrates the role of insurance as a substitute for health stock.

The coefficients for family size vary in sign and significance for health measures. This pattern suggests two interpretations. A negative relationship may indicate that as the number of family members declines, additional resources become available for use in the production of health or maintenance of a preferred health level. Alternatively, a positive correlation may reflect that health levels of the family unit are complements. The negative relationship of medical expenditures to family size lends support to the proposition that family unit health levels are complementary.

Dummy variables were included in the estimating equations to account for the differences in health demands attributable to characteristics such as race, marital status, and occupation. In terms of race, nonwhites were found to have a larger health stock measured by functional status, but perceived their health status, relative to their peers, as lower. The number of restricted days was lower for whites except among the health-related retired. These findings seem to coincide with the demand for medical care. Employed whites spent 24 to

13. See Grossman [7, p. 46, n. 6].

123 percent more on medical care than did nonwhites over the survey period. Retired and health-related retired whites expended an average of 68 to 79 percent more on health care, respectively, than did nonwhites.

The findings on marital status and health demands lend support to the earlier interpretation that the health levels of adult family members are complements.[14] Married individuals were found to have higher levels of mental and physical functioning and a higher perception of their health status, H, than nonmarrieds. The number of restricted days also fell over the survey period for marrieds. The better health status of married individuals is further reflected in their declining level of medical expenditures.

The differences in health stock and needs among occupational groups revealed that employed and former professional (white collar) workers perceived their health status as better than that of individuals in blue collar occupations. White collar workers' physical functioning, however, was lower as was their mental functioning. In contrast, retired professionals were found to have a higher level of mental well being than nonprofessionals. Health-related retired professionals had the greatest number of restricted days, and medical expenditures ranged from 34 to 56 percent higher for individuals involved in white collar occupations compared to those in blue collar jobs over the survey period.

In looking at the demand for health and medical care in later life it is necessary to consider the role of existing health stocks and health expenditure patterns. Individuals demand a certain amount of health capital and medical care to maintain a level of health that is constantly depreciating with age in latter life. The five different measures of health used as dependent variables to estimate the demand curves for health were entered as one-period lagged variables representing additional explanatory variables in the various demand equations for the second and third rounds.[15] Interpretation of these lagged terms is difficult because all other variables are held constant across equations. For this analysis, the following explanations could be used to account for the partial effects of the lagged terms. The coefficients of the lagged term for medical outlays indicate the proportion of expenditures necessary to offset the increasing effects of health depreciation associated with normal aging. An example might be the purchase of additional medication for a chronic condition or improved corrective lenses. The lagged health status coefficient represents the degree to which an individual perceives his health has changed based on purely subjective factors. The restricted days coefficient indicates the impact of random events such as short-term acute illnesses or an accident upon health stock and medical needs. Finally, the lagged

---

14. Parsons and others have found that spouse's education is an important determinant of male health. See [7].

15. Two-period lagged terms were also estimated but proved not to provide any additional information.

functional measures indicate the amount of appreciation or depreciation of health in terms of functioning associated with normal aging.

In looking at the lagged variables over the last two rounds, it is apparent that measures of prior health are significant in determining the demand for health and medical care. Previous health status appears to be the most significant factor across all three groups. For workers, previous levels of mental well being and restricted activity days are consistently significant factors. For retired individuals the functional scales and restricted activity days are significant factors in determining health demands, whereas for health-related retired, no lagged terms except previous health status were found to be consistently significant. Generally, these lagged coefficients can be viewed as the effect of each measure of health upon present health status. Because of the interrelation and feedback effects among the lagged terms, however, the coefficients do not express accurately the total effect of each lagged health measure upon present health levels.[16] One can obtain some indication of the importance of the lagged variables in determining the factors underlying changes in health by comparing the size of and changes in the coefficients over the survey period and between groups. One should consider the interpretations of these findings carefully, however.

Gross Investment Production Function

Table 7 presents the estimates of the gross investment production functions for selected sample groups.[17] These estimates can be used along with the reduced-form parameters to help explain individual behavior regarding the demand for health and medical care. They also provide some justification for the economic significance of the explanatory variables used. For example, the positive correlation between the various health measures and age (except the health status variable) indicates a positive relationship between the depreciation rate and the stock of health capital. Being aware of scale reversals, we note that the negative medical care elasticities of the functional scales reflect the observed gross positive correlation between medical care and sick time. The negative correlation between the health status and flow measures of health with respect to medical care reflects the positive relationship between medical care and the depreciation rate.

16. Use of a variance components model might be an appropriate way to determine the partial and total effects of each variable upon the various health measures, but such an approach is beyond the scope of this paper.

17. The estimates for the other sample groups were similar. Two-stage OLS analysis was also done first estimating the demand curve for medical care. The predicted values of M were then used in the estimation of the production function. Because of the variance in the estimates due to the set of variables excluded from the second stage, the OLS estimates have been used for interpretation.

Table 7. *Gross investment production functions of individuals with positive sick time*

Dependent variable	Sample group	ln M	ln Y	ln FS	R	ln IS	ED	Age	R²
ln PH	B1	−.015 (−7.4)ᵃ	.001 (1.05)	−.017 (−1.6)	.013 (.82)	.002 (.83)	.008 (6.14)	.003 (1.13)	.04
	B2	−.008 (−2.54)	.001 (.54)	−.03 (−1.65)	−.0005 (−.02)	−.004 (−.12)	.001 (−.5)	.005 (.92)	.04
	R2	−.033 (−9.23)	.006 (2.61)	−.038 (−1.73)	.10 (3.14)	−.003 (−.74)	.025 (9.92)	.033 (6.00)	.06
	HR2	−.027 (−4.29)	.008 (1.84)	.023 (.66)	.091 (1.83)	.0002 (.03)	.013 (2.73)	.080 (.82)	.05
ln MH	B2	.0005 (.34)	.0007 (−.94)	.005 (−.62)	.002 (.16)	.002 (1.64)	.003 (3.09)	.009 (4.17)	.02
	R2	−.01 (−.499)	−.001 (−.96)	−.04 (−3.28)	.023 (1.30)	.005 (2.27)	.05 (3.31)	.030 (9.72)	.04
	HR2	−.009 (−1.94)	.004 (1.23)	.041 (1.65)	.083 (2.33)	.002 (−.36)	.012 (3.40)	.016 (2.25)	.05
ln H	B2	−.013 (−7.44)	.001 (−.15)	.007 (−.69)	.004 (−.26)	.0009 (−.54)	.008 (6.81)	.003 (.91)	.04
	R2	−.023 (−10.9)	.004 (2.91)	−.012 (−.89)	.006 (.30)	.007 (−3.19)	.019 (12.08)	.009 (2.87)	.07
	HR2	−.019 (−4.26)	.003 (.88)	.034 (1.33)	.002 (.06)	.005 (−.96)	.007 (2.02)	.001 (.16)	.04
−ln RAD	B2	−.187 (−13.9)	−.0001 (−.02)	−.081 (−1.26)	.159 (1.72)	.002 (−.20)	.012 (1.71)	−.003 (−.16)	.12
	R2	−.135 (−16.4)	.01 (2.36)	.011 (−.25)	.122 (1.92)	.008 (−.96)	.046 (8.8)	−.019 (1.74)	.10
	HR2	−.167 (−10.2)	.018 (1.87)	.048 (−.57)	.079 (.66)	.016 (−.98)	.007 (.63)	−.047 (2.04)	.18

ᵃ *t* values are in parentheses, and intercepts are not shown.
Source: [9].

Elasticity

In order to assess the influence of changes in the rate of return on investment in health and its impact on the decline in health stock, the elasticity of the MEC schedule was estimated for each of the three sample groups. The elasticity parameter was estimated using the production function for healthy days where the elasticity, $E = (1/1+C)$. Grossman assumed that the best estimate of E is .5, i.e., $C = 1$. The estimated coefficients from the sample groups were tested at the .05 level of confidence on a two-tailed test to determine if they were significantly different from one. Elasticities of the MEC schedule were found to be significantly different for employed individuals. They were .66, .81, and .58, respectively, for the three rounds. The elasticity coefficients for both groups of retired workers differed in the last round, being .64 for retirees and .71 for health-related retirees.

These larger elasticities for retirees indicate that the amount of health capital demanded has been reduced because the portion of health capital that can be offset by a given amount of investment has declined. For older individuals this lower rate of return reflects the increase in the depreciation rate with age. These estimates of E can be employed to compute $\tilde{\delta}$, the continuously compounded rate of increase in the depreciation rate over the life cycle.[18] Since the depreciation rate rises with age, $\tilde{\delta}$ should increase over the three rounds. Defining health in terms of the physical functioning scale employed, individuals' average yearly rate of increase in the depreciation rate is .62 percent compared to 4.1 percent for retired and 2.9 percent for health-related retired. The average rates based on the mental well being measure are .73 percent for employed, .9 percent for retired, and 1.9 percent for health-related retired. For the health status measure, the average rates are .82 percent for employed, and 2.4 percent and .5 percent for retired and health-related retired, respectively. The flow measure, $-RAD$, yields an average rate of 2.2 percent for employed, 2.4 percent for retired, and 2.8 percent for health-related retired.

Comparison among sample groups of these rates of change in the depreciation of health capital reveals some interesting patterns. Workers are found to have the lowest rates in relation to each measure of health. Retired individuals, however, have a greater rate of increase in terms of the physical and health status measures than do health-related retirees. These differences may reflect differential patterns of adjustment between the two retired groups. In a comparison of the rates generated by the different health measures, two patterns are found. Across the three sample groups the rates based on the physical and health status measures follow the same pattern. The similarity of these rates across employment groups suggests that an individual's perception of changes in health more closely parallels his physical functioning ability than the other measures of health. It is also of interest that the rates for mental well being and the flow of healthy days parallel each other across employment groups.

The decline in health capital and the rate of increase in the decline indicate that retirees experience a larger and faster decrease than do workers. These differences reflect the two groups' variances in characteristics such as age and education, inputs used in the production of health. For example, the mean age of retirees is approximately 15 months higher than that of workers. If one corrects for this differential, the decline in retirees' health capital in terms of physical functioning falls from .9 percent per year to .75 percent. Similarly, the decline in health capital based on the other measures of health also is reduced from 2 to 14 percent.[19] The incorporation of other characteristic differences

18. The percentage rate of decrease in the stock of health over the life cycle is estimated with the equation

$$\bar{H}_i = -s_i E_i \tilde{\delta}_i,$$

where s_i is the share of depreciation in the cost of health capital, E_i is the elasticity of the MEC schedule and $\tilde{\delta}$ is the rate of depreciation.

19. The reduction in the decline in the depreciation of health capital adjusted for age differentials for retirees was 17 percent for physical health, 14 percent for mental well being, 7 percent for health status, 8 percent for restricted activity days, and 5 percent for medical care.

in the determination of the levels of health capital would provide a means of identifying the effects of shifts in employment status, net of these characteristic differences, upon the demand for health and medical care. The technique of indirect standardization enables one to calculate the effect of characteristics differentials between groups. The following section uses this method to examine the variation in health between workers and retirees.

Group Standardizations

Regression analysis identified the factors that account for the variation in the levels of the stock of health capital and medical expenditures. The variation also can be illustrated by examining the differences among the sample groups' averages on each of the variables represented as outcomes in the model. Such an approach enables one to test the hypothesis that variations in health demands are the result of differences in levels of characteristic inputs among the sample groups. The evaluation is done by substituting the means of the independent variables of one group, for example retirees, into the regression equation for another group—employed. This yields a calculated value of the dependent variable for use in group comparisons.[20] In effect, the question answered by this operation is this: suppose the sample group of employed males had socioeconomic characteristics equal to the average for the sample group of retirees, what would be the best estimate of their stock of health and medical care demands? Similarly, the substitution of the employed groups' mean characteristics into the regression equations for retirees generates an estimate of health levels and demands based upon the proposition that retirees have an average level of socioeconomic traits equal to that of workers.

Table 8 presents selected comparisons among the sample groups for each round and longitudinal comparisons between the employed and retired groups.[21] The five alternative measures of health are used to generate a multiple set of the necessary regression coefficients for the analysis. The odd-numbered columns in Table 8 present the predicted values for the alternative health measures based on the basic regression model.[22] The even-numbered columns present the calculated values of the health measures for one group, for example B2, when the mean characteristics of the group immediately below in the table are used. Comparing the employed group, B1, with the group already retired in the first period, R1, we find that for the B1 group, the difference between columns 1

20. These values reflect the calculated relationship in the neighborhood of the mean.
21. The sample groups, *R1* and *HR1*, are the individuals that make up the groups *R2* and *HR2* in round 2, respectively. They were broken into groups for round 1 to look at their differences from other respondents as specific subgroups of the working population.
22. These values are estimated on the regression equation without the lag terms entered as independent variables.

Table 8. Differences in means between employed, retired, and health-related retired males for health measures generated by indirect standardization

Dependent variable	Round 1			Round 2			Round 3			Cross-round			Cross-round		
	Group	Column (1)	(2)	Group	Column (3)	(4)	Group	Column (5)	(6)	Group	Column (7)	(8)	Group	Column (9)	(10)
ln M	B1	4.09	4.03	B2	3.72	4.10	B3	4.02	3.84	B1	4.09	4.00	R1	4.19	4.67
	R1	4.19	4.38	R2	3.86	3.9	R3	4.03	3.94	B2	3.72	3.76	R2	3.86	3.61
	R1	4.19	4.94	R2	3.86	.398	R3	4.03	3.93	B2	3.73	3.83	R2	3.86	3.90
	HR1	4.33	4.8	HR2	4.54	4.7	HR3	5.01	4.58	B3	4.02	3.87	R3	4.03	3.18
ln PH	B1	.812	.836	B2	.452	.455	B3	1.86	1.83	B1	.812	.824	R1	.727	.755
	R1	.727	.741	R2	.499	.492	R3	.696	.612	B2	.452	.456	R2	.452	.444
	R1	.727	.651	R2	.499	.496	R3	.696	.606	B2	.452	.467	R2	.452	.468
	HR1	.752	.704	HR2	.243	.102	HR3	.334	.486	B3	1.86	1.84	R3	.696	.660
ln H	B1	.439	.445	B2	.051	.054	B3	-.027	-.007	B1	.439	.484	R1	.299	.334
	R1	.299	.359	R2	-.055	-.066	R3	-.168	.026	B2	.051	.055	R2	-.055	-.054
	R1	.299	.337	R2	-.055	-.637	R3	-.168	-.222	B2	.051	.026	R2	-.055	-.046
	HR1	.304	.325	HR2	-.168	-.174	HR3	-.426	-.354	B3	-.027	-.011	R3	-.168	-.312
ln MH	B1	.091	.097	B2	.096	.089	B3	.009	.037	B1	.091	.099	R1	.072	.085
	R1	.071	.075	R2	.226	.177	R3	.261	.253	B2	.095	.064	R2	.226	.113
	R1	.071	.129	R2	.226	.206	R3	.261	.256	B2	.095	.086	R2	.226	.183
	HR1	.104	.083	HR2	.021	.048	HR3	.226	.208	B3	.009	.039	R3	.261	.262
-ln RAD	B1	-3.14	-3.81	B2	-1.62	-1.59	B3	-1.80	-1.79	B1	-3.14	-4.09	R1	-3.21	-3.22
	R1	-3.21	-3.19	R2	-1.97	-1.95	R3	-2.13	-2.13	B2	-1.62	-1.56	R2	-1.97	-1.82
	R1	-3.21	-3.25	R2	-1.97	-1.94	R3	-2.13	-2.15	B2	-1.62	-1.57	R2	-1.97	-1.91
	HR1	-3.22	-3.24	HR2	-2.27	-2.24	HR3	-2.67	-2.65	B3	-1.80	-1.77	R3	-2.13	-2.12

Source: Estimates are based on predicted values calculated from [9].

and 2, 4.09–4.03, illustrates the effect upon the value of medical care, M, for employed individuals by giving them the mean characteristics of retirees. For retirees, R1, the difference between columns 1 and 2, 419–4.38, shows the effect upon the value of medical care demands of substituting the mean characteristics of workers for retirees. In this case, retirees and workers with retiree characteristics had lowered predicted values of medical demands than retirees with workers' characteristics and workers, respectively. Thus, it appears that characteristics associated with retirees lower medical care demands. By comparing the way health is produced, however, the difference between the two groups' values in column 1, 4.19–4.09, and column 2, 4.38–4.03, reveals that retirees are less efficient in their production of health and demand more medical care, than do workers.

In economic terminology, the difference between the values of column 1 and column 2 for one sample group is analogous to the changes in the quantity of health care demanded due to a change in price. Therefore, one must examine the change in demand when the price of inputs such as own time, market goods, and income change. The differences in column 1 and column 2 between two groups is similar to the change in demand due to a shift in one of the determinants of demand, here represented as a change in the production function. This means that the differences in demand reflect the effect of giving one group the productive capability of another group.

Comparisons between the sample groups revealed a fluctuating pattern of health demands. Using the indirect standardization technique discussed above, workers given retirees' mean characteristics for each round were found to have a higher level of health stock than were workers as measured by the health status variable, H. This higher assessment, however, is contradicted by a decline in health in two of the three rounds as indicated by the fall in both functional scales, no significant change in the production of healthy days measured by $-RAD$s, and an increase in medical outlays. The comparisons between retirees and retirees with workers' mean characteristics over the three rounds revealed a somewhat similar pattern. The level of health measured by H for retirees characterized as workers increased and medical expenditures rose. The functional scales showed a slight improvement in the latter rounds, but the flow measure, $-RAD$s, indicated no change between the groups. Evaluating the differences in health and medical care demands from a productive viewpoint, individuals defined or characterized as retired were found to be less efficient on the scales of mental health, MH, health status, H, and flow measure, $-RAD$, yet more efficient in relation to the physical functional measure. Such findings may indicate that retirees perceive their health status as better because of a higher level of physical functioning. The elimination of job stress could account for this pattern. The apparent lack of complementarity of the health status measure with the other measures, however, again raises the question as to what the self-assessed measure explains.

The comparisons between retired and health-related retired individuals also revealed a conflicting pattern of health levels and demands. Health-related retirees given retirees' mean characteristics were found to have a higher demand for medical care, yet a greater stock of health capital in terms of the mental, health status, and flow measures than health-related retired individuals over the three rounds. In two of the three rounds, however, the physical functioning measure indicated a lower level of health capital. Retirees given the mean characteristics of health-related retired individuals revealed higher medical care demands and greater stocks of health capital as measured by mental and health status variables over two rounds. Interestingly, the health-related retired were found to be more efficient in their production of health than were retirees in terms of the functional scales for two rounds.

The lack of a large discernible negative shift in health stocks, combined with significantly higher medical demands for the individuals characterized or defined as health-related retirees, might be explained in two ways. First, individual demands for health capital and medical care have been more structurally defined by a health limitation. Thus the necessary inputs and required outputs of the individual's production function for health captial are more readily known. In addition, such individuals are eligible for supplemental financial and medical benefits that provide additional inputs into the production process. A second reason is that health-related retirees have adjusted their activities, preceptions, and expectations in accordance with their health limitations, whereas retirees have made such adjustments only infrequently because of acute illness or injury.

The cross-wave comparisons of workers and retirees provide some additional information to clarify the health-retirement relationship. For both groups, the level of health capital fell as measured by the self-assessed health variable reflecting the depreciation of health with age. In terms of mental functioning, the level of health capital declined for retirees but improved for workers. The overall level of medical expenditures was lower for retirees in conjunction with higher levels of physical functioning. The highest levels of medical expenditures for retirees paralleled the lowest levels of physical functioning and the highest self-assessments of health. Workers' highest medical expenditures also paralleled the highest health self-assessments, but the lowest levels of mental functioning. Based on these findings it appears that the variance in the characteristics of the different sample groups accounts for much of the difference in health demands. The lack of any consistent pattern correlating individuals defined or characterized as retired with lower health stocks or significantly greater demands for medical care suggests that retirement does not lead to a poorer state of health.

Summary

The demand for health capital and medical care among older adults changes over the life cycle. To ascertain the degree of change, health must be defined and measured. Throughout this paper five alternative definitions of health have been used to estimate the demand for health. In a comparison of the predictive ability of each measure, as indicated by the coefficient of multiple determination, R^2, correct signs and significant coefficients, one finds that two measures, mental well being and self-assessed health status, cause difficulty in explaining the proposed causal relationships of the model. Both are self-assessed measures, which makes them subject to measurement error. This is compounded by the fact that the concept of mental well being is difficult to measure empirically. Moreover, the causal relationships between the various explanatory variables and mental well being are not known as pertains to health. Thus, the interpretation of this measure should be used cautiously. Predicted values and correlations based on the self-assessed health status measure are inconsistent. One finds that the age coefficients based on the health status variable indicate an increase in health capital with age and a corresponding decline in gross investments in health for all individuals. The age-specific levels of health as predicted by health status indicate health-related retirees have higher levels of health capital than do workers and non-health-related retired individuals. Further, the higher levels of demand for medical care for workers and retirees correspond to the highest levels of self-assessment. Because of these conflicting findings, emphasis should be placed on the health measures more attuned to quantification, objective measurement, and consistency in terms of the model's causal relationships.

In conclusion, the use of the different health measures provided alternative ways to estimate and analyze changes in the demand for health. The findings of this analysis suggest that the positive correlation of age with health depreciation rate is the one underlying relationship that helps explain the basic reason for retirees altering their demand for health and medical care. This decline in health is strongly correlated with various socioeconomic traits that affect an individual's ability to be an efficient producer of health. For example, retirees were found to be older and have less educational training than employed persons. Such differences in the characteristic inputs of health production generate higher user costs and lower returns to gross investments, resulting in lower health stocks and poorer health. The impact of these differentials in socioeconomic characteristics then, rather than employment status, was found to be a primary reason, along with age, for changes in the demand for health. Thus, there appears to be little justification for the proposition that retirement leads to poor health.

Appendix A. The Demand for Health

In Grossman's [3] investment model, the optimal stock of health capital is that stock that maximizes the individual's intertemporal utility function:

$$U = U(\phi_0 H_0, \ldots, \phi_n H_n, Z_0, \ldots, Z_n), \tag{A.1}$$

where

H_o = inherited stock of health,
H_i = stock of health in period i,
ϕ_i = flow of health services per unit stock, and
Z_i = total consumption of an aggregate commodity in period i.[23]

Gross investment in health and the aggregate commodity is assumed to be produced according to the following (homogeneous of degree 1) production functions:

$$I_i = I(M_i,\ TH_i,\ E_i), \tag{A.2}$$
$$Z_i = Z(S_i,\ T_i,\ E_i), \tag{A.3}$$

where

M_i = medical care input in period i,
TH_i = own time spent producing health in period i,
X_i = goods input used to produce the aggregate commodity Z in period i,
T_i = time input in the production of the aggregate commodity in period i, and
E_i = the stock of human capital in year i.

The marginal and average cost of gross investment in health capital, π_i, can be calculated in terms of the observable variables W_i (the wage rate), P (the price of medical care), and E (the education of the consumer). This is done by solving simultaneously the equations describing the total cost of gross investments in health (A.4), the production function for gross investments in health (A.5), and the first-order cost-minimization conditions in the production of health (A.6).

$$\pi_i I_i = PM_i + W_i TH_i \tag{A.4}$$
$$\ln I_i = \alpha \ln M_i + (1 - \alpha) \ln TH_i + r_H E, \tag{A.5}$$

where

$$r_H = \frac{\partial \ln I_i}{\partial E}.$$

$$\frac{P}{MP_M} - \frac{W_i}{MP_{TH_i}} \quad \text{or} \quad \frac{P}{W} = \frac{\alpha}{1-\alpha} \frac{TH_i}{M_i} \tag{A.6}$$

the marginal cost of gross investment in health, π_i:

$$\ln \pi_i = (1 - \alpha) \ln W + \alpha \ln P - r_H E. \tag{A.7}$$

23. The aggregate commodity is defined to include all goods that enter the utility function except healthy days.

Substitution of the expressions for δ_i and π_i from Equations (B.2) (Appendix B) and (A.7) into Equation (B.1) (Appendix B) gives the following reduced form for the health stock demand curve:

$$\ln H_i = \alpha\epsilon \ln W_i - \alpha\epsilon \ln P + r_H E - \delta\epsilon i - \epsilon \ln \delta_o. \tag{A.8}$$

To implement the model empirically, the demand for the stock of health must be converted to a demand for the flow of services. Health indices such as reduced activity days *(RAD)* should be expressed as negative measures of health flows in the demand curve. The requirement that all available time must be allocated to some activity yields the following identity:

$$TW_i + T_i + TH_i + TL_i = \Omega$$

for all *i*, which can be written as

$$h_i + TL_i = \Omega$$

or

$$TL_i = \Omega - h_i = 365 - h_i.$$

Using the production function for healthy days, we obtain

$$TL_i = BH_i^{-c} \text{ or } -\ln RAD_i = -\ln B + C \ln H_i.$$

Substitution of the above equation for $\ln H_i$ yields the following demand curve for the service flow from health stock:

$$-\ln RAD_i = CB_R \ln R + C\alpha\epsilon \ln W_i + Cr_H E - C\delta\epsilon i - C\epsilon \ln \delta_o, \tag{A.9}$$

where $\ln R$ is the logarithm of full wealth. The inclusion of full wealth, or income, in the health flow demand curve rests on the assumption that the utility gained from good health is not negligible.

Appendix B. Empirical Application

This appendix describes the procedures followed by Grossman to implement empirically his theoretical model of the demand for health. The demand curve for the stock of health is derived from the equation that equates user cost with the marginal efficiency of health capital,

$$\ln \frac{W_i G_i}{\pi_i} = \ln (r - \tilde{\pi}_i + \delta_i).$$

The conversion of health stock, H_i, to the observable variable healthy days, h_i, is accomplished by the selection of the following production function for healthy days, $h_i = 365 - BH_i^{-c}$. This function generates a diminishing marginal product of health in producing healthy days, a condition necessary for a down-ward sloping MEC schedule, and gives

$$G_i = \frac{\partial h_i}{\partial H_i} = BC \, H_i^{-(c+1)}.$$

If one assumes a zero interest rate and constant marginal costs over time (i.e., $\pi_i = 1$), we obtain the following demand curve for the stock of health:

$$\ln H_i = \epsilon \ln W_i - \epsilon \ln \delta_i - \epsilon \ln \pi_i, \tag{B.1}$$

where ϵ is the elasticity of the marginal efficiency of capital schedule.

Both δ_i and π_i are unobservable in Equation (B.1), the demand curve for the stock of health. It is necessary to convert both δ_i and π_i into observable variables. The following form for the depreciation rate on the stock of health capital is used, $\delta_i = \delta_o \, e^{\delta_i}$ or, equivalently,

$$\ln \delta_i = \ln \delta_o + \delta_i.$$

Investment in health capital is subject to depreciation. Net investment in the stock of health equals gross investment minus depreciation, $H_{i+1} - H_i = I_i - \delta_i H_i$, where δ_i is the depreciation rate on the stock of health capital in period i. This equation states that the stock of health in any period $k > i$ can be written as a function of the stock of health in period i, H_i, previous depreciation rates, and previous health investment.

The individual is faced with a time constraint that requires him to allocate all of his time to some activity. Letting TT represent the total amount of time in any period, the time constraint can be written as:

$$TT = TW_i + T_i + TH_i + TL_i, \tag{B.3}$$

where TW_i represents hours of work and TL_i represents the time lost from market and nonmarket activities due to illness. It is important to distinguish sick time, TL_i, from TH_i, the time allocated to the production of health. Sick time is assumed to be entirely lost; it cannot be used in either nonmarket or market production.[24]

The individual also is constrained in that the present value of lifetime earnings and nonwage income must equal the sum of the present value of lifetime consumption. This constraint can be written as

$$\sum_{i=0}^{n} \frac{(PM_i + FX_i)}{(1+r)^i} = \sum_{i=0}^{n} \frac{W_i \, TW_i}{(1+r)^i} + A_o, \tag{B.4}$$

where

---

24. This assumption is made primarily to avoid the consideration of joint production in the household, a problem that is difficult both theoretically and empirically.

$P =$ price of medical care assumed constant in all time periods,

$F =$ price of the aggregate commodity assumed constant in all time periods,

$W_i =$ wage rate in period i,

$TW_i =$ time worked in period, i,

$A_o =$ initial assets, and

$r =$ rate of interest.

Solving Equation (B.3) for TW_i, these restrictions can be written in terms of full wealth, $W_i TT$, spent in producing health, the aggregate commodity and time lost due to sickness as follows:[25]

$$\sum_{i=0}^{n} \frac{\{PN_i + FX_i + W_i(T_i + TH_i + TL_i)\}}{(1 + r)^i} + \sum_{i=0}^{n} \frac{W_i TT}{(1 + r)^i} + A_o. \tag{B.5}$$

The total cost of gross investment in health, $PM_i + W_i TH_i$, can be written as $\pi_i I_i$, and the total cost of producing the aggregate commodity, $FX_i + W_i T_i$, can be replaced by $C_i Z_i$, where π_i and C_i are the average and marginal costs, respectively, of producing health and the aggregate commodity.[26]

The first-order condition necessary to find the optimum stock of health in period i comes from the differentiation of the Lagrangian containing the intertemporal utility function with respect to gross investment.

$$G_i[W_i + (UH_i/\lambda)(1 + r)^i] = \pi_{i-1}(r - \tilde{\pi}_{i-1} + \delta_i), \tag{B.6}$$

where

$h_i =$ the number of healthy days, $(\Omega - TL_i)$, in period i,

$Uh_i =$ the partial derivative of the utility function with respect to healthy days in period i;

$G_i =$ the marginal product of the stock of health in the production of healthy days, and

$\pi_{i-1} =$ the percentage rate of change in the marginal cost of producing health,

$$\left(\tilde{\pi}_{i=1} = \frac{\pi_i - \pi_{i-1}}{\pi_{i-1}} \right)$$

$R =$ lifetime full wealth,

$$\sum_{i=0}^{n} \frac{W\Omega}{(1 + r)^i} + A_o.$$

25. The total gross investment quantities I_i and Z_i are used rather than the individual inputs in the production functions because of the empirical difficulties in obtaining data that allow the separation of TH_i and T_i.

26. The equality of average and marginal cost in the product of both health and the aggregate commodity results from the first-degree homogeneity of the production functions for both commodities.

By dividing by π_{i-1}, the left side of Equation (B.6) is the marginal efficiency of health capital, MEC. The MEC schedule consists of the monetary rate of return on psychic components of utility,

$$\frac{G_i(Uh_i/\lambda)(1+r)^i}{\pi_{i-1}},$$

and the rate of return in the labor market, π_{i-1}, derived from health capital. The right side of Equation (B.6) is the user cost of health capital, consisting of the rate at which interest income is foregone, r, the rate of capital gain or loss, $\tilde{\pi} - 1$, and the rate of depreciation, δ. The optimal stock of health capital is that stock where the marginal efficiency of capital equals the user cost of capital.

Appendix C. Functional Scales

The questions used for calculating the mental and physical health scales were q55; q110a, b; q54; q71; q72a, b, c; q73a, b, c; q63c; q70a (1969 Questionnaire).

For each health dimension, the following scale was used:

Rating	Level of functioning
1	excellent
2	good
3	mildly impaired
4	moderately impaired
5	severely impaired
6	totally impaired

To make scoring uniform, responses of 4 on q54 and 1102 were converted to a value of 3 creating the following ratings.

Rating	Condition
1	No more than one question may have a 2 response
2	(a) No response poorer than 2, or (b) One 3 response if remainder are 1, or (c) One 3 response, plus one 1 response, the rest 2's
3	(a) One 3 response, the rest 2's, or (b) Two 3 responses, plus one 1 response, and one 2 (if the fourth question is applicable)
4	Two or more 3 responses, no 1 responses

These ratings originally were modified by response to q144a, but discontinuation of this question in subsequent rounds necessitated its removal.

The following combinations of responses to the eight items on physical health were assigned the following ratings:

Rating	Condition
1	Self-assessed health better than that of others, no mobility or activity limitations, full-time work possible or being performed.
2	Self-assessed health better than that of others, or same as that of others; may have some mobility or activity limitations but can, or does, work full time.
3	Self-assessed health worse than that of others; may have some mobility or activity limitations, but can, or does, work full time.
4	At most may be able to work part time; unable to go outside and/or use public transportation unaided, but is not housebound.
5	Cannot, and does not, do any work; housebound.

These ratings were modified if the respondent spent 14 or more nights in a hospital in the previous year or had postponed medical treatment. The respondent scale value was increased by one rating point indicating a poorer state of health. The use of 14 days of hospitalization as a modifier is based upon the average number of days persons aged 45–64 spent in a hospital in 1968.[27] Two weeks of hospitalization also appears to be the guide used by medical practitioners in determining whether a previous health condition has an impact on health a year later.[28] Treatment postponement indicates that there is a health problem that needs attention, indicating that the respondent is not as well as reported. Finally, if a respondent received disability payments because of determined physical impairments, his rating also was adjusted to reflect the influence of this physical health disability.

27. See Fillenbaum and Maddox [2].
28. Ibid.

References

[1] Binstock, R. H., and E. Shanas, *Aging and the Social Sciences* (New York: Van Nostrand Reinhold Company, 1976).

[2] Fillenbaum, G. G., and G. L. Maddox, *Assessing the Functional State of LRHS Participants* (Durham, N.C.: Center for Aging and Human Development, 1977).

[3] Grossman, Michael, *The Demand for Health: A Theoretical and Empirical Investigation* (New York: National Bureau of Economic Research, Inc., 1972).

[4] Maddox, G. L., and E. B. Douglass, "Self-assessment of Health: A Longitudinal Study of Elderly Subjects," *Journal of Health and Social Behavior,* 14 (Fall 1973), 87–93.

[5] Martin, J., and A. Doran, "Evidence Concerning the Relationship Between Health and Retirement," *Sociological Review,* 14 (Nov. 1966), 340–342.

[6] Ostfeld, A., "Frequency and Nature of Health Problems of Retired Persons," pp. 83–96 in F. M. Carp (Ed.), *The Retirement Process,* Public Health Service Publication No. 1778 (Washington, D.C.: U.S. Government Printing Office, 1968).

[7] Parsons, D. O., "Health, Family Structure and Labor Supply," *American Economic Review,* 67 (Sept. 1977), 703–711.

[8] Reynolds, W. J., W. A. Rushing and D. L. Miles, "The Validation of a Functional Status Index," *Journal of Health and Social Behavior,* 15 (Fall 1974), 24–38.

[9] Social Security Administration, *Longitudinal Retirement History Study,* 1969–1973 (Washington, D.C.: U.S. Government Printing Office).

[10] Streib, G. F., and C. J. Schneider, *Retirement in American Society* (London and Ithaca, N.Y.: Cornell University Press, 1971).

[11] Thompson, W., and G. F. Streib, "Situational Determinants: Health and Economic Deprivation in Retirement," *Journal of Social Issues,* 14 (Mar. 1958), 20–32.

[12] Wonnacott, R. J., and T. H. Wonnacott, *Econometrics* (New York: John Wiley & Sons, Inc., 1970).

Retirement Patterns of Self-Employed Workers *Joseph F. Quinn*

According to census estimates, the proportion of the nonagricultural labor force that is self-employed has been decreasing steadily. Since 1940, for instance, the percentage of men who are self-employed has fallen from 14.8 percent to 7.7 percent (1970), while the proportion of self-employed women has decreased from 7.4 to 3.4 percent in the same time period.[1] Older workers, comprise a disproportionate share of the self-employed. David Smallwood [3] reports that in 1976 over 28 percent of workers 65 and over covered by social security were self-employed compared to less than 6 percent of those under 30. The progression with age is monotonic and shows a marked jump around age 60. In the data used for this research (men and nonmarried women aged 58–63), over 12 percent of employed men and over 6 percent of the women described themselves as self-employed. This cross-sectional age trend probably is the result of both cohort and longitudinal effects. The first refers to the fact that since the relative size of the self-employed sector is shrinking, one might expect a larger proportion of the older cohorts, at any given time, to be self-employed. Compounding this situation, however, may be a tendency for some of the members of any given cohort to move from wage and salary employment to self-employment in their later years for reasons described below.

The self-employed work in an institutional environment substantially different from that of wage and salary workers. The self-employed generally are not affected by compulsory retirement rules, and are much less likely to be covered by pension plans. In addition, the self-employed are less constrained by institutional rules concerning vacation time and the length of the work week, and should be more able to vary the amount and kind of labor supplied. The lack of compulsory retirement provisions and the relative flexibility with respect to hours suggest that the self-employed may be more able to withdraw gradually from the labor force than their wage and salary counterparts. Given the psychological and financial trauma that often accompanies a sudden and complete retirement, this option to withdraw slowly may be an important advantage of self-employed status. These advantages may induce career self-employed individuals to remain in the labor force longer than those in wage and salary jobs,

This research was supported by a grant from the Social Security Administration and was begun while I was a visitor at the Institute for Research on Poverty at the University of Wisconsin—Madison. I would like to thank Steve Woodbury, Joel Bolnick, and Karen McCormick for their assistance.

1. See [5, Table 80]. The percentages are proportions of the nonagricultural sector. Prior to 1966, the population included workers over 13; since then, it has included only workers over 15.

and may induce some of the latter to shift to the self-employed sector in later years.

In previous studies of retirement issues, the self-employed are usually either excluded completely from the analysis, or included with the much larger number of wage and salary workers. In the former case, nothing is learned about the retirement decisions of the self-employed. In the latter, any unique relationships are swamped by the rest of the sample. In this research we concentrate specifically on the retirement patterns of the self-employed, and in particular on the extent and correlates of gradual labor force withdrawal.

Frequently during the analysis we will attempt to differentiate between two types of self-employed—career and recent. The former are respondents who have spent a major or significant portion of their work lives as self-employed individuals. The latter are workers who only recently have become self-employed, and who may be using their new employment as a form of partial retirement. Although it is difficult to differentiate these two groups clearly, we have decided on the following operational definition: an individual is considered as "career" self-employed if he or she

    i. Is currently self-employed, and has worked at that job for eleven or more years, or

    ii. Is currently self-employed, and was also self-employed on the last job, or

    iii. Is currently out of the labor force, but was self-employed on the last job for eleven or more years, or

    iv. Was self-employed on the longest job of his or her career.

Anyone who does not fit into one of these categories, and who is self-employed on the current job, or out of the labor force but self-employed on the last job, is classified as "recent" self-employed. According to this definition, 87.5 percent of our sample of white married men are "career" self-employed; the remaining 12.5 percent are "recent." The latter percentage, though small, does offer some support for the longitudinal explanation of the cross-sectional age trend mentioned above.

The self-employed are an important group for analysis for at least two reasons. Despite declining numbers, they still represent a significant proportion of the work force and one that is disproportionately comprised of older workers. Due to well-known demographic trends, the ratio of older to younger workers is expected to grow, resulting in continued financial problems for the social security system. These problems might be alleviated if more older workers were to move from full-time employment to partial retirement (some via self-employment), rather than directly to complete labor force withdrawal as is usually the case. At present, the self-employed are more likely to do this, and we may be able to learn about this phenomenon by observing their retirement patterns. A second, related reason for studying the self-employed stems from recently legislated changes in early retirement laws. These provisions, delaying mandatory retire-ment from 65 to 70, will remove a constraint from the decisions of many workers aged 65–69. We may be able to gain some insight into how they will react by studying a group currently without such constraints, namely, those who work for themselves. This assumes, however, that the self-employed and wage and salary workers are similar enough in other respects (in utility functions) that such extrapolation is meaningful. This, unfortunately, may not be the case.

In the sections below, we first present a description of the data we have utilized, and, via cross-tabulations, the sample of self-employed individuals we have extracted. The distributions are frequently compared to those of the much larger number of wage and salary workers. The empirical sections consist of a discussion of the wage determinants of self-employed workers, and the correlates of labor force status, self-defined retirement status (a three-way breakdown) and hours of work. Finally, we end with a discussion of the implications of these results for the future, given the demographic trends mentioned above.

Data Source and Sample

The sample for this research is drawn from the 1969 wave of the Social Security Administration's Retirement History Study (RHS), and consists of 833 white married men aged 58–63 in 1969. Each man was either self-employed in 1969, or out of the labor force but self-employed on his last job.[2] We have eliminated the self-employed in agricultural occupations and those who were bedridden or housebound. The wage and salary sample, used for comparison purposes, includes 4845 white married men. Again, we have excluded agricultural occupations, and the bedridden and housebound. In all the cross-tabulations, the observations are weighted, so that the numbers and proportions represent population estimates.

The nonagricultural self-employed are found in all industries and occupa-tions. Among this group, over 60 percent are managers or professionals (mostly managers)—a figure much higher than the 25 percent for wage and salary work-ers (Table 1). The self-employed are less likely to be craftsmen, and much less likely to be operatives, than others. Compared to the career self-employed, the recent self-employed have an occupational distribution closer to that of the wage and salary personnel. They are less likely than the long-term self-employed to be professionals or managers, and more likely to be in sales, crafts, or laborer occupations.

Industrial breakdowns also show considerable contrast. The self-employed

2. In this self-employed category, there were also 69 white nonmarried men, 122 white nonmar-ried women, and a total of 53 nonwhites. To allow complete interaction between race, sex, and marital status and the other variables, these demographic groups were not combined. This research is based only on the largest subsample, white married men.

Table 1. *Occupation and industry, white married men aged 58–63, 1969*

Occupation and industry	Self-employed			Wage and salary
	All	Career	Recent	
Total number (thousands)	493.5	432.2	61.3	2878.6
Occupation (percent)[a]				
Total	100.0	100.0	100.0	100.0
Professional	13.1	14.2	5.9	10.0
Manager	47.8	49.4	35.9	15.0
Sales	7.7	7.1	12.4	5.1
Crafts	17.6	16.2	27.6	28.2
Operatives	5.2	5.0	6.9	20.7
Service	4.4	4.7	1.9	8.0
Laborers	2.4	1.5	8.5	6.2
Others[b]	1.7	1.9	0.9	6.9
Industry (percent)				
Total	100.0	100.0	100.0	100.0
Agriculture, forestry, mining	3.3	2.8	6.6	2.3
Construction	14.4	13.4	21.9	10.6
Manufacturing	5.8	5.5	7.6	36.7
Transportation, communications, public utilities	3.4	3.2	4.8	10.5
Trade	36.0	36.7	31.1	13.0
Finance, insurance, real estate	6.1	6.3	4.8	4.8
Service (except professional)	19.5	19.8	17.2	4.8
Professional service	10.9	12.0	2.9	9.5
Unknown	0.7	0.4	3.0	0.2
Public administration	0.0	0.0	0.0	7.6

[a] Sample excludes respondents reporting farmer, farm manager, farm laborer, or farm foreman as their occupation.
[b] Clerical, private household, and unknown.
Source: [4].

are much less frequently found in manufacturing, and almost never in public administration, and are much more frequently in the trade and service sectors (nearly 67 percent). The largest differences between career and recent self-employed are found in professional service (nearly all career) and construction (disproportionately recent) industries.

Overall, nearly 10 percent of this self-employed population is out of the labor force (Table 2). Although this figure is not dramatically different from the 12.9 percent of wage and salary workers, there are substantially different patterns by age. In the wage and salary sector, there is a noticeable jump between the 60–61-year-olds and those 62–63. This does not occur among the self-employed, where the age progression is smoother. The recent self-employed are more likely to be out of the labor force than are the career self-employed (15.1 vs. 8.9 percent), a fact that may reflect the relatively high failure rate of new businesses.

Table 2. *Labor force status, white married men aged 58–63, by age, 1969*

Labor force status	Total	Age 58–59	Age 60–61	Age 62–63
Self-employed—all				
Total (thousands)	493.5	178.7	156.7	158.1
In labor force	90.3%	92.5%	90.2%	87.9%
Out of labor force	9.7%	7.5%	9.8%	12.1%
Self-employed—career				
Total (thousands)	432.2	156.7	134.9	140.6
In labor force	91.1%	93.3%	91.2%	88.4%
Out of labor force	8.9%	6.7%	8.8%	11.6%
Self-employed—recent				
Total (thousands)	61.3	22.0[a]	21.8[a]	17.5[a]
In labor force	84.9%	86.8%	84.1%	83.5%
Out of labor force	15.1%	13.2%	15.9%	16.5%
Wage and salary workers				
Total (thousands)	2878.6	1061.3	955.2	862.0
In labor force	87.1%	93.1%	88.0%	78.8%
Out of labor force	12.9%	6.9%	12.0%	21.2%

[a] Based on between 25 and 50 observations.
Source: [4].

A further disaggregation by health status is revealing, and indicates the tremendous importance of health.[3] Of the self-employed with a health condition that limits the type or amount of work they can do, over 21 percent have withdrawn from the labor force (Table 3). Among those with no such limitation, fewer than 4 percent are out. As in the aggregate, there is no dramatic jump in labor force withdrawal among those aged 62–63.

The latter finding suggests that social security eligibility may be less important as a labor force status determinant for the self-employed than it is for wage and salary workers. A more direct approach to the social security question is to look directly at current social security status. We have defined as "currently eligible" anyone who either is receiving social security benefits or expects to receive them in the future and is currently at least 62 years old.[4] Overall, there is a much higher percentage of those currently eligible for social security who are out of the labor force (20.7 percent) than there is among those who are ineligible (5.0 percent). When we disaggregate by health status, we find that the same pattern applies in each subgroup (Table 4). Among those with some health limitation, over 36 percent of the eligibles are out of the labor force, whereas only 11 percent of those currently ineligible are out of the labor force.

3. This dichotomous health status variable was based on the answer to the following survey question: Does your health limit the kind or amount of work or housework you can do?
4. It is important to emphasize that social security (or pension) eligibility refers to *current* eligibility, not to mere coverage or participation in a program. A respondent who currently is eligible would immediately be eligible for benefits if he were to withdraw from the labor force.

Table 3. *Labor force status, white married men aged 58–63, by age and health status, 1969*

Labor force status	Total	Age 58–59	Age 60–61	Age 62–63
Self-employed—all				
No health limitation				
Total (thousands)	317.7	118.0	106.4	93.3
In labor force	96.6%	98.5%	96.2%	94.6%
Out of labor force	3.4%	1.5%	3.8%	5.4%
Some health limitation				
Total (thousands)	175.9	60.7	50.3	64.8
In labor force	78.9%	80.7%	77.6%	78.2%
Out of labor force	21.1%	19.3%	22.4%	21.8%
Wage and salary workers				
No health limitation				
Total (thousands)	2059.6	791.1	676.1	592.4
In labor force	95.2%	98.5%	96.9%	88.8%
Out of labor force	4.8%	1.5%	3.1%	11.2%
Some health limitation				
Total (thousands)	819.0	270.2	279.1	269.7
In labor force	66.9%	77.3%	66.5%	56.8%
Out of labor force	33.1%	22.7%	33.5%	43.2%

Source. [4].

Table 4. *Labor force status, white married men aged 58–63, by health and social security eligibility status, 1969*

Labor force status	Currently ineligible	Currently eligible	Perhaps eligible[a]
Self-employed—all			
No health limitation			
Total (thousands)	228.1	79.8	9.7[b]
In labor force	97.7%	92.9%	
Out of labor force	2.3%	7.1%	
Some health limitation			
Total (thousands)	102.1	69.8	3.9[b]
In labor force	89.0%	63.7%	
Out of labor force	11.0%	36.3%	
Wage and salary workers			
No health limitation			
Total (thousands)	1487.2	539.9	32.5
In labor force	97.8%	88.3%	
Out of labor force	2.2%	11.7%	
Some health limitation			
Total (thousands)	467.0	346.4	5.6[b]
In labor force	84.7%	42.5%	
Out of labor force	15.3%	57.5%	

[a] Men who are currently 62 or 63 years of age, and who don't know whether they expect to receive social security benefits in the future.

[b] Fewer than 25 observations.

Source: [4].

Table 5. *Labor force status, white married men aged 58–63, by pension eligibility status, 1969*

Labor force status	Currently ineligible	Currently eligible
Self-employed—all		
Total (thousands)	465.6	27.8[a]
In labor force	90.4%	87.7%
Out of labor force	9.6%	12.3%
Wage and salary workers		
Total (thousands)	2054.9	823.7
In labor force	90.5%	78.6%
Out of labor force	9.5%	21.4%

[a] Based on between 25 and 50 observations.
Source [4].

Of those in good health, the respective figures are 7.1 and 2.3 percent.[5] Although these are noticeable differences, they are smaller than the differences observed for wage and salary personnel. Here the proportion out of the labor force varies from 2.2 to 11.7 percent (for those with no health limitations), and from 15.3 to 57.5 percent (for the others), depending on social security eligibility status. More precise estimates of this effect will be obtained in the multivariate analysis described below.

Conclusions concerning pension eligibility are difficult to draw, since less than 6 percent of those self-employed (4.3 percent of the career and 15.5 percent of the recent) currently are eligible. Although more of those eligible are out of the labor force (and this is true for the career and recent subsets), the differences are small, and less than those for the wage and salary sector (Table 5). This is one case where the dichotomous labor force description (one is either in or out) is inadequate, since we find interesting pension effects when a trichotomous subjective retirement variable is used.

5. These figures appear to support the hypothesis of a social security effect, and therefore appear contradictory to the age patterns discussed above. The difference may be that these eligibility comparisons reflect at least three effects: a social security eligibility effect, an age effect, and a disability effect. The last occurs because those eligible for and receiving benefits via the disability provisions of the Social Security Act are defined as currently eligible, and, of course, are very likely to be out of the labor force. Since disabled beneficiaries can be less than 62, these respondents will both reduce the labor force participation contrast by age, and heighten it when the population is disaggregated by current social security eligibility status. Conclusions from the latter comparison should be drawn with some care, since the direction of causation is not solely from eligibility status to labor force participation. This is particularly true for the disabled eligibles, who in many cases are forced to retire by disabling conditions, and then turn to social security for benefits.

Among those with no health limitations, the disability complication should not arise, and only the social security eligibility and age effects remain. In this subsample, 2.3 percent of those currently ineligible and 7.1 percent of those eligible have withdrawn from the labor force, offering mild support for a social security effect (Table 4). Both age and eligibility status probably are correlated with other important determinants, so better estimates of their individual effects require multivariate analysis. This is discussed below.

Since we are interested in the reasons for retirement, we present in Table 6 the subjective reasons given for leaving their last jobs by those men out of the labor force. For the self-employed, the overwhelming response is health. Over 80 percent of those who answered named health, and most of the remainder simply claimed they wanted to retire. For wage and salary workers, these reasons also were the most frequent responses given, but the disparity was not as great. Overall, two-thirds named health (and the percentage grew with years out of the labor force), and nearly one-fourth claimed they wanted to retire. The importance of health, although perhaps overstated here, will be confirmed in the multivariate results.

Finally, we explore the importance of labor force status on the financial well being of the self-employed, and compare it to figures for wage and salary workers. Distributions of family income, disaggregated by labor force status of both husband and wife, are found in Table 7. On average, the self-employed have lower incomes than others. The medians are lower for all four subgroups (especially for families with the wife in the labor force), and there are substantially

Table 6. *Reasons for retiring from last regular job, white married men aged 58–63 who are out of the labor force, by years since last regular job, 1969*

Retirement reason	Total	Less than 3 years	3–6 years	More than 6 years
Self-employed—all				
Total (thousands)	47.9	18.9	21.0	8.0
Number answering	43.9	16.1	20.3[a]	7.5[b]
Health	80.4%	79.0%	79.9%	
Too old or wanted to retire	15.7%	14.0%	17.3%	
Pension or social security	0.0%	0.0%	0.0%	
Job terminated	2.6%	3.5%	2.8%	
Other[c]	1.3%	3.5%	0.0%	
Wage and salary workers				
Total (thousands)	370.7[d]	174.1	128.2	65.0
Number answering	352.9	164.4	124.7	63.8
Health	66.3%	50.5%	76.7%	86.5%
Too old or wanted to retire	24.2%	37.8%	15.9%	5.3%
Pension or social security	1.2%	1.4%	1.4%	0.0%
Job terminated	2.5%	3.5%	1.4%	1.9%
Other[c]	5.9%	6.8%	4.6%	6.4%

[a] Based on between 25 and 50 observations.

[b] Based on fewer than 25 observations.

[c] Compulsory, personal or other.

[d] Slightly larger than the sum of the three components because of a few respondents who did not answer the question on years since last job.

Source: [4].

Table 7. *Annual family income, white married men aged 58–63, by labor force status and wife's labor force status, 1969*

Income class	Spouse out of LF[a]		Spouse in LF[a]	
	Respondent out of LF (1)	Respondent in LF (2)	Respondent out of LF (3)	Respondent in LF (4)
Self-employed—all				
Total (thousands)	33.6	239.0	14.3	206.6
Reporting family income	20.2[b]	167.3	10.8[c]	141.8
$0–1,999	25.7%	7.2%		3.6%
2,000–4,999	43.1%	19.5%		18.7%
5,000–7,499	11.3%	20.6%		20.4%
7,500–9,999	5.7%	18.1%		16.7%
10,000–14,999	8.6%	16.4%		21.1%
15,000+	5.6%	18.2%		19.6%
(Median income)[d]	($4,240)	($7,830)	($4,893)	($8,368)
Wage and salary workers				
Total (thousands)	250.7	1507.0	120.1	1000.8
Reporting family income	191.9	1195.5	100.5	808.4
$0–1,999	16.2%	1.8%	4.1%	0.6%
2,000–4,999	39.0%	11.5%	23.5%	5.0%
5,000–7,499	18.5%	26.6%	24.8%	13.5%
7,500–9,999	13.7%	25.2%	24.5%	21.3%
10,000–14,999	9.0%	22.9%	17.4%	38.6%
15,000+	3.6%	11.9%	5.7%	21.1%
(Median income)[e]	($4,589)	($8,496)	($7,254)	($11,256)

[a] LF = labor force.
[b] Based on between 25 and 50 observations.
[c] Fewer than 25 observations.
[d] Computed with $500 intervals.
[e] Computed with $2,500 intervals.
Source: [4].

more self-employed in each subgroup in the lowest two income intervals (less than $5000). In families where the self-employed husband is in the labor market, the wife's labor force status makes very little difference in the distribution. This is probably because the wife often works in the business, rather than drawing a separate paycheck, as would a wage and salary spouse.

As mentioned above, this dichotomous description of retirement status (in or out of the labor force) overlooks the possibility of gradual labor force withdrawal, a phenomenon that may be important among the self-employed. To investigate this, we utilize a three-way subjective characterization in which respondents describe themselves as either completely retired, partly retired, or not retired. Over 20 percent of this self-employed sample consider themselves retired (Table 8). Eight percent consider themselves completely retired, 12 percent describe themselves as partly retired, and nearly 80 percent report they are not retired. Among recent self-employed, the percentage retired is even

Table 8. *Subjective retirement status, white married men aged 58–63, by labor force status, 1969*

Labor force status	Total	Completely retired	Partly retired	Not retired
Self-employed—all[a]				
Total (thousands)	493.0	40.8	61.3	390.9
(Horizontal percent)	(100.0)	(8.3)	(12.4)	(79.3)
In labor force	90.3%	11.0%	86.7%	99.1%
Out of labor force	9.7%	89.0%	13.3%	0.9%
Self-employed—career				
Total (thousands)	431.7	31.2	53.6	346.9
(Horizontal percent)	(100.0)	(7.2)	(12.4)	(80.4)
In labor force	91.0%	5.4%	85.9%	99.5%
Out of labor force	9.0%	94.6%	14.1%	0.5%
Self-employed—recent				
Total (thousands)	61.3	9.7[b]	7.6[b]	44.0
(Horizontal percent)	(100.0)	(15.8)	(12.4)	(71.8)
In labor force	84.9%			96.0%
Out of labor force	15.1%			4.0%
Wage and salary workers				
Total (thousands)	2877.3	338.6	151.6	2387.1
(Horizontal percent)	(100.0)	(11.8)	(5.3)	(83.0)
In labor force	87.1%	4.6%	76.2%	99.5%
Out of labor force	12.9%	95.4%	23.8%	0.5%

[a] The number of self-employed is slightly less than in previous tables because of one respondent who did not answer the subjective retirement status question. This is true for all tables that include this variable.
[b] Fewer than 25 observations.
Source: [4].

higher—nearly 30 percent. These patterns are quite different from those of wage and salary workers. Among the latter, only 17 percent are retired, and these are disproportionately completely retired. Only 5 percent of the wage and salary workers are partly retired, compared to 12 percent of both groups of self-employed.

Since the respondents may define partial retirement in a number of ways, it is useful to compare this dimension with more objective measures of labor supply. As Table 8 illustrates, subjective retirement status correlates highly with labor force status. Almost all of those "not retired" are in the labor force, and most of those "completely" retired are out. Among the partly retired, there is more diversity. Seven-eighths of the self-employed and three-fourths of the wage and salary respondents were in the labor force at the time of the survey.

In Table 9, we have estimated annual hours of work, and our figures suggest that the completely retired, partly retired, and those not retired are very different groups. Among the self-employed who are not retired at all, we estimate that 82 percent work more than 2,000 hours per year, over 50 percent work 2,500

Table 9. *Annual hours of work, white married men aged 58–63, by subjective retirement status*

Hours of work	Total	Completely retired	Partly retired	Not retired
Self-employed—all				
Total (thousands)	493.0	40.8	61.3	391.0
Reporting annual hours	446.6	40.8	55.6	350.1
0 hours	11.3%	(89.0%)	15.7%	1.5%
1–499	1.4%	4.2%	5.1%	0.5%
500–999	3.5%	4.1%	10.4%	2.4%
1,000–1,499	5.2%	1.3%	(20.0%)	3.4%
1,500–1,999	10.9%	0.0%	22.0%	10.5%
2,000–2,499	(26.5%)[a]	0.0%	15.8%	31.3%
2,500–2,999	16.4%	0.0%	3.2%	(20.3%)
3,000+	24.8%	1.4%	7.9%	30.2
Wage and salary workers				
Total (thousands)	2877.3	338.6	151.6	2387.1
Reporting annual hours	2736.1	335.3	140.9	2260.0
0 hours	14.5%	(96.6%)	26.4%	1.6%
1–499	0.4%	0.3%	8.5%	2.1%
500–999	1.0%	0.3%	11.0%	0.5%
1,000–1,499	2.0%	0.9%	(14.7%)	1.4%
1,500–1,999	6.4%	0.2%	11.8%	7.0%
2,000–2,499	(61.7%)	1.2%	21.8%	(73.2%)
2,500–2,999	8.4%	0.3%	3.7%	9.9%
3,000+	5.0%	0.2%	2.0%	5.9%

[a] Parentheses denote interval containing median hours.
Source: [4].

hours or more, and nearly one-third work over 3,000 hours. The median is slightly over 2,500 hours. Even the partly retired appear to put in long hours. Over one-fourth have estimated annual hours over 2,000 and two-thirds work 1,000 hours or more, with a median of around 1,500 hours. Over 90 percent of those who describe themselves as completely retired supply 0 hours, and of those who are in the labor force, nearly all work less than 1,000 hours per year.[6]

6. Because of the derivation of the annual hours estimates, these distributions may exaggerate the annual labor supply of some of the self-employed, especially for the partly retired. All respondents were asked how many hours per week they usually worked at their job. We have combined this with an estimate of weeks per year to arrive at our annual hours figure.

When asked about earnings, respondents could answer in any time unit, from per hour to per year. Those who answered per year (that is, reported an annual salary) were then asked how many weeks per year they usually worked. For these individuals, nearly 58 percent of the self-employed sample, the annual hours estimate is simply the product of hours per week and weeks per year. Those who reported a monthly salary, another 7 percent of the sample, were asked how many months per year they worked, and we have estimated their annual hours as 4.33 (weeks/month) times (months/year) times (hours/week). The other 35 percent of the self-employed sample, however, were asked neither about weeks or months per year. In the absence of these data, we have assumed full-year work, and have multiplied our hours per week figure by 52. For those

Table 10. *Subjective retirement status, white married men aged 58–63, by health status and age, 1969*

Retirement status	Total	Aged 58–59	Aged 60–61	Aged 62–63
Self-employed—all				
No health limitation				
Total (thousands)	317.1	118.0	106.4	92.8
Completely retired	2.3%	0.5%	2.2%	4.8%
Partly retired	9.1%	5.4%	10.5%	12.1%
Not retired	88.6%	94.1%	87.3%	83.1%
Some health limitation				
Total (thousands)	175.9	60.7	50.3	64.8
Completely retired	19.0%	16.3%	19.0%	21.6%
Partly retired	18.4%	18.3%	17.5%	19.2%
Not retired	62.6%	65.4%	63.5%	59.2%
Wage and salary workers				
No health limitation				
Total (thousands)	2058.3	791.1	674.9	592.3
Completely retired	4.3%	1.1%	2.9%	10.2%
Partly retired	3.4%	1.5%	3.5%	5.9%
Not retired	92.3%	97.4%	93.6%	84.0%
Some health limitation				
Total (thousands)	819.0	270.2	279.1	269.7
Completely retired	30.5%	20.6%	30.8%	40.2%
Partly retired	9.9%	7.2%	7.7%	14.9%
Not retired	59.6%	72.2%	61.5%	44.9%

Source: [4].

The self-employed hours distribution is considerably higher than the wage and salary distribution, which is dominated by the tremendous mode of full time workers around 2,000 hours. Two-thirds of self-employed workers have estimated annual hours of over 2,000, as have one-fourth of the partly retired. Despite some errors in measurement noted in footnote 7, the self-employed appear to be an extremely hard-working group, working long hours frequently at relatively low wages.

Table 10 illustrates again that health is an important determinant of retire-

---

whose labor supply reduction consists of reducing weeks per year rather than hours per week, this calculation will result in an overestimation of annual labor supply.

We can get an indication of the reasonableness of the full-year assumption by looking at the distribution of weeks per year and months per year of the "annual" and "monthly" self-employed respondents, the only ones asked these questions. Overall, 83 percent of the "annual" respondents reported that they worked 50 to 52 weeks, and 84 percent of the "monthly" respondents claimed they worked 12 months per year. Among the partly retired subset who are more likely to be supplying reduced amounts of labor than were those not retired at all, the analogous percentages are 73 and 67 percent. If these percentages can be applied to those other than the "annual" and "monthly" individuals, this indicates that the full-year assumption has some merit, but will nonetheless result in an overestimation of annual labor supply for a small number of primarily partly retired respondents.

ment status and that the percentage of the population retired (both completely and partly) rises with age. Among the self-employed with some health limitation, over one-third consider themselves retired compared to only 11 percent of the others. In all age categories, the retired who have good health are primarily partly retired, whereas among the retired who have health limitations, the distribution is even. For all age-health cells, partial retirement is much more likely among self-employed than among wage and salary workers; complete retirement is less so.

In Tables 11 and 12, we expand on earlier tables concerning social security and pension eligibility, using the trichotomous retirement status variable. As before, the probability of being retired is always higher among those currently eligible for social security, and the difference is much greater among those with a health limitation (Table 11). Among the self-employed, in contrast to wage and salary workers, partial retirement is always more frequent than complete retirement, except among the relatively small group of self-employed (14 percent)

Table 11. *Subjective retirement status, white married men aged 58–63, by health and social security eligibility status, 1969*

Retirement status	Currently ineligible	Currently eligible	Perhaps eligible[a]
Self-employed—all			
No health limitation			
Total (thousands)	227.6	79.8	9.7[b]
Completely retired	1.3%	5.6%	
Partly retired	8.0%	12.0%	
Not retired	90.7%	82.4%	
Some health limitation			
Total (thousands)	102.1	69.8	4.0[b]
Completely retired	8.1%	36.1%	
Partly retired	19.5%	17.1%	
Not retired	72.4%	46.9%	
Wage and salary workers			
No health limitation			
Total (thousands)	1486.0	539.9	32.5
Completely retired	2.0%	10.4%	
Partly retired	2.4%	6.1%	
Not retired	95.6%	83.5%	
Some health limitation			
Total (thousands)	467.0	346.4	5.6[b]
Completely retired	12.8%	54.7%	
Partly retired	7.8%	12.6%	
Not retired	79.4%	32.7%	

[a] Men who are 62 or 63 years of age, who "don't know" whether they expect to receive social security benefits in the future.
[b] Fewer than 25 observations.
Source: [4].

Table 12. *Subjective retirement status, white married men aged 58–63, by pension eligibility status, 1969*

Retirement status	Currently ineligible	Currently eligible
Self-employed—all		
Total (thousands)	465.6	27.4[a]
Completely retired	7.7%	18.7%
Partly retired	11.3%	32.2%
Not retired	81.0%	49.2%
Self-employed—career		
Total (thousands)	413.8	17.9[a]
Completely retired	7.0%	12.7%
Partly retired	11.7%	29.2%
Not retired	81.3%	58.2%
Self-employed—recent		
Total (thousands)	51.8	9.5[b]
Completely retired	13.2%	
Partly retired	7.8%	
Not retired	79.0%	
Wage and salary workers		
Total (thousands)	2053.7	823.6
Completely retired	8.3%	20.4%
Partly retired	4.7%	6.7%
Not retired	81.0%	72.9%

[a] Based on between 25 and 50 observations.
[b] Fewer than 25 observations.
Source: [4].

who have health limitations and currently are eligible for social security. Of this group, over half are retired, and two-thirds of those completely retired.

The pension results are interesting, particularly in light of the fact that little emerged in the dichotomous table (Table 5). Table 12 suggests that pension eligibility may have an effect on the labor supply decisions of the self-employed, but it is primarily toward inducing a movement to partial retirement status, not a movement out of the labor force.[7] Of the self-employed eligible for a pension, nearly one-third are partially retired, and another 19 percent totally retired, compared to only 11 and 8 percent, respectively, of those not eligible. This is quite different from the wage and salary sector where the effect appears to be the inducement of complete retirement.

7. Much of the difference by pension status is probably a true labor supply effect, reflecting the different amounts of labor supplied by the two eligibility groups. It is also possible, however, that certain people who are receiving pensions from previous employment consider themselves partly retired solely *because* of this pension receipt, even though they continue to work full time. The effect, in this case, would be on only the self-perception of their retirement status, rather than on their labor supply, and this would be a much less interesting and less important effect.

Table 13. *Total assets, white married men aged 58–63, by subjective retirement status*

Assets	Total	Completely retired	Partly retired	Not retired
Self-employed—all				
Total (thousands)	493.0	40.8	61.3	390.9
Reporting total assets	292.4	24.5[a]	36.2	231.8
$neg–4,999	6.6%	20.6%	4.6%	5.5%
5,000–9,999	7.8%	9.1%	12.5%	6.9%
10,000–19,999	10.0%	9.2%	11.0%	10.0%
20,000–29,999	12.4%	(16.5%)	7.9%	12.7%
30,000–49,999	(16.9%)[b]	11.9%	11.2%	(18.4%)
50,000–74,999	13.4%	6.7%	(11.1%)	14.4%
75,000–99,999	11.6%	6.9%	14.5%	11.6%
100,000+	21.2%	19.0%	27.2%	20.5%
Wage and salary workers				
Total (thousands)	2873.3	338.7	151.0	2383.6
Reporting total assets	1950.2	230.2	97.8	1672.2
$neg–4,999	12.3%	20.6%	21.5%	10.6%
5,000–9,999	11.1%	12.6%	8.7%	11.0%
10,000–19,999	19.5%	(18.3%)	17.6%	19.8%
20,000–29,999	(16.2%)	13.5%	(9.4%)	(17.0%)
30,000–49,999	19.7%	16.1%	15.9%	20.4%
50,000–74,999	9.3%	6.2%	10.2%	9.7%
75,000–99,999	4.4%	5.5%	3.5%	4.3%
100,000+	7.6%	7.2%	13.2%	7.2%

[a] Based on between 25 and 50 observations.
[b] Parentheses denote interval containing median.
Source: [4].

In Table 13 we compare the wealth distributions of self-employed and wage and salary workers by subjective retirement status.[8] Of those reporting assets, the self-employed are by far the wealthier. Their median wealth is over $40,000, compared to less than $25,000 for wage and salary workers. Among the self-employed, those partly retired are the wealthiest, with a median of over $50,000 per year and over a quarter in the over $100,000 category. The median of those not retired is slightly under $50,000, whereas for those completely retired, it is near $25,000. These wealth differences between those partly and completely retired suggest that the decision to retire may more often be voluntary for those partly retired. This hypothesis is supported by tabulations on the type of and reasons for retirement. Nearly 86 percent of those completely retired describe the end of their last regular job as unexpected, and 84 percent gave health as the retirement reason. Among the partly retired, nearly 44 percent

8. Wealth is defined as total financial assets plus the net equity in a home, business, farm, or real estate. In each case, mortgages and other debts owed have been subtracted from estimated market value.

claimed the cessation was planned, fewer than half named health as the reason, whereas over one-third said either they wanted to retire or were getting too old to work.

In summary, these tables indicate that partial retirement is a viable option among self-employed of early retirement age (58–63), and that it is more commonly chosen than is complete retirement. Because these are self-employed people, even those partly retired often work long hours, though noticeably fewer hours than those not retired. The incidence of partial retirement appears to increase with age (especially among those with good health), and is more prevalent among the respondents with health limitations. The likelihood of partial retirement appears positively correlated with social security and (especially) pension eligibility status. As with nearly all conclusions concerning retirement, health is extremely important, and many of the relationships appear quite different in separate health status subgroups.

In the wage and salary sector, partial retirement is much less common. This is probably because wage and salary workers have less discretion over hours supplied (either hours per week or weeks per year) and often may be forced to change jobs in order to reduce their labor supply. Faced with this option, many may simply withdraw completely. Also, private pensions require retirement from the covered job, and sometimes withdrawal from the industry. For the self-employed fortunate enough to have a pension, such a constraint would not exist, since eligibility, in most cases, stems from a previous job.

Model and Methodology

Cross-tabulations of a sample can be enlightening and suggestive, but they suffer from the fact that explanatory variables are usually correlated, and very few are held constant in any given table. We therefore present some multivariate regressions and logit estimates in which we attempt to identify the determinants of labor force and subjective retirement status as well as hours of work. These labor supply equations are based on a simple economic model of family behavior in which the husband and wife supply the hours of work (H_i) that maximize a family utility function subject to an income constraint.[9] From this model we derive labor supply equations for each household member in which hours supplied is a function of the wage rates facing both, the potential flow of unearned income (the amount that would accrue if neither person worked at all), and other arguments such as health status and number of dependents that reflect differences in utility functions. Finally, since this is a national sample, we have experimented with geographic variables, including SMSA (Standard Metropoli-

9. This model is outlined in more detail in Quinn [1].

tan Statistical Area) and regional dummies and measures of general business conditions.

In the first equations, the dependent labor supply variable has been collapsed into a dichotomous or trichotomous variable reflecting either labor force or subjective retirement status. In regressions on such variables, the predicted value for an individual is best interpreted as the *probability* of a particular state, and the coefficients as *changes* in the probability associated with unit changes in the explanatory variables. Because probabilities logically are bounded by 0 and 1, certain problems arise when dichotomous variables are analyzed in a regression framework. These can be alleviated by the use of nonlinear logit techniques; this is discussed below.

Specific problems arise with two of the explanatory variables. Potential family unearned income is a measure of the income flow that the family would enjoy if neither member worked, and it should include potential retirement benefits. Unfortunately, these are not available in the data. Rather than use actual retirement benefits, a clearly endogenous variable, we have reduced the social security and pension components to dichotomous eligibility variables, added an interaction between the two, and redefined the income variable as asset income only (rent, interest, dividends, and an imputed rent an owner-occupied housing).

The second problem concerns the wage term. If self-employed people do not face an infinitely elastic demand curve for their labor, then their marginal wage rate (and average wage rate, which is all we can measure here) depends on the amount of labor supplied, and therefore is endogenous. Its use will then result in biased coefficients. A standard econometric response is an instrumental variables technique, in which the actual wage is replaced by a predicted wage imputed on the basis of exogenous characteristics. This approach also solves the problem that some of the sample is out of the labor force, and therefore no wage rate can be derived from data on workers' current jobs.

In the next section, we present a brief discussion of the wage equation for self-employed men. Although this is of some interest in itself, the results are used primarily to impute wages in the labor supply results below.

Wage Equation

The wage equations below are based on a human capital view of wage determination.[10] We hypothesize that an individual's wage depends on his productivity, which is assumed to be a function of certain measurable characteristics such as education, training, experience, and health status.

In the equation chosen, we include three measures of human capital, education, experience (years at the current job), and health (a dummy reflecting

10. For a more complete description of the wage model, see Quinn [2].

the existence of a health limitation). The first two measures are entered in interval dummy form to allow nonlinearities and, in the case of education, diploma effects. The experience term can be viewed in at least two ways. First, it may proxy the accumulation of human capital—the individual gets better at the job over time. This interpretation should, but does not, include any relevant years of experience on previous jobs. A second view, however, is that it may reflect, in the case of the self-employed, the development of a clientele. We suspect both effects will be captured. In an attempt to differentiate the training and the clientele effects, we also included a more direct measure of training—that of specific vocational training. Despite the fact that this variable had been very significant in previous work with wage and salary employees, it was never significant in the self-employed wage equations, and is not included in the equations reported here.

We expanded the human capital model to include geographic variables (SMSA and four regional dummies, and a price index), and a measure of business conditions (the local employment rate). Only the SMSA dummy and a variable indicating residence in the South were significant. Finally, we ran equations with and without industrial and occupational dummies, and utilized the equations in which they were included.

The specification chosen was log-linear. In this case, the regression coefficients estimate the percentage change (rather than absolute change) in the wage rate associated with a one-unit change in the explanatory variable. The coefficients appear in Table 14.[11]

The education coefficients are reasonable and significant. There is a steady wage increase with increased education, and no evidence of the wage dip at the postgraduate level often observed with wage and salary samples. Workers with postgraduate education earn an average of over 67 percent more than those with a high school degree, who in turn earn over 20 percent more than those with less education.[12] There is evidence of strong college and high school diploma effects, and evidently no payoff for 1–3 years of college. This result is somewhat puzzling, since one would expect that diploma effects, with their signaling capabilities, would be less important in the self-employed sector.

The last three tenure variables are highly significant, indicating that returns are higher after being in business ten years. They rise further through twenty years, and then appear to taper off after that. Not surprisingly, those with health limitations earn less—almost 25 percent less—than those in good health.

11. The regression contains all those currently self-employed individuals with sufficient data to derive an hourly wage rate, and those who had been out of the labor force for fewer than five years for whom a wage could be derived from their last (self-employed) job. In the latter cases, the wages were inflated to 1969 wage levels.

12. The spread in the education coefficients is even greater when industry and occupation are excluded. This suggests that part of the payoff to education may be movement into higher paying industries and occupations. If so, the education coefficients in Table 14 underestimate this effect. Our goal, however, is to predict wages, not calculate the return to education.

Table 14. *Wage equation, white married self-employed men aged 58–63: dependent variable — 1n [wage(cents/hour)]*

Variable	Coefficient	t statistic
Years of education		
0–8	−.216	2.41
9–11	−.236	2.31
12	(—)	(—)
13–15	−.016	0.12
16	.294	2.04
17+	.666	3.86
Years at current job		
0–2	(—)	(—)
3–5	.031	0.20
6–10	.206	1.49
11–15	.350	2.57
16–20	.451	3.28
21+	.423	3.68
Existence of health		
limitation (0, 1)	−.249	3.55
Residence in the South	−.219	2.81
Residence in an SMSA	.307	4.53
Occupation		
Professional	.469	2.40
Managerial	.184	1.18
Sales	.031	0.15
Crafts	−.001	0.00
Operative	(—)	(—)
Other	.125	0.71
Industry		
Construction	.097	0.57
Manufacturing	(—)	(—)
Trade	−.402	2.80
Finance, insurance,		
real estate	.271	1.37
Service	−.219	1.47
Other	.088	0.47
Constant	5.329	
R^2	.33	
N	586	

Source: [4].

The geographic variables are both significant, which indicates that hourly returns are lower in the South and higher in SMSAs. Since these are money wages, these coefficients probably reflect cost-of-living differences, but they may also reflect business conditions. The occupational coefficients suggest that professionals and, to a lesser degree managers, tend to earn more than others. The variance of the manager coefficient occurs because that occupation encompasses a wide range of self-employed jobs, from the manager of a large self-owned firm to the proprietor of a corner grocery store. Within industries, wages appear to be highest in finance, insurance, and real estate, and lowest in the trade and service industries.

This equation explains a third of the interpersonal variation in the log of wages. This is a reasonable R^2 for a sample that already has been disaggregated by race, sex, and marital status.

Labor Supply Equations

Labor force status equations appear in Table 15. The dependent variable is labor force status, with 1 denoting in the labor force.[13] These equations indicate that it is more difficult to predict labor force status for the self-employed than for the wage and salary population. In the aggregate equation (column 1), five variables are significant (at the 5 percent, one-sided level). As in nearly all retirement research, health status plays a prominent role. The coefficient estimate here suggests that the probability of labor force participation drops nearly 14 points for those with health limitations. In addition, current social security eligibility is significant, and indicates the probability of labor force participation is over 12 points lower if one is currently eligible.[14] Although the coefficients on pension eligibility and the interaction term are insignificant, probably because of the small number of self-employed persons eligible for a pension and the even smaller number of persons eligible for both, the point estimates indicate that the effects of social security and pension eligibility are more than additive, and that an individual eligible for both has a labor force participation probability 20 points lower than he would if he were eligible for neither. The direction of the interaction is similar to that found in previous research on the non-self-employed population. The dependents term is insignificant, although the sign is as expected—the presence of dependents tends to increase the probability of labor force participation.[15] As we will see below, this tendency is confirmed in the hours equation. Finally, labor force participation probabilities are lower in the South. This coefficient (-0.042) undoubtedly overstates the causational

13. There are two changes from the functional form discussed in Section 3. First, the spouse's wage was not significant, and was dropped from the equations. Similarly, the labor market (or business conditions) indicators were consistently insignificant, suggesting the local business conditions, at least in 1969, were not an important factor. (This result should be interpreted with caution, since 1969 was a year of extremely high business activity.)

14. The sample contains a small number (16) of respondents who are receiving social security benefits, yet are less than 62 years old. Presumably these men are eligible via the disability provisions, although, oddly, five are in the labor force, and seven do not consider themselves completely retired. When these men are deleted from the aggregate equation, the health and social security terms drop slightly in magnitude, but remain highly significant. The other coefficients change very little, although the wage term does slip under the 5 percent significance level.

15. The dependents variable was entered both as a dummy, and as the number of dependents. In neither form was it significant.

Table 15. *Labor force status equations, white married self-employed men aged 58–63: dependent variable — labor force status (0, 1)*

Variable	All (1)	No health limitation (2)	Some health limitation (3)
Health limitation (0, 1)	−.138 (6.43)[a]	— —	— —
Eligible for social security (0, 1)	−.124 (5.65)	−.036 (1.90)	−.252 (5.27)
Eligible for pension (0, 1)	.050 (0.87)	.029 (0.41)	.094 (0.63)
Eligible for both (0, 1)	−.127 (1.48)	−.192 (2.49)	−.087 (0.46)
Dependents (0, 1)	.013 (0.55)	.016 (0.71)	.008 (0.13)
Imputed wage ($/hour)	.010 (1.86)	.005 (1.23)	.034 (2.02)
Asset income ($000/year)	−.008 (2.86)	−.005 (2.10)	−.014 (2.42)
South (0, 1)	−.042 (1.79)	−.022 (1.07)	−.060 (1.18)
Constant	.975	.963	.840
R^2	.14	.04	.12
N	836	534	302

[a] t statistics are in parentheses.
Source: [4].

influence of living in the South, since in many cases, this variable will be picking up the joint decision to retire and move to the South.

The wage and asset income variables are both significant and have the expected signs.[16] Labor force participation probabilities rise with an increase in the wage rate, and fall as the flow of asset income rises. Because the wage rate reported by a self-employed individual may contain a return to capital, we experimented also with an adjusted rate, for which we subtracted an imputed return to capital from the annual earnings before converting to an hourly rate.[17] The results using an imputed adjusted rate (based on an adjusted wage rate equation similar to that in the previous section of this paper) were almost identical, although the t statistic of the coefficient and the R^2 of the equation were slightly lower in the adjusted case.

Table 15 also illustrates the importance of health as an interactive term. When we disaggregate the self-employed sample by health status, we see two very different subgroups. In general, those with health limitations are more responsive to the explanatory dimensions. The clearest example is social security eligibility—the −.124 coefficient in the aggregate equation is an average of a small but significant effect among the healthy (−0.036), and a very large effect among the others (−0.252). Similarly, the health impaired have larger coefficients for both wage and asset income, suggesting more response to these factors. The one interesting exception is the social security–pension interaction term,

16. For 133 respondents (16 percent of the sample), the asset income data are missing. These data gaps were handled by the technique of pairwise deletion, in which each of the components of the $X'X$ (or correlation) matrix is estimated with only those observations with complete data on the two variables in question.

17. The logit coefficients are not reproduced here, but are available from the author.

which is large and significant for the healthy, and neither large nor significant for the others. This implies that for those in good health, neither social security nor pension eligibility alone has much impact, but eligibility for both does reduce the labor force participation probability by almost 20 points. The qualitative nature of these disaggregated results is very similar to results found among wage and salary workers [1].

As mentioned previously, the use of labor force status ignores an important dimension of the retirement process—partial retirement. Of the self-employed in this sample, 12 percent labeled themselves as partially retired, and on average worked considerably fewer hours than those not retired. In the regressions below, we analyze correlates of the three retirement status categories.

Since the coefficients in these equations refer to probability changes, and since the sum of the three predicted probabilities for any individual (that is, for any set of explanatory variables) should sum to one, there are restrictions on the coefficients in these equations. In particular, if

$$COMPRET = \alpha_0 + \Sigma \alpha_i X_i + \epsilon_1,$$
$$PARTRET = \beta_0 + \Sigma \beta_i X_i + \epsilon_2,$$
$$NOTRET = \gamma_0 + \Sigma \gamma_i X_i + \epsilon_3,$$

then we should find

$$\alpha_0 + \beta_0 + \gamma_0 = 1,$$

and

$$\alpha_i + \beta_i + \gamma_i = 0 \text{ for all } i \neq 0.$$

Fortunately, as long as we include a constant term, these restrictions will hold automatically in the OLS regression estimates.

As in the labor force status equations above, health status appears to be extremely important in the retirement decisions of the self-employed (Table 16). A health limitation increases the probability of being completely or partly retired, by 13 and 8 percentage points respectively, and therefore reduces the probability of being "not retired" by 21 points. Current social security eligibility is also important. It increases significantly the probability of being completely retired, and reduces the likelihood of being "not retired." There is no net effect in the partial retirement equation, perhaps because social security eligibility causes offsetting flows—into partial retirement from "not retired" status, and out of partial retirement into complete retirement.

The pension terms are most interesting here. Only two are significant, and they suggest that pension eligibility induces individuals out of "not retired" status into *partial* retirement. Since it does not seem to induce the self-employed into complete retirement (the coefficient is positive, but very insignificant), this effect did not show up in the labor force status equations. Of the interaction terms, only the coefficient in the "completely retired" equation is significant,

Table 16. *Subjective retirement status equations, white married self-employed men aged 58–63*

Variable	Completely retired (1)	Partly retired (2)	Not retired (3)
Health limitation (0, 1)	.128 (6.51)[a]	.083 (3.31)	−.211 (7.35)
Eligible for social security (0, 1)	.129 (6.41)	.016 (0.64)	−.146 (4.94)
Eligible for pension (0, 1)	.009 (0.17)	.262 (3.91)	−.271 (3.54)
Eligible for both (0, 1)	.181 (2.31)	−.120 (1.19)	−.061 (0.54)
Dependents (0, 1)	−.004 (0.17)	−.057 (2.02)	.061 (1.89)
Imputed wage ($/hour)	−.007 (1.57)	−.002 (0.28)	.009 (1.31)
Asset income ($000/year)	.006 (2.32)	.004 (1.21)	−.009 (2.63)
South (0, 1)	.064 (3.00)	.002 (0.01)	−.067 (2.14)
Constant	−.004	.092	.911
R^2	.17	.05	.17
N	836	836	836

[a] *t* statistics are in parentheses.
Source: [4].

indicating that eligibility for both social security and another pension dramatically increases the probability of complete retirement. This is consistent with the results in the labor force status equations.

The wage terms are all insignificant, but the point estimates suggest that high wages tend to make complete retirement, and to a lesser degree, partial retirement, less likely. Two of the asset terms are significant, and indicate that a high flow of asset income induces both complete and partial retirement. The dependents coefficients, insignificant in all the labor force status results, are now significant in two equations. The presence of dependents does not appear to affect the decision to retire completely; rather it seems to affect the extent of labor supply among those in the labor force by lowering significantly the probability that one is partly retired (−0.057), and increasing the chances of being "not retired" (0.061). The South coefficients illustrate that self-employed people in the South are much more likely to be completely retired, and much less likely to be "not retired" than are those workers living elsewhere.

We also ran retirement status equations for the two health subsets. Since the qualitative results are quite similar to the labor force status results already discussed, the coefficients are not reproduced here. In general, in the equations explaining the probabilities of being completely retired and not retired, the coefficients are larger in the subset with the health limitation. As before, the social security-pension interaction term is significant in explaining the complete retirement of those in good health, and insignificant (though larger in magnitude, in this case) for the others. In the partial retirement equation, very few variables are significant in the disaggregated equations. The most notable exception is pension eligibility, which is very large (.318) and highly significant in explaining partial retirement of those in good health. Among those with health limitations, it is not significant.

Logit equations for each of the dichotomous dependent variables also were run, and comparisons of predicted probabilities from the logit and regression estimate were made. The samples with which the logit coefficients were estimated are not the same as those used in the regressions since the logit program has no mechanism for handling missing data. Therefore, all those respondents with data missing on asset income were excluded from the logit runs, leaving a sample of 699—down 16 percent from the full 836 used in the regressions. Despite this difference in samples, the qualitative results are quite similar. With only three exceptions, all of the coefficients significant in the regressions were significant in the logit runs, and in only one of the three cases was the sign of a significant coefficient reversed. The logit runs confirm the importance of health and social security eligibility on the retirement decisions of these men, and the large impact of pension eligibility on the partial retirement decision. One of the three exceptions noted above concerned the influence of the social security-pension interaction term on the decision to retire completely. In the regression (Table 16), it was positive and significant, suggesting a strong positive interaction; in the logit run, it was negative and insignificant, with quite different implications. The explanation may be because in eliminating those with missing asset data, we lost 5 out of the 21 respondents eligible for both social security and a pension. With such small numbers, the loss of a few observations can change point estimates significantly.

As a more objective check on the logit and regression runs, we calculated predicted probabilities for the four dependent variables for four hypothetical individuals. The four are all assumed to be ineligible for a pension, to have no dependents, to live outside the South, and to have wage and asset income flows of $3 per hour and $1000 per year. They differ in health and social security eligibility status. Two regression probabilities are shown—one derived from the aggregate regression, and the other from the regression on the appropriate health subset. As is shown in Table 17, the differences in predicted probabilities generally are quite small. Most differences are two percentage points or less, and the maximum is .07. One surprising result is that the predictions from the health subset equations (with, in effect, complete interaction between health and the other variables) are not always closer to the logit estimates than are those from the aggregate. Although they usually are closer, in six of the sixteen comparisons here, they are not. Four of these six occur in the final column, in which the respondent has a health limitation and is eligible for social security. Despite some minor differences, we suggest that the logit estimates tend to confirm the results drawn above.

We have argued that people can alter their labor supply by withdrawing from the labor force, or by remaining in the labor force and moving to a state of partial retirement. We have discussed some of the correlates of retirement

Table 17. *Predicted probabilities from regression and preliminary logit results,
white married males, self-employed*

Source	Health limitation? Eligible for social security?	No No	No Yes	Yes No	Yes Yes
Predicted probability[a]					
Labor force status					
Logit		.98	.93	.91	.73
Aggregate regression[b]		1.00	.87	.86	.73
Appropriate health regression[c]		.97	.94	.93	.68
Completely retired					
Logit		.01	.05	.04	.24
Aggregate regression[d]		−.02	.11	.11	.24
Appropriate health regression[e]		.01	.04	.03	.29
Partly retired					
Logit		.09	.10	.15	.16
Aggregate regression[f]		.09	.11	.17	.19
Appropriate health regression[e]		.07	.11	.22	.20
Not retired					
Logit		.92	.81	.79	.58
Aggregate regression[g]		.93	.78	.72	.57
Appropriate health regression[e]		.92	.85	.76	.51

  [a] Assuming the individual is ineligible for a pension, has no dependents, does not live in the South, has an imputed wage of $3 per hour and asset income of $1,000 per year.
  [b] Table 15, col. 1.
  [c] Table 15, col. 2 or 3.
  [d] Table 16, col. 1.
  [e] Available from the author.
  [f] Table 16, col. 2.
  [g] Table 16, col. 3.
  Source: [4].

status, using a subjective self-classification. In this section we present some preliminary results with a more direct measure of the degree of labor force participation—annual hours of work. Although it does have the advantage of objectivity, this measure has at least three shortcomings. First, there are errors in the measurement of this variable, especially for the partly retired, since the survey question on weeks of work per year was not asked of all respondents (see footnote 6). Second, the variable hours of work does not uniquely measure retirement status. The same number of annual hours of work may represent customary full-time labor supply for some, but a drastic reduction in effort for others. Finally, we lose the approximately 10 percent of the sample who are in the labor force but for whom we cannot derive an estimate of annual hours from the data.

    With these caveats in mind, we present hours equations in Table 18, for those self-employed with known positive hours. The R^2 levels for all three equations (aggregate, and by health status) are very low, indicating that most of the interpersonal variation remains unexplained. There are some significant coefficients. In the aggregate equation, the health term is highly significant,

Table 18. *Annual hours of work equations, white married self-employed men aged 58–63 with positive hours of work, 1969*

Variable	All	No health limitation	Some health limitation
Health limitation (0, 1)	−294 (3.67)[a]		
Eligible for social security (0, 1)	− 57 (0.69)	− 42 (0.45)	− 81 (0.49)
Eligible for pension (0, 1)	162 (0.79)	74 (0.34)	397 (0.83)
Eligible for both (0, 1)	−597 (1.82)	37 (0.09)	−1198 (1.94)
Dependents (0, 1)	177 (2.05)	238 (2.50)	50 (0.27)
Imputed wage ($/hour)	− 46 (2.32)	− 41 (2.02)	− 114 (2.06)
Asset income ($000/year)	− 3 (0.31)	0 (0.00)	2 (0.12)
South	− 80 (0.92)	−137 (1.34)	− 57 (0.34)
SMSA	−106 (1.36)	− 3 (0.04)	− 270 (1.73)
Constant	2797	2702	2777
(Mean hours)	(2498)	(2574)	(2320)
R^2	.05	.03	.09
N	666	458	208

[a] *t* statistics are in parentheses.
Source: [4].

suggesting that self-employed men with health limitations work nearly 300 fewer hours per year than those without health limitations. The individual social security and pension effects are not significant, but the interaction term is. The point estimate for the effect of eligibility for both is nearly −500 hours, or about 10 hours per week. The dependents term is significant and positive, which confirms the interpretation offered above for the dependents coefficients in Table 16. There is evidence of a small negative wage effect, and no evidence of a significant influence of asset income.

When we disaggregate by health, we find that the social security and pension terms remain insignificant, and that the interaction effect seems to fall predominately on those in relatively poor health. This is the opposite of what was found in the labor force status equations (Table 15), where eligibility for both social security and a pension induced labor force withdrawal among those in good health. Among those with good health who decide to remain in the labor force, it appears the interaction has little effect. The dependents term is significant only for those in good health, and a backward-bending wage effect is found for both groups.

We also ran hours equations with industrial and occupational dummies. Together they raised the R^2 in the aggregate equation to .21, and suggested a wide diversity in annual labor supply. Compared with the reference occupational category of operatives, annual supply is 205 hours greater for managers and another 120 hours greater for professionals. Sales workers, on the other hand, work nearly 300 hours less than the reference group. Among industries, the trade coefficient is very large and significant suggesting nearly 600 extra hours over the reference industry (manufacturing). Construction workers work nearly

300 hours less than the reference group (perhaps reflecting the effects of bad weather), whereas those in finance, insurance, and real estate and other service industries work about 200 hours more.

When we compare the results in Tables 16 (subjective retirement status) and 18 (annual hours), we find the pension results puzzling. The retirement status coefficients suggest that pension eligibility alone induces a movement from "not retired" to "partly retired," but this does not show up at all in the hours equation. In the hours equation, it is eligibility for both that appears important (for those with a health limitation, at least), whereas this term is insignificant (and negative) in the partial retirement equation. At present, the explanation for this is not clear.

The social security results, on the other hand, do appear consistent. In Table 16, we see a movement to complete retirement (for most, 0 hours) from "not retired," and, not surprisingly, no significant effect on the annual hours of those who remain in the labor force.

Summary

The self-employed sector in the United States economy is a declining one, but one that is disproportionately populated by older workers. This is because (a) older workers are from cohorts in which self-employment once was more prevalent, and (b) some workers shift into self-employment in their later years. In the RHS sample with which we have worked, we estimate that approximately 12 percent of the self-employed have recently become so. The labor supply and retirement patterns of the self-employed are different from those of wage and salary workers. The distribution of annual hours worked is much higher for the self-employed, and they are much more likely to describe themselves as partly retired (12.4 percent vs. only 5.3 percent of wage and salary workers). Although a respondent's categorization of himself as partly retired is subjective, the partly retired do have hours of work distributions that are distinct from those of the completely retired and not retired individuals.

The tables and regressions revealed some important correlates of partial retirement status. Its probability increases with increased age of the respondent (for both self-employed and wage and salary workers), and was more likely among those with health conditions that limit the type or amount of work they could do. Among the self-employed, the partial retirement probability was strongly affected by the availability of a private pension. This result appeared in the tabular, regression, and logit results. Social security eligibility did not appear important, perhaps because it produces offsetting flows—into partial retirement from the not retired state, and into complete from partial retirement.

In the future, retirement patterns will become increasingly important as the proportion of the population in the older cohorts grows during the latter part of the century. If current trends toward earlier retirement continue or accelerate, severe funding problems are predicted for the social security system. These problems would be reduced if a larger proportion of the retirement aged population were to remain in the labor force and continue to work on a full- or part-time basis.

Although it is risky to extrapolate over time on the basis of cross-sectional results, the research presented here may be useful in a discussion of future retirement trends in two ways. The first concerns future retirement patterns of the self-employed, and the second, the patterns of the much larger group of wage and salary workers.

Forecasting the future size of the self-employed population is difficult, especially since we have not focused on why people become self-employed, but only on what those who are self-employed do. On one hand, the relative growth of the retirement age population over time, ceteris paribus, should increase the number of self-employed, if a constant (or increasing) proportion of wage and salary workers becomes self-employed near the end of the work life. If this occurs, we may see an increase in the frequency of partial retirement, since it is more common among the self-employed. On the other hand, these transitions to self-employment may decrease with the delay of mandatory retirement to age 70 for most workers. This will occur if these late-career transitions were prompted by the prospect of an involuntary mandatory retirement. Many of these workers may find themselves ready for complete labor force withdrawal by 70. This influence will be compounded by the generally lower proportions of younger cohort workers who are currently self-employed.

Within the self-employed sector, whatever its size, there is a reason to expect an increase in the extent of partial retirement if growth continues in the percentage of the population covered by pensions (often from a previous job). If the large impact of pension eligibility on the probability of partial retirement continues, a larger proportion of the self-employed will be influenced to opt for a transitional period. (This factor could be reversed if the administrative requirements of ERISA significantly reduce the extent of pension coverage.)

The overall trend in the number of partly retired self-employed people therefore is unclear. Whatever its direction, its overall impact on the economy and on the social security system will be small relative to the impact of wage and salary trends. This is the second topic on which this research may be helpful. It is tempting to extrapolate from the experience of the relatively unconstrained self-employed to the preferences of wage and salary workers. If one were to do so, one would conclude that there may be an unmet demand for partial retirement among wage and salary workers. This demand may increase as the age of compulsory retirement is pushed forward to 70. Since the business community generally was opposed to this legislative change (and presumably to full-time work to age 70), we may see an increase in hours flexibility and in gradual labor force withdrawal to the mutual benefit of both employer and employee.

Such extrapolations, however, are dangerous since self-employed and wage and salary workers may come from populations with quite different tastes. How relevant is the behavior of a self-employed real estate agent to the decision of a 30-year veteran of the assembly line? The self-employed are more likely to be in lines of work that they find interesting, and therefore probably are more likely to want to continue working. In addition, those self-employed who have moved to partial retirement generally have moved down from an hours distribution quite different from that of the average full-time wage and salary worker. This also makes it less likely that the preferences of one group provide a useful guide to the behavior of the other.

In summary, we have found evidence that partial retirement is a viable option for the self-employed, and, in fact, in this age group (58–63), it is more common than complete retirement. Partial retirement is much less frequent among wage and salary workers. If recent trends in pension coverage continue, we predict that the importance of partial retirement among the self-employed will grow. Future trends in the relative size of the self-employed population, unfortunately, are difficult to predict. We may be able to learn something about the effect of reduced labor market constraints (hours of work or mandatory retirement) on the behavior of wage and salary workers by studying the self-employed, but we caution that differences between the two groups make this a difficult undertaking.

References

[1] Quinn, Joseph F., "Microeconomic Determinants of Early Retirement: A Cross-Sectional View of White Married Men," *Journal of Human Resources,* 12 (Summer 1977), 329–346.

[2] ———, "Wage Determination and Discrimination Among Older Workers," *Journal of Gerontology,* 34 (September 1979), 728–735.

[3] Smallwood, David, "A Preliminary Investigation into the Nature and Causes of Retirement by the Self-Employed," Department of Economics, North Carolina State University, 1977 (mimeo).

[4] Social Security Administration, *Retirement History Study* (Washington, D.C.: U.S. Government Printing Office, 1969).

[5] U.S. Bureau of the Census, Census of the Population, 1970, Vol. 1, *Characteristics of the Population, Part I* (Washington, D.C.: U.S. Government Printing Office, 1973).

Individual Retirement Decisions: Discussion *H. Gregg Lewis*

It is instructive, I think, for those interested in retirement policy and population aging to look at the data on the labor force participation rates of U.S. males by age over a long period of time—back to 1890. For the period 1890–1955, I use the figures provided by Gertrude Bancroft [1]; for the period 1955–77 my figures are from the *Employment and Training Report of the President, 1978* [3]. There are some incomparabilities between the data from these two sources, but they are only a minor hindrance to examining the trends in the data.

Consider first the labor force participation rates of U.S. white males 25–44 years of age. The two sources of data indicate that in 1890, less than 4 percent—perhaps as few as 2 percent—of these males were *not* labor force participants. A small fraction of these nonparticipants were in school, I conjecture; another fraction, how large I do not know, surely consisted of males who were permanently incapable of market work. A larger fraction, I suspect, consisted of males temporarily unable to work. The residual fraction, probably small, included workers discouraged after unsuccessful searches for employment and a few playboys. The bulk of the nonparticipants surely were in that status for real health reasons.

From 1890 to about 1960 there was no trend in the nonparticipation rate of these 25–44-year-olds. However, in recent years, say 1960–77, the *non-participation* rates of these white males has risen by about two percentage points, approximately doubling the nonparticipation rate.

Surely in the period since 1890 the real health, including its energy and stamina aspects, of U.S. white males 25–44, has had an upward trend. Why then has their nonparticipation rate not trended downward? The effect of the upward trend in health, in my judgment, has been offset and recently more than offset by the effects of three other forces: (a) an increased fraction of 25–44-year-olds in school full time; (b) the upward trend in real income with which some temporarily ailing males bought nonparticipating rest that they would not otherwise have bought; and (c) especially recently, the proliferation of sick leave and disability pay programs both public and private.

The story for white males 45–54 years of age is much the same as for their 25–44 counterparts except in two respects: (a) their nonparticipation rate, 1890–1965 was about two percentage points higher; and (b) the recent (1960–77) upward movement of the rate was greater—about four, rather than two, percentage points—than the earlier period. (For both groups of men, the 1960–77 change amounted approximately to a doubling of the nonparticipation rate.) Given the age difference and the associated worsening of health, the greater nonparticipation rate for men aged 45–54 than for those aged 25–44 is not surprising.

The story for 55–64-year-old men is not very different. There is only a hint of an upward trend in their nonparticipation rate before 1960 and again an approximate doubling of their nonparticipation rate between 1960 and 1977. Their nonparticipation rate, not surprisingly, was considerably higher than for younger men.

The story for men 65 and over starts out in 1890 in a not very startling way: their nonparticipation rate was roughly .30, probably about three times as large as that for men aged 55–64. A substantial portion of this rise of nonparticipation with age was a result of the associated worsening of health. But surely part of the rise reflected increased wealth per dependent, and market wages falling with age. After 1890 the story of the 65-and-over men is very different from that for the younger men—there is a very sharp upward trend in their nonparticipation rate. By 1940 the rate had almost doubled to about .55; in 1960 the rate was .66 and in 1977 it was .80.

Participation rates, of course, are crude measures of labor force participation. I would prefer annual hours worked per year or even average hours worked per week, but such data are not available by sex and age. In 1890 average hours worked per week in the United States was roughly 60 and the participation rate for males 65 and over was about .70. I am going to assume that in all years average working hours per week for working men 65 and over was some unknown but constant fraction of average hours in the economy. Let me call the fraction λ. Then in 1890 average hours per week for both participants and nonparticipants is roughly 42λ. For 1940 the participation rate was about .44 and the average hours worked about 40. The corresponding figures for 1977 were .20 and 36. Hence, we have the following very crude estimates of average hours per week of participation for males aged 65 and over:

1890	42λ
1940	17.8λ
1975	7.2λ.

Between 1890 and 1940 hours of participation dropped at the rate of 4.8λ per decade; the corresponding decline in 1940–1977 was about 2.9λ per decade. Thus, in absolute terms, the decline per decade was about 1.7 times as large before 1940 as it was after 1940. In percentage terms, the decline was about 1.7 percent per year from 1890 to 1940 and about 2.5 percent per year—or about 1.5 times larger than 1.7—in the 1940–77 period.

Thus, the decline in labor force participation of men aged 65 and over measured as a decline in the labor force participation *rate,* or in average weekly hours, was of the same order of magnitude before the New Deal legislation (Social Security, Fair Labor Standards Acts) and later legislation dealing with "welfare" and well before private pension arrangements became important as that following this legislation and these arrangements. Surely an explanation of the downtrend in participation in the 1939–1978 period should be helpful in explaining, though perhaps with some relabeling or repackaging of variables, the 1890–1940 downtrend. Furthermore, accounting for cross-section differences in extent of labor force participation among older males in, say, 1969, should also account about as well for such differences in 1929 and even 1899.

What is the explanation for these trends and cross-sectional differences? I begin with health status and its associated dimensions of energy, stamina, ambition, and the like. Surely current and recent health status and the associated health status expectations are and have been important variables explaining differences among older men in the extent of their labor force participation. Furthermore, although I suspect that if we had good scales for measuring health, for our purposes, the data would show that the distribution of older men of given ages has shifted toward better health. I doubt that the role of health would have diminished much as a labor force participation factor because of interactions with real income. Thus, I begin with the expectation that health status differences, even among men 58–63 years of age in 1969, were important in explaining their extent of labor force participation.

What does Quinn find? Does he confirm my expectations? He does, although there are some problems with interpreting what he has found. In the first place he has eliminated from his sample "bedridden and housebound" men. We do not know how many were so eliminated or even whether they were all *non*participants, although I presume they were. The effect of this elimination is to reduce the estimated impact of poor health on nonparticipation. Second, health status is self-reported, which raises what I call the "economics of talk" problem. Because persons, I think quite generally, try to make their "talk"— the way they answer questions—consistent among themselves and consistent with their actions, "talk" is an endogenous variable in the model system. Thus, health talk may be the consequence rather than the cause of labor force participation actions. For this reason, I suspect that there may be an upward bias to the health status coefficient in numerical terms, especially in the participation rate regression.

What Quinn estimates can be summarized simply:

1. The regression for all workers reported in Table 15 implies that for self-employed males 58–63 in 1969 the labor force participation rate for those reporting a health limitation, other things the same, was 13.8 percentage points lower than for those reporting no health limitation (36 percent reported a health limitation). The actual difference in the labor force participation rate between the two health status groups was about 18 percentage points.

However, among "the other things the same" in Table 15 is the "imputed wage." Furthermore, Quinn's wage equation reported in Table 14 implies that those with a self-reported health limitation, other things the same, earn a wage that is 22 (not 25 as he states) percent lower than that of those not so reporting.

Unfortunately he does not tell us the mean wage of those without a health limitation. Let me assume that it was $5 an hour. Twenty-two percent of this is $1.10. Now plug a negative $1.10 into the equation in Table 15 opposite "imputed wage" and there is an additional drop of 1.1 percentage points in the participation rates of those with health limitations.

2. The regression for all workers reported in Table 18 implies that among self-employed males 58–63 in 1969 with positive hours of work in 1969, those with health limitations will work 294 fewer hours. But again, the health limitation affects the imputed wage. If the mean wage of those with no health limitation was $5 per hour, the effect of the health limitation through the wage is about a positive 51 hours, making the total effect 294 − 51, or 243 hours.

But health is not the only factor explaining differences in the labor force participation among older men, and I have already said that it surely explains very little of the strong upward trend of nonparticipation among males aged 65 and over.

What is the explanation for this upward trend, especially before 1940 when we cannot easily cite private pensions and New Deal legislation as *the* variables doing the work? Twenty-one years ago I would have answered the question as follows, I suspect.

First, because the over-64-years-of-age class is open-ended, I would search for more age detail; for example, 65–69, 70–74 in order to be sure that the trend was not to any large extent due to a shift in the distribution by age in this open-ended class.

Second, I would have looked for what I will call "class of worker" effects within the 65–69, 70–74, etc. classes. We know that there was a very strong downward trend from 1890 to 1940 and of course thereafter in the fraction of males whose primary occupation was that of farm entrepreneurs and to some extent also of proprietors of Mama and Papa grocery stores and other retail, wholesale, and service establishments. Self-employment, as Quinn has emphasized, has the virtue that one can reduce his hours or weeks of work fairly easily without having to change employers—that is, without having to search for part-time work with another employer, losing human capital specific to the previous employment in the process. (Minimum wages set by law or trade unions after the 1930s, I strongly suspect, have made this search process an even more difficult one for older wage and salary workers. And so-called "compulsory" retirement arrangements surely have produced more such search and loss of human capital than otherwise would have occurred.)

Third, I would be very surprised if these two factors went very far in explaining the marked pre-1940 downtrend in the extent of labor force participation by the over-64 age group. Twenty-one years ago in a piece titled "Hours of Work and Hours of Leisure" [2] (leisure then being the name given to nonmarket activities), I argued that the U.S. supply of male labor to market activities, measured as a fraction of the lifetime spent in these activities, was a backward-bending function of the lifetime or permanent real wage. As the lifetime real wage rises over long periods of time, the fraction of the male lifetime spent in labor market activities will fall. This fall will occur along each of several dimensions of lifetime hours, although not necessarily in equal ratio among the dimensions.

1. Hours of work per day fell from an average of about ten in 1890 to an average of about eight in 1940.
2. Days of work per week during working weeks fell roughly from about six to about five so that hours per week fell from about 60 to about 40 from 1890 to 1940.

    It should be noted that since 1940 there has been little tendency for hours worked per day on working days to fall below eight and for days worked per week in working weeks to fall below five. What little movement downward there has been since 1940 has been because of a slight increase in holiday days off. There is, by the way, an important puzzle here as to why there was such a marked downward trend from 1890 to 1940 and so little from 1940 to date.
3. Weeks worked per year in working years fell but little, I judge, from 1890 to 1940, and since 1940 have, I suspect, fallen, though probably no more than 10 percent. Moreover, this dimension is one in which I would expect slow decline at best for specific human capital reasons in the future.
4. Years worked per lifetime, if one counts school years as work years for our purposes and I think they should, have fallen both before 1940 and after, judging from the labor force participation data. Furthermore, for specific human capital reasons, I would expect the reduction in years per lifetime to take the form of earlier retirement rather than that of an increased frequency of year-long and half-year-long vacations in middle life. Certainly the labor force participation rate data support this view.

A few attempts have been made to test this view against U.S. time-series data with results that are not a resounding confirmation of it. The theory seems to work much better before 1940 than after. The testing, however, is hampered by the absence of data that correspond closely either to the concept of lifetime labor supply or that of the lifetime real wage. For this reason, I am not persuaded that the position I took 21 years ago is really quite wrong. However, the human capital revolution has taken place meanwhile, and I would now give a greater role to schooling than I gave earlier. Elementary schooling is, in large part I think, not appreciably specialized to market rather than to household activities, but above that level it becomes increasingly oriented to the market. Thus, as the fraction of cohorts completing high school, college, and even graduate school has increased, human capital has become increasingly specialized to the market.

Are Quinn's findings consistent with the position I took 21 years ago? Certainly not directly. He uses recent cross-section data that pertain only to workers at or near retirement age rather than to the working lifetimes of these workers. And translation of the theory I held 21 years into one for such a cross section is not altogether obvious. For example, it is surely clear that the wage earned by a 58-year-old in 1963 or what he would have earned had he worked in 1963 is not necessarily a good measure of his lifetime wage.

Suppose that we had a *large* micro-data set for older males, say those aged 58–63, with data comparable to those used by Quinn, but pertaining to, say, 1929, instead of 1969. Also suppose that our left-hand variable were a current— i.e., 1929—labor supply variable: annual hours worked, weeks worked in 1929, or even labor force status. What would I then want for right-hand variables?

First of all, because I am sure that age strongly interacts in effects on the left-hand variables with other right-hand variables, I would fit equations by single years of age if I could. Hence, assume, for example, that I am fitting an equation for 63-year-olds.

Second, notice that up to this point *property* income has played no role in my thinking. The reason is quite simple. The present value of a person's wealth when young, except for a very few fortunate persons, consists inconsequentially of his property income. Put differently: the wealth in property that an individual has at age 63 consists almost wholly of assets accumulated in earlier years from savings from his and his spouse's earnings. Thus, at age 63 his property wealth reflects his lifetime wage much more than it reflects property that he had at age 20. For this reason, lacking retrospective data on his *real* wage before age 63, property wealth stands in, in my 1957 view, for the lifetime wage.

However, property wealth even in 1929 for a 63-year-old, was not simply the amount in a passbook savings account, and I think that an additional dollar of wealth in savings accounts might very well not have had the same effect on his labor supply as an additional dollar in life insurance, or in a house, or in an oil painting, or in an annuity to become effective at age 65 or at any age of his choice. Thus, I would group the wealth items into several distinct classes. In particular, I suspect that the larger the fraction of wealth held in real form (houses, paintings, etc.), the stronger are the family's tastes for market goods relative to household time and hence the more likely is labor force participation. Indeed, the problem of using property wealth as a stand-in for the lifetime wage is a general one because of the taste factor. Consider two males with the same lifetime wage profile, but different tastes. Surely the one with greater tastes for market goods relative to household time will tend to work a *larger* fraction of his lifetime and accumulate more wealth. Thus, in the cross-section comparison one needs to look for variables proxying tastes. One of these may be schooling.

But now let's shift gears. It is 1969, not 1929, and the men are 1969's 63-year-olds. Things have changed. In 1929 we would have been little concerned with pension schemes except, perhaps annuities. But in 1969 pension arrangements were common and of considerable variety. Some 1969 pension schemes would have fitted under the 1929 rubric: property wealth, annuities. But what of the nonvested pension to begin at age 65 for a man 63 years old if he stays with his employer for two more years? Surely, if the pension is not negligible, it provides an incentive to stay working for the employer rather than to retire. If the age at which pension payments were to begin had been, say, 62, instead of 65, then in effect it would have become vested, and we would treat that wealth in the same fashion as a 1929 annuity, except that if getting it were contingent on leaving the employment (compulsory retirement), we would be inclined to strengthen our prediction that it will cause a decline in extent of labor market activities, the more so, the larger the pension. Thus, pensions in my scheme fit under the property wealth or lifetime wage heading, but the handling of their variety requires careful specification.

The same applies to social security. Here's a man 63 in 1969 who can become fully insured by continuing to work another year. Surely the social security incentive is to continue to work. (This is a special incentive not present for a man who has never been covered by social security.) Here's another man 63 years old who is already fully insured and, therefore could, if he chose, be receiving benefits. Should he do so? That is, what is his optimum strategy and what does this strategy imply about his hours of work? This question is not a simple one for the following reasons:

1. By *deferring* receipt of benefits he will surely increase the monthly benefit amount (while receiving benefits for fewer months), but not by *actuarial* amounts of increase, and he is likely to increase the earnings base on which benefits are calculated, especially during inflation.
2. Second, the amount he receives once he starts receiving benefits is not independent of his earnings until he is considerably older, and the amount of his earnings tax depends both on the amount he earns per year and on how the earnings are spread over the months of the year.

I have proxied, imperfectly to be sure, the lifetime wage by property wealth. In the present context, do I still want a wage variable or variables? The answer is surely yes. What I would like is something like the ratio of the current market or potential wage to the average of this over the remaining years of the lifetime with the expectation that this variable would be positively related to labor supply. I would probably have to settle for the current wage, along with a variable or variables that would pick up current labor market conditions in the area in which the man lived. But what would I do about the men for whom the current wage was not available with all of the attendant selectivity bias problems? Well, I'd probably predict the wage from an auxiliary equation and be unhappy about having to do it.

Of course, there would be some other variables: schooling, probably; number of dependents, probably; class of worker, probably; and perhaps some more, but not many. I would focus my attention on what I have called the wealth variables and the wage variable or variables.

But now it is time to go back to the question: Do Quinn's findings make sense? That is, do they confirm my expectations? Quinn's findings do for the most part, though his proxies for the pension and social security wealth variables are crude. An increase in asset income, a reduction in number of dependents, and being eligible for social security reduce both participation and hours worked (among workers). However, the *average* effect of asset income on both hours and participation may not have been very big. The greater puzzle to me is pension eligibility. Among those *not* eligible for social security, being eligible for pension *increases* both hours of work among workers and labor force participation rates, whereas it has the opposite effect among those eligible for social security. I am also a bit puzzled by the finding that an increase in the *imputed* wage increases the participation rate but reduces hours of work. The imputed wage, however, is a relatively poor proxy for the current market wage, and, of course, in the hours-of-work equation all of those with zero hours were left out.

References

[1] Bancroft, Gertrude, *The American Labor Force: Its Growth and Changing Composition* (New York: John Wiley & Sons, Inc., 1958).
[2] Lewis, H. Gregg, "Hours of Work and Hours of Leisure," pp. 1–11 in L. Reid Tripp (Ed.), *Proceedings of the Ninth Annual Meeting* (Madison: Industrial Relations Research Association, 1957).
[3] U.S. Department of Labor, *Employment and Training Report of the President* (Washington, D.C.: U.S. Government Printing Office, 1978).

Labor Supply

Secular Changes in Female Job Aspirations   *Solomon W. Polachek*

Concern has been voiced over and over again about the soundness of the social security system. The problem centers on the capability of the working population to support transfer payments to the nonworking aged. Given current population trends, it is easy to see the reason for such concern. The tendency toward lower fertility during the last several decades has diminished the ratio of working persons to those not working. In 1930 the ratio was 7.54 workers to every person in the country over 65. In 1976 the figure had slipped to 4.23 workers, and the prognosis is for continued decline—to 3.89 in 1990, and even lower in the next century. Such a large decrease will place a tremendous burden on the earnings that the working must devote to supporting the aged.

This awesome responsibility on the work force is being eased by an increase in the number of working women. Female labor force participation rates have advanced tenfold over the last fifty years and are still rising. These figures mean not only that the total number of working women has increased, and probably can be expected to increase still further in the future, but also that more women are spending more of their lives in the work force. Assuming that job aspirations are related to the expected length of one's working life, then the increased number of working years may provide incentives for women employees to achieve better paying, higher responsibility jobs, and thereby ease further the social security burden of the working population.

This chapter concentrates only on this last aspect of the complicated problem of the changing structure of the work force. It examines only the impact of increased female labor force participation on the occupational aspirations of women, so as to predict changes in women's occupational distributions. It is hoped that the methods and ideas in this limited study will be of use to others in their efforts to arrive at a fuller comprehension of both expected changes in occupational structure and their impact on the welfare of the aged.

The chapter offers first a rationale for expecting female job aspirations to be related to lifetime labor force participation. Within this section are descriptions of the economic concepts needed to make this assertion, namely, descriptions of the earnings profile, the concept of discontinuous labor force participation, and how being out of the labor force causes atrophy of wage potentials that differs among occupations. A cost minimization model is presented illustrating the relationship between life-cycle labor force participation and occupational choice. Finally, empirical estimates are provided to measure this relationship, and from these estimates projections are obtained of the impact of increased labor force participation on occupational aspirations.

Relationship Between Lifetime Labor Force Behavior and Labor Market Aspirations

Some Preliminaries

For the purposes of this study, labor market aspirations are defined to be the occupation one wishes to achieve at a particular life-cycle phase. Such aspirations are based solely on individual preferences but presume as given the constraints each individual may face as a member of society. Not all groups face the same constraints. If access to jobs varies by population strata, then the career aspirations of these population subgroups may be affected. For example, it has been alleged that much of the cross-sectional difference in occupational structure can be attributed to discrimination. Women and blacks presumably are, to a large extent, forced into the more menial occupations, and at these job levels their aspirations cease.

This chapter takes societal values as exogenous, current discrimination levels as given, and asks how women's individual occupational aspirations are related to their lifetime labor force participation. It is hypothesized that those women with the most continuous labor force participation have the highest occupational aspirations, holding discrimination levels and other constraints constant. If correct, this cross-sectional assertion can be applied to predict time-series changes in occupational aspirations motivated by the secular increases in female labor force behavior. To the extent that macroeconomic considerations do not act to limit these aspirations so that the economy is able to absorb an influx of new workers to prestigious occupations, the cross-sectional estimates can be translated into predictions of the impact of women's changing labor force participation patterns on their occupational distribution.

Data

Two sets of data are used so as to provide robustness. The first is the National Longitudinal Survey (NLS), Mature Women 30–44 [7]; the second, the University of Michigan Income Dynamics Panel (IDP) [2]. Both are national samples that contain retrospective work history information as well as detailed information on occupation and demographic characteristics. Both are also well documented in the current literature.[1] A random sample of 518 white women was

---

1. These samples were drawn randomly from the tape. They were purposely kept moderate in size to prevent exorbitant computer costs. To maintain compatability between the two samples, the IDP sample was limited to women 30–50 years old; it is described in [2]. A description of the NLS data is contained in Parnes [7].

chosen from the NLS and 482 from the IDP. The samples are similar with almost identical mean variable values. The one compatibility problem is that the NLS classifies occupations in census one-digit categories, whereas the IDP uses its own codes. This difference is not crucial since the logit technique used in the following estimates treats categories as unordered polytomous variables.

Occupation should by no means be construed as a concept telling all there is to know about one's labor force status. Yet the concept of occupation cannot be ignored because embodied within it is information about wages and the socioeconomic status of individuals. Data on occupation probably are more prevalent than any other statistics defining one's economic well being. Sociologists and economists utilize occupational data to compare economic position across demographic groups. In fact, although not explicitly considered, the results of this paper can be used to help explain socioeconomic differences by sex brought about by the apparent occupational segregation observed in the United States and other economies [9].

In this paper occupation is defined in terms of very broad categories.[2] This is advantageous for at least two reasons. First, it is consistent with Welch and Maclennan [15], who claim that 98 percent of the wage variance captured by 298 census occupational titles could be explained by condensation of the titles into nine broad categories. Second, it minimizes biases caused by possible occupational mobility.

The paper now turns to providing a detailed justification of the initial hypothesis asserting the relationship between continuous labor force participation and occupational choice. This entails a digression to explain "earnings profiles," how earnings profiles can vary by occupation, and finally, the relationship between occupational aspirations and labor force participation.

The Earnings Function

The graph of an individual's wages at each age *(t)* of the life cycle is known as an earning's profile.[3] (See Figure 1.) Typically, earnings profiles are concave functions rising quickly initially and then leveling off.[4] To be most appropriate, the earnings function should be fitted with longitudinal data so as to reflect age-wage points of given individuals. In practice, cross-sectional estimates predominate.[5] Thus, it is usually assumed that intracohort effects are negligible.

2. For the NLS data these are (1) professional, (2) managerial, (3) clerical, (4) sales, (5) craft, (6) operative, (7) household worker, and (8) service. For the IDP data there are (1) professional, (2) managerial, (3) clerical-sales, (4) operative, and (5) unskilled.

3. Often annual earnings are used on the vertical axis instead of wage rates.

4. When annual earnings are used, the profile often falls because of decreased work hours at higher wages.

5. Recent longitudinal data sets have permitted estimation based on pooled cross-section time-series data. Such analyses obtain measures of intercohort as well as intracohort effects.

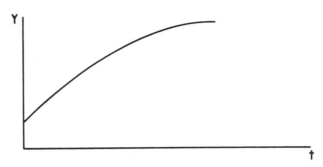

Figure 1. *Age-earnings profile*

Given the above caveat, the slope of an earnings profile reflects the rate at which wages change over a lifetime. The steep slope at the initial labor market entry implies rapid wage growth. The flatter segment at the end of the life cycle is indicative of the slow rate at which wages rise for older workers.

Earnings and Discontinuous Labor Force Participation

Implicit in the construction of the age-earnings profile is the tacit assumption of a continuous work history. One is assumed to work each and every year since graduation from school. For white male workers this assumption does not seem too unreasonable. For other strata such as women, however, unemployment spells as well as periods of intermittent labor force participation must be taken into account.

Aside from the obvious period of zero earnings, dropping out of the labor force has two direct effects, both culminating in potential wage losses. They manifest themselves during the period out of the labor force, but are observable only upon reentry.[6] Assume a person drops out of the labor force for $(t_2 - t_1)$ years (Figure 2). The total wage loss can be described as the difference in wages received upon labor market reentry (Y_{t_2}) and wages that would have been received if no work interruption had occurred $(Y_{t_2}{}^*)$. This wage gap is broken down into the two effects. Define Y_{t_1} to be one's wage just prior to dropping out of the labor market. The first effect is the pure depreciation in wages $(Y_{t_2} - Y_{t_1})$ caused by intermittent participation. The second is the loss in earnings power caused by the loss of seniority $(Y_{t_1} - Y_{t_2}{}^*)$. This latter effect measures the potential wage loss caused by wages not rising as they would if one had

---

6. Since this wage loss is observed only for those reentering the labor market, a possible "selectivity" bias exists in its measurement. However, if those women who do not reenter the labor force are the ones with the greater losses in market earnings power (otherwise they would reenter the labor force), then conventional estimates would *underestimate* the effect of intermittent labor force participation.

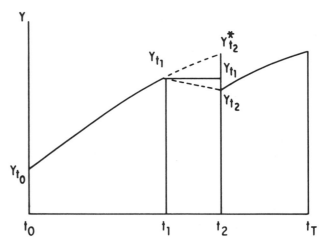

Figure 2. *Age-earnings profile: the case of discontinuous labor-force participation*

remained in the labor force.[7] Each of these factors is important in its own right. For our purposes, however, we concentrate on both effects and define the combined effect to be the "atrophy" of earnings power caused by intermittent labor force participation.

Occupation and the Earnings Profile

Occupations are not identical.[8] Each possesses unique labor market characteristics. For example, some occupations require large amounts of training. Others require significant skill maintenance to prevent skill deterioration over the life cycle.[9] Each of these occupational attributes manifests itself by affecting the shape of the earnings profile. Those occupations with large amounts of on-the-job training result in steep age-earnings profiles. Those requiring large

7. There is evidence that $Y_{t_1} - Y_{t_2}^*$ is an underestimate; for example, Polachek [8] and Sandell and Shapiro [11], assuming that the slope $(Y_{t_1} - Y_{t_0})$ would be flatter for those with expectations of dropping out of the labor force. A lower slope implies that *observed* estimates of $Y_{t_1} - Y_{t_2}^*$ are smaller in magnitude than would be the case if expectations of $t_2 - t_1$ approached zero.

8. This is especially true for broad one-digit occupational categories.

9. Other kinds of job characteristics typical of the occupation may exist. Examples include physical skills inherent in some kinds of work, health hazards, and even seasonality of jobs. Given the existence of compensationing wage differentials, these characteristics should also affect wage levels and, hence, the age-earnings profile. However, since we are interested solely in the relationship between labor force participation and occupation, we can ignore explicit consideration of these aspects, even though as shall be illustrated, they are implicitly dealt with in that they affect the shape of the earnings profile and, therefore, the total wage loss associated with intermittent participation.

amounts of skill maintenance no doubt have high obsolescence and more concave profiles.

In each of these cases continuous labor force participation is important. Put differently, dropping out of the labor force necessitates wage losses associated with training difficiencies and skill obsolescence. The atrophy concept previously defined represents a shorthand summary measure of the effects on wage potential. If occupational differences exist as described, then these age-earnings profile differences show up as differing atrophy rates. Occupations in which training is most important have the highest atrophy rates. Relatively low atrophy rates are associated with occupations in which training and skill maintenance are relatively unimportant. It is assumed that each occupation has a unique atrophy rate. Thus, knowing an atrophy rate implies knowledge of a particular occupation. Because levels of atrophy affect occupational earnings, wages in each occupation can be described uniquely as a function of atrophy (δ). We wish to show that job choice is related both to occupational atrophy rates and to time out of the labor force.

Atrophy Rates: Are Occupations Different?

No readily available data exist measuring atrophy in each occupation. Therefore, atrophy is estimated using techniques roughly similar to the techniques developed in Mincer and Polachek [5]. Measures are obtained from the δ_j coefficient of the following equation.

$$\ln Y_j = \alpha_{oj} + \alpha_{1j}S + \delta_j H + \alpha_{2j}\underline{X} + \epsilon, \quad j = 1, \ldots, M \qquad (1)$$

where

$Y_j \equiv$ hourly wage rate,
$S \equiv$ years of schooling,

$$H \equiv \left(\frac{T-N}{T}\right) \text{ percent home time,}$$

$\underline{X} \equiv$ a vector of other standardizing variables, and
$j \equiv$ an index for each of M occupations.

The δ coefficient measures the impact on wages of being out of the labor force a greater percentage of one's lifetime. By referring to Figure 2 it can be seen that embedded within the coefficient is the direct loss of earnings power caused by intermittent labor force participation $(Y_{t_2} - Y_{t_1})$ *as well as* the loss in earnings power caused by lost seniority $(Y_{t_1} - Y_{t_2}{}^*)$.

Estimates are given in Table 1. It is important to note that the net effect of intermittent labor force participation is negative for each occupation, and remains so under various specifications of (1). Chow tests reveal significant differences across occupations.

Table 1. *Estimated atrophy rates by occupation*

	Data source	
Occupation	NLS[a]	IDP[a]
Professional	−.1357	−.27
Managerial	−.5313	−.42
Clerical	−.3623 ⎫	−.24
Sales	−.2813 ⎭	
Craft	−.4436	_[b]
Operative	−.1115	−.18
Household work	.3868[c] ⎫	−.15
Service	−.2326 ⎭	

[a] NLS = National Longitudinal Survey [7] and IDP = Income Dynamics Panel [2].
[b] Sample too small to obtain estimate.
[c] Not significantly different from zero.
Source: [2, 7].

Life-Cycle Labor Force Participation

Labor force intermittency represents movement into and out of the labor market. Total time out of the labor market varies across the population. Perhaps the greatest diversity in life-cycle labor force participation exists among women. Table 2 is presented to illustrate this variation. The data indicate the total number of years spent in the labor force as a fraction of the total possible years that could be spent at work. Note that never-married women are in the labor force most (over 90 percent for those with college and graduate school). Married women with spouses present work least.

Table 2. *Percentage lifetime labor force participation by marital status and education*

	Education			
Marital status	Elementary	High school	College	Graduate school
	(percent)			
Married, spouse present	27.4	33.8	36.4	50.0
Married, spouse absent	28.3	33.4	54.1	NC[a]
Widowed	31.7	32.4	44.9	56.5
Divorced	38.1	51.8	62.4	50.0
Separated	46.1	47.5	49.6	68.2
Never married	28.2	66.9	88.9	97.2
Total	30.1	36.9	41.4	59.1

[a]NC = not calculated (too few observations).
Note.—Life-time labor force participation = total years worked divided by total exposure (age minus education minus 6) to the labor force.
Source: [7].

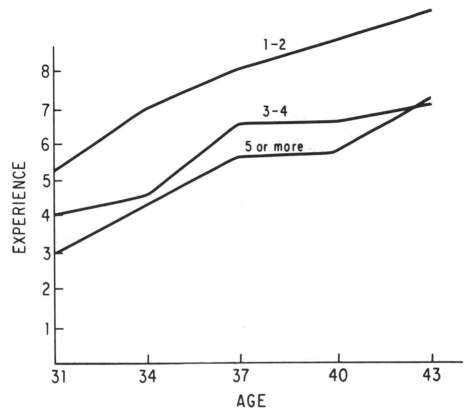

Figure 3. *Experience of married spouse present females cross-classified by number of children*

Other factors are also important. The impact of children on labor force behavior is illustrated in Figure 3. As can be seen, the presence of children strongly decreases women's working years. Typically, men as a group work more continuously. Their labor force participation relative to that of women is given in Figure 4.

Relationship between Life-Cycle Labor Force Participation and Occupational Choice

Given the assumption that an occupation can be characterized by its earnings profile, and given the fact that individuals, especially women, vary in lifetime labor force participation, is there a sorting among individuals based on one's

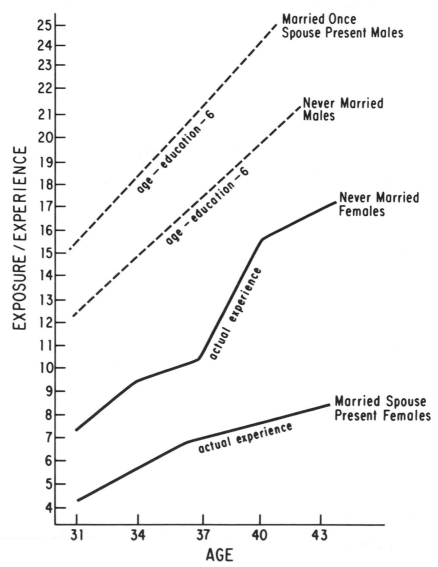

Figure 4. *Age exposure/experience profiles*

life-cycle labor force participation *and* the atrophy rate of one's optimal occupation? That is, do those persons with expectations of higher labor force activity have different job aspirations from those with low labor force expectations? This section seeks to answer this question. If such a relationship is plausible, then a rationale exists for the type of forecast originally postulated.

A Model of Occupational Choice: A Theoretical Relationship between Occupational Attributes and Continuous Labor Force Participation

Assume that women (and even men) are cognizant of their family plans, and hence have some idea of expected lifetime labor force participation. Thus, the number of years out of the labor force (presumably for family responsibilities) is known and is treated as an exogenous variable. Further assume that occupational choice is based on the now standard condition of lifetime income maximization.[10]

Define $E(\delta, h)$ to be one's average lifetime wage rate. It can be seen (from Figure 2) that $E(\delta, h)$ is positively related to initial wage (Y_{t_0}) and inversely related to atrophy (δ) and home time (h).[11] As an example, let

$$E(\delta, h) = w(\delta) - \delta h w(\delta),$$ (2)

where

$$E(\delta, h) \equiv \text{average lifetime wage in occupation characterized by atrophy } (\delta) \text{ and labor force intermittency } (h),$$

$$w(\delta) \equiv Y_{t_0}(\delta) \equiv \text{initial wage in occupation if no labor force intermittency would exist},$$

$$\delta \equiv \text{atrophy rate, and}$$

$$h \equiv \frac{(T-N)}{N} \equiv \text{percent of working years out of the labor force.}$$

Note that initial wage levels are assumed to be a function of (δ). This follows from the hedonic price literature developed by Sherwin Rosen [10]. The rationale is as follows. If atrophy implies lower earnings upon reentry to the labor market, then the market compensates wages of workers in occupations where the price of intermittency is high. Thus, it is assumed $\frac{\partial w}{\partial \delta} > 0$. Second-order conditions dictate that $\frac{\partial^2 w}{\partial \delta^2} < 0$.

Under the above assumptions, lifetime income is the product of years at work (N) and the average lifetime wage in the chosen occupation. Thus, lifetime earnings can be depicted as

$$NE(\delta, h) = N[w(\delta) - \frac{T-N}{N} \delta w(\delta)].$$ (3)

10. Note that the dual problem is to choose the occupation that minimizes the losses associated with intermittent labor force participation.
11. Life-cycle considerations would entail looking at wage and atrophy rates in *each* time period. At the cost of sacrificing implications about occupational mobility, we simplify to avoid undue mathematical complications. Further, we do not distinguish the effects of timing of intermittent labor force participation on occupational choice.

An individual chooses an occupation with atrophy (δ) so as to maximize (4) given her labor force expectations. Thus

$$\underset{\delta}{\text{Max}} \ [Nw(\delta) - \delta(T - N) \ w \ (\delta)].\tag{4}$$

First-order conditions dictate

$$Nw' = (T - N) \ (w + \delta w'),\tag{5}$$

where $w' = \dfrac{\partial w}{\partial \delta}$.

Equation (5) can be interpreted in terms of the standard marginality conditions. As indicated, one chooses an occupation with an atrophy rate such that the marginal loss of earnings during the work segment $[(T - N)(w + \delta w')]$ is exactly balanced by the marginal gain in lifetime earnings Nw'. These marginality conditions are illustrated in Figure 5.

In the case of full labor force participation $(T - N)$, the marginal cost curve vanishes, implying that occupational choice (depicted by optimal δ) is determined by the intersection of MR and the horizontal axis. In such a case, the individual standardizing characteristics (other than T, N) that influence the shape and position of MR are the sole determinants of occupation.

Effect of a Change in Lifetime Labor Force Participation

What changes in occupational choice result if lifetime labor force participation exogenously increases? The answer to this question can be obtained by differentiating equilibrium Equation (5) totally and perturbing the result by an exogenous increase in labor force participation. Rewriting (5) in its implicit form

$$F(\delta, \ N) = 0,\tag{6}$$

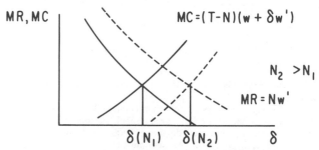

Figure 5. *Determination of optimal occupation*

and totally differentiating, yields

$$\frac{\partial F}{\partial \delta} \, d\delta + \frac{\partial F}{\partial N} \, dN = 0.$$

Solving for $\dfrac{d\delta}{dN}$ yields

$$\frac{d\delta}{dN} = - \frac{\overset{>0}{\dfrac{\partial F}{\partial N_i}}}{\underset{<0}{\dfrac{\partial F}{\partial \delta}}} > 0, \tag{8}$$

where from (5) we have

$$\frac{\partial F}{\partial N} = w' + w + \delta w' > 0.$$

The denominator $\left(\dfrac{\partial F}{\partial \delta}\right)$ is negative because of the second-order conditions neces-

sary in the maximization of (2). Thus, $\dfrac{d\delta}{dN} > 0$. An increase in labor force

participation therefore implies a shift in the *MR* and *MC* curves (dashed lines in Figure 5) and hence, higher equilibrium atrophy rates.

The equations are important because they provide justification for the initially hypothesized forecasts of occupational distribution based on changing life-cycle labor force participation. In addition, they identify high atrophy occupations as those most sensitive to changes in lifetime labor force participation. Referring to Table 1, we note that the currently rising life-cycle labor force participation implies shifts toward the managerial-professional occupations and away from the more menial jobs. We now embark on measuring these qualitative predictions.

Estimation

Lifetime Labor Force Participation and Occupational Choice

Occupation is a discrete nonordered variable. This implies that any a priori ranking of occupations can only be arbitrary. Given its polytomous nonordered nature, traditional econometric approaches do not yield efficient estimates of the impact of causal factors such as labor force intermittency on occupation.[12]

---

12. See Theil [14] for a more detailed explanation of the shortcomings of OLS estimates.

Instead, since occupational groupings can be broken into mutually exclusive categories, logistic or probit approaches can be applied.

This paper utilizes a logit specification in which the determination of occupation can be viewed as a system of $(M-1)$ independent equations.

$$\ln \frac{P_{jt}}{P_{lt}} = X_t \, \beta_j,$$ (9)

Where

> $j \equiv 2, \ldots , M$ (the number of occupations),
> $t \equiv$ the observation index,
> $X \equiv$ a vector of independent factors affecting the logit $\equiv$ (c, s, e, h),
> $c \equiv$ constant,
> $S \equiv$ years of schooling,
> $e \equiv$ exposure to the labor market (age minus S minus 6.0) so as to adjust for occupational change caused by the natural aging process, and
> $h \equiv$ years not in the labor force.

Each coefficient β of the β_j vector can be interpreted as the partial impact of the independent variable on the logarithm of the odds ratio of being in occupation j relative to some base occupation. Equation (9) can be estimated

Table 3. *Multiple logit model of occupational choice (asymptotic* t-*ratios in parentheses)* $N = 518$[a]

Dependent variable[b]	Independent variables[b]				
	c	m	s	e	h
$\ln \dfrac{P(OC_2)}{P(OC_1)}$	6.027 (2.28)	0.845 (1.053)	−.593 (−3.481)	−.028 (−.421)	−1.217 (−1.407)
$\ln \dfrac{P(OC_3)}{P(OC_1)}$	1.612 (1.25)	0.356 (0.91)	−.210 (−2.80)	0.093 (3.07)	0.657 (1.41)
$\ln \dfrac{P(OC_4)}{P(OC_1)}$	0.203 (0.10)	−.462 (−.74)	−.375 (−3.10)	0.154 (3.28)	2.375 (3.00)
$\ln \dfrac{P(OC_5)}{P(OC_1)}$	1.499 (0.35)	−.437 (−.33)	−.451 (1.61)	0.066 (0.63)	1.095 (0.63)
$\ln \dfrac{P(OC_6)}{P(OC_1)}$	7.147 (4.36)	−.156 (−.19)	−.813 (−7.78)	0.107 (2.65)	1.299 (2.07)
$\ln \dfrac{P(OC_7)}{P(OC_1)}$	4.155 (1.16)	−.237 (−.19)	−.845 (−4.11)	0.110 (1.12)	2.461 (1.53)
$\ln \dfrac{P(OC_8)}{P(OC_1)}$	4.667 (2.80)	−.018 (−.04)	−.577 (−5.47)	0.084 (2.11)	1.558 (2.46)

[a] Random sample from NLS data.
[b] Variable definitions: $OC_1 \equiv$ professional; $OC_2 \equiv$ managerial; $OC_3 \equiv$ clerical; $OC_4 \equiv$ sales; $OC_5 \equiv$ craft; $OC_6 \equiv$ operative; $OC_7 \equiv$ household worker; $OC_8 \equiv$ services (excluding household); $c \equiv$ constant; $m \equiv$ marital status (1 $\equiv$ married): $s \equiv$ years of schooling; $e \equiv$ exposure (A-S-6); $h \equiv$ home time (measured continuously).

Table 4. *Multiple logit equations for occupational choice, white married women (IDP data) N = 482*

Dependent variable	Independent variables[a]			
	c	*s*	*e*	*h*
ln (managerial/professional)	.416 (.21)	−.219 (−1.87)	.075 (1.68)	−.035 (−.92)
ln (clerical/professional)	2.664 (2.46)	−.242 (−3.76)	.047 (1.73)	.043 (1.88)
ln (operative/professional)	6.812 (4.84)	−.649 (−6.97)	.065 (1.95)	−.010 (−.38)
ln (unskilled/professional)	6.208 (4.57)	−.574 (−6.47)	−.005 (−1.47)	.099 (3.46)

[a] Independent variables definitions: c = constant; s = years of schooling; e = labor force exposure; h = years of exposure *not* in the labor force (home time).

by maximum likelihood techniques.[13] for both data sets.[14] As predicted, the results in Tables 3 and 4 illustrate a strong relationship between life-cycle labor force participation and occupational choice. The *h* coefficients can be interpreted as the effect of greater time out of the labor force upon the odds of being in occupation *j* relative to being professional. As can be seen, more time out of the labor force increases the probability of being in all except managerial (and possibly operative) occupations relative to being in professional occupations. This result holds for *both* data sets. Looking at the relative magnitudes of the coefficients, more labor force intermittency increases the odds of being both unskilled and a household service worker relative to being clerical and salesworkers; and to being clerical and salesworkers relative to operatives or nonhousehold service workers. Indeed, continuous labor force participation is most important for managerial and professional workers.[15] Those persons with the least continu-

13. The likelihood function is

$$L = \prod_{t\in\Omega_1} P_{t1} \prod_{t\in\Omega_2} P_{t2} \cdots \prod_{t\in\Omega_M} P_{tM},$$

where the *P*'s are defined above and Ω_i represents each possible occupation. The program used was developed by Peter Schmidt and Robert Strauss [13] and is comparable except for the normalization to techniques of Theil [14], and McFadden [3].

14. The probability of an individual being in any occupation can be calculated as:

$$P_{1t} = \frac{1}{1 + \sum_{j=2}^{M} \exp(X_t\beta_j)}$$

$$P_{it} = \frac{e^{X_t\beta_i}}{1 + \sum_{j=2}^{M} \exp(X_t\beta_j)} \quad i = 2, \ldots, M.$$

15. The results for professional workers are not as strong as expected. The reason is that nurses and teachers are included. Experiments leaving out these groups improved the results.

ous labor force participation are least likely to be in managerial occupations. Thus, it is established that even after adjusting for marital status, age, and education *among white women,* differences in life-cycle labor force behavior patterns are associated with the probability of being in a given occupation.[16] Yet, as indicated, the relationship differs among occupations.

Atrophy, Occupation, and Time Out of the Labor Force: Corroborative Results

According to the theory outlined, it is claimed that each occupation has a unique atrophy rate. Further, those individuals with expectations of higher time out of the labor force would face relatively large wage losses in occupations with high atrophy rates. Thus, a negative correlation is predicted between atrophy (Table 1) and the home time coefficients (Tables 3 and 4). Table 5 presents the correlation coefficients between occupational atrophy rates and the home time coefficients. Note that as predicted, these correlations are *strongly* negative indicating that those persons with higher home time have higher probabilities of being in occupations with lower atrophy rates. Again, this result holds for *both* data sets.

Table 5. *Simple correlation between atrophy and home time coefficients*

Data source	Correlation (atrophy rate and home time coefficient)
NLS	−.37
IDP	−.71

The above correlations are based on coefficients computed across broad occupational categories. Rather than rely on such an aggregation, it is possible to perform similar computations based on individual data. Occupational atrophy rates are assigned to each woman on the basis of her occupation. Appropriately weighted[17] OLS regressions run over both entire samples using individual data yield:

$$\delta = 0.086 - .001h + .0009e + .011s - .006y \quad R^2 = .20$$
$$(4.1) \quad (-2.8) \quad (1.7) \quad (9.3) \quad (-.9)$$

(IDP) (10)

and

$$\delta = .132 - .0043h + .0015e + .005s + .040m + .003S_m \quad R^2 = .03$$
$$(4.08) \quad (2.15) \quad (3.23) \quad (4.23) \quad (2.77)$$

(NLS) (11)

16. The sample pertains *only* to females. Thus, home time coefficients are not measuring sex discrimination.
17. See Gary Saxanhouse [12].

where *t* values are in parentheses,

$h \equiv$ years home time (T-N),

$e \equiv$ labor market exposure,

$s \equiv$ years of schooling,

$y \equiv$ the existence of young children in the household,

$m \equiv$ marital status, and

$S_m \equiv$ parental education.

Again, as depicted above, a strong inverse correlation exists between time out of the labor force *(h)* and atrophy (δ).

Projections

It is not atypical to apply cross-sectional analysis to predict time-series changes.[18] If we assume that the cross-sectional estimates reasonably represent occupational choices, they can be used for time-series projections. This is the procedure followed for both data sets.

The multiple logit estimates relating labor force participation to occupation are used on the assumption of a diminishing trend of time out of the labor force *(h)*. Since the purpose of this paper is to emphasize technique rather than to make an exact forecast, the radical assumption of full female labor force participation is made. An occupational probability density function (pdf) is obtained for each woman using the coefficients of Tables 3 and 4 with the assumption that $h = 0$. Aggregation of all individual probabilities yields a projected population-wide occupational pdf.

Both sets of data yield the same results (Table 6). Decreasing home time implies a doubling of women in managerial occupations (from 3 to 7 percent of women in the NLS and 4.6 to 8.8 percent in the IDP), about a 30 percent increase of women in professional occupations (from 14 to 19 percent in the NLS and 18.5 to 23.6 percent in the IDP), and a 25 to 60 percent decline of women in unskilled jobs (14 to 9.5 percent in the NLS and 19.3 to 7.4 percent in the IDP).

Qualifications

With this as with all work, numerous qualifications are in order. A partial list is presented. (1) These projections ignore the economy's ability to absorb more employees in professional-type occupations. Because macroeconomic variables are not explicitly considered, it would be best to view the forecasts as a measure of expected changes in female occupational *aspirations* as opposed to

18. For example, see J. Mincer [4].

Table 6. *Projected female occupational distribution*

Occupation	Actual	Projected
	(percent)	
NLS		
Professional	14	19
Managerial	3	7
Clerical	46	49
Sales	7	3
Craft	0.9	0.8
Operative	15	13
Household	1	0.5
Service	13	9
Total	99.9	101.3
IDP		
Professional	18.5	23.6
Managerial	4.6	8.8
Clerical-sales	41.3	34.2
Operative	16.4	26.0
Unskilled	19.3	7.4
Total	100.0	100.0

actual occupational choice. (2) Precise estimates of h were not presented. Thus, our occupational estimates are indicative only of directionality. (3) It should be noted that estimates of h are needed for men as well as women. Although we have concentrated on increased female labor force participation, we cannot ignore the secular decline in male labor force participation. With these declines there probably would be a shift in male occupations toward blue collar jobs. Such trends perhaps may even be strong enough to enable the economy to absorb increased numbers of women in the professional-type occupations already discussed. Finally, (4) no account was taken of the simultaneity that may exist between occupational and lifetime labor force participation. Whereas this study assumes that exogenous labor force behavior affects occupational choice, it is conceivable that the causality may work in the other direction. If this paper were concerned only with unbiased coefficient estimation, then simultaneous equation techniques would have to be invoked. However, the multiple logit used in this chapter is appropriate, given an objective of forecasting purely occupational distribution.

Summary, Conclusions, and Extensions

The purpose of this study was to develop the beginnings of a methodology by which to project female occupational choice. A model was postulated illustrating the importance of continuous life-cycle labor force participation on occupational choice. This was done by illustrating a sorting of occupational and individual attributes and the differing atrophy rates of occupations. Those with the most atrophy are least amenable to intermittent labor force participation. Consequently, women expecting long home time segments are postulated to choose jobs with the least atrophy. This hypothesis is formed on the basis of analyzing the relationship between occupation and life-cycle labor force participation. Multiple logit analysis was used to ascertain this relationship and to obtain projections of female occupational aspirations given decreased trends in female labor force intermittency.

Although we have dealt specifically with women's occupational distribution, our model has wider applicability in that it can be viewed as a generalization of the hedonic index approach, capable of obtaining derived demand curves for occupational characteristics. Further, though obtaining a derived demand curve for the occupational characteristic atrophy was our concern, other characteristics could also have been considered. In the case of females, Doescher [1] illustrates how the number and spacing of children are related to flexibility of hours as well as atrophy.

In addition, we need not have concentrated on women. For example, occupational safety could have been considered and related to individual risk aversion. In this case, family characteristics (e.g., family size) may increase risk aversion so that heads of large households may "purchase" relatively safer jobs, ceteris paribus. Declining family size (holding income and other variables constant) may lead to a decline in occupational safety.

The model presented is only an initial step toward forecasting labor market changes. Other population attributes and other job characteristics as well as macroeconomic considerations should be incorporated. Once all this is done, more precise estimates would be achieved, which could then be used to measure more accurately the effects of changing demographic trends on labor market conditions, and finally, on the social security burden on those of working age.

References

[1] Doescher, Tabitha, "Occupation and Fertility," Ph.D. dissertation, University of North Carolina at Chapel Hill, in progress.

[2] Institute for Social Research, University of Michigan. *A Panel Study of Income Dynamics: 9th Wave of Household Heads and Wives* (Ann Arbor, 1976).

[3] McFadden, Daniel, "Conditional Logit Analysis of Qualitative Choice Behavior" in Paul Zarembka (Ed.), *Frontiers in Econonometrics* (New York: Academic Press, 1974), pp. 105–142.

[4] Mincer, Jacob, "Labor Force Participation of Married Women," in *Aspects of Labor Economics: A Conference of the Universities-National Bureau Committee for Economic Research,* NBER Special Conference Series 14 (Princeton: Princeton University Press, 1962).

[5] Mincer, Jacob, and Solomon Polachek, "Family Investments in Human Capital: Earnings of Women," *Journal of Political Economy* 82 (March/April 1974), S76–S108.

[6] Parnes, Herbert S., *Dual Careers,* Vol. 1, Manpower Research Monograph No. 21 (Washington, D.C.: U.S. Government Printing Office, 1970).

[7] Parnes, Herbert S., *National Longitudinal Survey, Mature Women, 30–44* (Columbus, O.: Center for Human Resource Research, 1972).

[8] Polachek, Solomon William, "Potential Biases in Measuring Male-Female Discrimination," *Journal of Human Resources,* 10 (Spring 1975), 205–229.

[9] Polachek, Solomon William, "Occupational Segregation: Theory, Evidence, and a Prognosis" in Cynthia Lloyd (Ed.), *Women in the Labor Market* (New York: Columbia University Press, 1979), 137–157.

[10] Rosen, Sherwin, "Hedonic Prices and Implicit Markets: Product Differentiation in Pure Competition," *Journal of Political Economy,* 82 (Jan./Feb. 1974), 34–55.

[11] Sandell, Steven, and David Shapiro, "Women's Incorrect Expectations and Their Labor Market Consequences," paper presented at Western Economics Association meetings, San Francisco, June 1977.

[12] Saxonhouse, Gary R., "Estimated Parameters as Dependent Variables," *American Economic Review,* 66 (Mar. 1976), 178–183.

[13] Schmidt, Peter, and Robert Strauss, "Estimation of Models with Jointly Dependent Qualitative Variables: The Simultaneous Logit Approach," paper presented at the Econometrics Society meetings, San Francisco, Dec. 1974.

[14] Theil, Henri, "A Multinational Extension of the Linear Logit Model," *International Economic Review,* 10 (Oct. 1969), 251–259.

[15] Welch, Finis, and Iva Maclennan, "The Census Occupational Taxonomy: How Much Information Does It Contain?" prepared for The Department of Health, Education, and Welfare and The Department of Labor, R-1849-HEW/DOL (Santa Monica: Rand Corporation, 1976).

Retirement in Dual-Career Families   *Kathryn Anderson, Robert L. Clark and Thomas Johnson*

The retirement decision is one of the most important life-cycle decisions for each worker, and the pattern of labor force withdrawal has significant macro-economic implications. The sharp increase in female labor market activity during the last thirty years may affect future retirement decisions as couples in which both spouses have spent considerable time in the labor force approach the retirement years. This paper specifically addresses the influence of wives' market activities on their husbands' retirement decisions and conversely, the role of the male-oriented variables in determining female labor supply. The results of the examination of family retirement decisions will have implications for the future flow of benefits and taxes resulting from the nation's pension system.

The importance of this research lies in the rapid growth of two-earner families in the United States. This changing career orientation of married women has significant implications for rates of family formation, income distribution, measured unemployment rates, family time allocation and many other social and economic relationships. The continued labor force attachment of wives during their work life will significantly influence the meaning and timing of retirement.

In a dual-career family, the wife is more likely to have earned a private pension benefit and have a social security benefit that exceeds the benefits to the spouse of a worker. These pension benefits can be expected to influence the labor force participation decision of the wife and the husband as well. Eligibility for pension benefits by one family member tends to induce retirement through income effects of the benefits and through implicit wage reductions. Although not altering the value of market time of the spouse, the factors can be expected to affect their labor supply through increased family income and the relationship of the family member's time in household activities.

Studies of individual labor supply have expanded during the last two decades, and most empirical work has concentrated on individuals aged 55 and below, thus ignoring older workers. Those empirical studies that have examined the labor supply of older workers have employed as explanatory variables pension-related factors, health status, aggregate economic characteristics, financial and wage variables, and individual and family characteristics. The pension-related effects are usually among the dominant factors influencing labor force participation, and they include social security benefits, the earnings test, age of eligibility, private pension and compulsory retirement. In previous studies, however, the simultaneous determination of labor supply of older dual-career families has not been analyzed. Such an analysis would be based in the context of several types of labor supply literature. In the next few pages, we briefly review this literature as it concerns the retirement decision and labor supply of married women.

Pension benefits provide a flow of income to individuals that is not derived from current market work. The availability of these benefits may induce reductions in labor supply. The receipt of these benefits may, however, be contingent on modifications in individual work patterns [6, 4, 23]. The earnings test for social security and the required retirement from the specific job to receive appropriate pension effectively reduce the market wage which, in turn, tends to reduce labor force participation and hours of work [4, 6, 21]. In many cases, the size of pension benefits may be increased by delayed retirement. Burkhauser [7] notes that the present value of pension benefits is a significant factor determining retirement.

Health impairments may reduce a worker's market productivity and therefore, the market wage rate that he can command. In addition they may also increase the onerousness of work. The anticipated result is that health limitations decrease labor market activity. The importance of health in the retirement decision has been illustrated in a series of surveys of the elderly [28, 3, 20], as well as in econometric studies by Quinn [23] and Burkhauser [7].[1] The consensus of previous research indicates that these two factors—existence of pension income and the health status of workers—usually exert the dominant influence of the labor supply of older workers, and Quinn [23] finds evidence supporting a strong interactive effect between the two. However, it is also important to note at this point that the reasons for retirement may change with advancing age.

Studies of the labor supply decisions of married women find evidence supporting a simultaneous decision-making process within the family unit. Family resource constraints consist of the potential earnings of each spouse and of nonwage income. Wives have three alternative uses of their time: leisure, market work, and home production. The optimal allocation of time will depend on their home and market productivity, the relative productivity of their husband's time in home and market production, and other income. Mincer [19] and Kosters [17] provided much of the early theoretical framework for labor supply models of married women.

Employing the Mincer framework, Cain [8] reported negative correlation between wives' time in the market and husbands' incomes. This result supporting Mincer's earlier estimates indicates that husbands' and wives' times are substitutes in the home production process. (Also see Bowen and Finegan [6], and Kalachek and Raines [15].) Somewhat different findings are reported by Wales and Woodland [27], and Kniesner [16], who estimate that the leisure time of the husband and wife are complements. These studies usually find positive responses by married women to their own wage rates. Measures of home productivity, such as number of small children, tend to be negatively correlated with

---

1. For a detailed review of the factors determining the labor force participation of the elderly, see Clark, Kreps, and Spengler [9].

labor supply [11, 5]. Papers by Ashenfelter and Heckman [2] and Schultz [25] support the general finding that women are more responsive than males to own wage changes and are characterized by an upward sloping supply curve.

The decision by married women to enter the labor force is the result of utility-maximizing behavior that compares the costs and benefits of participating in the market relative to the net benefits of home production and leisure. In general, female labor force participation responds positively to increases in their own wage but negatively to increases in income and fertility.[2] Recently, McElroy and Horney [18] have illustrated that family time allocation decisions can be placed in a bargaining framework. In this model, it is important to know which family member is the recipient of nonwage income. Such a finding has added significance for older families in which pension benefits comprise an increasing proportion of family income.

Modeling and Simulation

The model of the family that we use to explore the implications of dual careers is a life-cycle model that begins after the marriage partners have established a family. In this section, we describe the model in a nontechnical manner. A more mathematical treatment will be available in a later report. Because of the nonlinearity and complexity of the model, analytical solutions cannot be obtained in closed form. Therefore, a simulation procedure is used to explore the implications of the model for different market opportunities and characteristics of the marriage partners. The two polar cases that will be simulated first are (a) no comparative advantage between the partners in home and market work, and (b) one spouse has a strong comparative advantage in market work. Because of limitations on the number of statements that can be used in the simulation routine, the characteristics of pension plans must be approximated in a manner that is much less elegant than we have been able to achieve for an individual decision manner.

A Life-Cycle Model with Two Productive Family Members

The objective of the family is to maximize the present value of the stream of utility over the family horizon. This requires that all goods be valued by a single utility functional. The analysis is simplified and exposition is clarified by constructing this functional in two stages. First, we assume that all utility of family members is derived from a single composite, home-produced commodity that we call Zeds.[3] Thus, the objective is to maximize the present value of

---

2. For a more detailed review of the research concerning female labor supply, see Anderson [1].
3. It has become traditional to refer to units of human capital as Eds denoted by *E*. Since our composite commodity is produced in a manner similar to the production of Eds, the nomenclature seems appropriate.

the consumption of Zeds over the lifetime plus the utility of financial assets left as bequests. We assume that the lifetime is fixed and known.[4] Next, we assume that Zeds are produced according to a neoclassical production function with three inputs. The inputs are (1) a good purchased in the market, (2) the human capital-augmented time or effort of the husband, and (3) the human capital-augmented time or effort of the wife.[5] The production function used is discussed more fully in the appendix to this chapter. The form used for this production function allows the effort of husband and wife to be either substitutes or complements depending upon the value of a parameter and the amount of effort put into home production.

The utility, at the beginning of the planning period, of leaving a bequest is taken to be a logarithmic function of the bequest. Studies of risk have shown that the logarithmic utility function has reasonable properties. The primary advantage of the logarithmic form for our study is that it prevents plans to end life in debt since as the bequest approaches zero, the logarithm approaches minus infinity.

Each spouse also has an opportunity to work in the market. Each can rent his human capital for a fixed rate R, which means that his wage rate is R times the stock of human capital.[6] Even if the rental rate is equal for the two partners, the wage rates may differ because of different levels of human capital possessed by the partners. This means that one spouse may have a comparative advantage in market work even though the coefficients on husband's and wife's efforts in the home production function are equal and the market rental rates are equal.

Each spouse begins marriage with an initial stock of human capital. Each spouse's stock of human capital changes at a rate that depends upon the effort he or she devotes to producing more human capital. Human capital also depreciates at a constant rate for each spouse.[7] Human capital production is a very

---

4. Thus, the objective is to maximize the functional

$$J = \int_0^T e^{-\rho t} U[Z(t)]\, dt + W[B(t)].$$

This formulation has either of two interpretations. Either (a) both marriage partners anticipate death at the same moment T, or (b) support of the surviving marriage partner is planned for and provided through the bequest function $W[B(T)]$.

5. The effort of the ith spouse in producing Zeds is written $K_{ih} = s_{ih} E_i$, where s_{ih} is the fraction of the moment at time t which is spent in producing Zeds and E_i is the human capital stock of the ith spouse.

6. The ith spouse produces income at the rate $R_i E_i s_{im} = R_i K_{im}$ where s_{im} is the fraction of the moment spent working in the market.

7. Each spouse i begins the marriage at $t = 0$ with an initial stock of human capital, $E_i(0)$. His or her stock of human capital then changes according to the differential equation

$$\dot{E}_i = Q_i(K_{il}, D_i) - \delta_i E_i,$$

where $\dot{E}_i$ is the time rate of change of E_i, Q_i is the rate at which E_i is produced, $K_{il} = s_{il} E_i$ is the effort devoted to producing more human capital, D_i is the input purchased, and δ_i is the rate of depreciation of E_i.

individualistic enterprise with each spouse's human capital produced through a combination of his own effort and a purchased input. At this time we do not plan to generalize to allow inputs from one spouse to affect directly the production of human capital of the other.

The main use of the life-cycle model and the simulation algorithm for obtaining solutions of the necessary conditions for optimal control in the model will be to investigate the effects of different relationships among these parameters on the retirement decision of the marriage partners. The limiting case is with both marriage partners being completely equal; i.e., they begin marriage with equal stocks of human capital, they have identical production functions for augmenting their human capital, their market rental rates are equal, and they have identical coefficients in the home production function. There is no limiting case of inequality of comparative advantage since this can arise from several different sources and the parameters may be varied continuously.

We will investigate the effects of comparative advantage first by varying the parameters in one activity at a time. Thus, from the base case of complete equality we will have one spouse begin with a smaller stock of human capital. This corresponds to the tradition of wives being younger than their husbands. Even though husband and wife have completed the same number of years of formal schooling, the extra years of experience of the husband could result in his having a larger stock of human capital at marriage. Another route for exploration will be to move to different coefficients in the production of the home commodity. The effects of different market rental rates for human capital will also be explored. This is the case that might be termed discrimination since we have not postulated any reason why a unit of human capital possessed by one spouse should be less productive in the market than a unit possessed by the other.

When postulating differences in human capital endowments it is important to be careful to distinguish between achievement and ability. Achievement is an apt term for the quantity of human capital possessed by an individual at a given time. Two persons might have different levels of achievement because they began with smaller endowments, because they have devoted a smaller proportion of their resources to investment in their human capital, or because they are less efficient at producing human capital with given inputs. Ability is an apt term for differences in efficiency in producing output with given inputs.[8]

---

8. Suppose that the human capital production is a Cobb-Douglas form

$$Q_i = \beta_{io} K_{il}{}^{\beta i1} D_i{}^{\beta i2}.$$

Clearly, a larger β_{io} or a larger sum $\beta_{i1} + \beta_{i2}$, with β_{i1}/β_{i2} constant would mean a greater output for given inputs and thus would represent greater ability. It is less clear how we should characterize differences in β_{i1}/β_{i2}. For estimates of β_{i1}/β_{i2} see Derrick and Johnson [10] and Johnson [14].

Use and Limitations of a Simulation Algorithm

The necessary conditions for maximization of the objective functional are obtained by application of the maximum principle.[9] These conditions are a set of differential equations subject to boundary value constraints. The complexity of the problem precludes solution of these equations in closed form. Therefore, we have used the Continuous System Modeling Program (CSMP) [26] to integrate the differential equations over the life cycle and obtain solutions that satisfy the boundary values through an iterative procedure.

Basically, the problem is to determine the correct values of the shadow prices at the beginning of the life cycle. The maximum principle says that we will follow the optimal path through time if at each moment we maximize the net returns while properly valuing changes to the state variables. The value of a unit change in a state variable is given by a shadow price, which is a function of time. In our problem there are three state variables, the human capital of spouse 1, the human capital of spouse 2, and the net stock of financial assets or bonds held. The system of necessary conditions includes a differential equation for each of the three shadow prices. Starting from initial values at the beginning of the life cycle, these differential equations tell us how to update each shadow price as we proceed through time. However, the boundary conditions to be satisfied are that the shadow price of each spouse's human capital must go to zero at the end of the planning horizon, and that the shadow price of financial assets at the end be equal to the marginal utility of bequests. Thus, we have to guess at what initial values the shadow prices, through the updating differential equations, will lead to the required terminal values. When our initial guesses of the shadow prices do not lead to the required terminal values, we must change our initial guesses and again simulate the life cycle.[10]

The major complication in the procedure is accounting for constraints and corner solutions. For example, each spouse has three activities among which a unit of time may be divided.[11] If each spouse devotes some fraction of each unit of time to every activity, we can fairly easily find the interior solution. We must, however, allow for each activity to be at its minimum value of zero. This requires special branching and consequent lengthening of the computer code.

9. See Intriligator [12] for an exposition of the maximum principle at the level of an advanced course in economic theory. For a more simplified exposition, see Perrin and Johnson [22]. The equations for the present problem are contained in a technical appendix that will be available upon request.

10. Of course, we follow a systematic procedure for changing our guesses. We first take small fixed steps in changing the initial guesses and from the results we estimate the partial derivatives of changes in terminal values with respect to changes in initial guesses. We then use a Newton-Raphson procedure with these partial derivatives to improve our initial guesses. This continues until we produce final results within specified limits of the required terminal conditions.

11. The fraction that spouse i spends in home production is s_{ih}, in production of human capital is s_{il}, and in market production is s_{im}. The constraint for spouse i is $s_{ih} + s_{il} + s_{im} = 1$.

Another complication arises as we follow the differential equations updating the shadow prices of human capital through the life cycle. The theory and elementary economic reasoning dictates that in the solution of the necessary condition equations, these shadow prices must be positive up until the last moment. The real complication, however, arises because the logarithm of each of these shadow prices appears in the computations. Thus, in the computer code we have to assure that these shadow prices never go below zero and include special branches when one of these shadow prices does go to zero before the last moment in one of the iterations during the search for the solution of the necessary condition equations.

These complications have caused our model code to press the limits of the CSMP simulation routine even in the simplest case of a two-person family. The CSMP routine allows a maximum of 600 "macro outputs" and we have 535 in our most basic problem. Therefore, we are going to be very limited in our ability to include realistic social security tax and benefit schemes in our algorithm.[12]

Treatment of Social Security, Health, and Other Extensions

Because of the limitations in the size of the CSMP routine, and on computer time costs, we will have to model effects of social security, mandatory retirement, changes in health, etc., by step changes in parameters or state variables. For example, mandatory retirement at t_m might be modeled as a step decrease in the market rental rate for human capital at t_m. A catastrophic health problem might be modeled as a step decrease in human capital affecting both market and home production.

When including any of these changes we have to be very careful to distinguish between anticipated and unanticipated changes. An anticipated change must be included in the model for life-cycle planning from the very beginning. Unanticipated changes, however, mean that the original plan must be terminated with whatever values of the variables exist at the time of the occurrence, and a new life-cycle plan formulated from that point to the end of the planning horizon. Of course, the remaining time in the planning horizon may be one of the parameters that can change unexpectedly.

In the initial version of our model we have the end time T corresponding to the simultaneous death of both marriage partners. Since wives typically have outlived husbands, it is very desirable to try to model a family life-cycle plan that would anticipate the survival of one partner beyond the death of the other.

---

12. One of our students, David Smallwood, is working on a life-cycle model of an individual and including a very representative social security system. This has greatly complicated the program for a single person.

It is not yet clear how much computational complexity this will add, so we can promise little more than that we will consider this extension.

Data Description

The data employed in this analysis are taken from the Retirement History Study conducted by the Social Security Administration. A national sample of

Table 1. *Summary of variables used*

Variable name	Distinction
LNWH	logarithm of current wages of the husband
AGEH	husband's current age
AGEH2	husband's age squared
REDUCI	husband's education
HLTH	= 1 if health limits husband's ability to work
	= 0 if health does not limit husband's ability to work
DUM69	= 1 if 1969
	= 0 otherwise
DUM71	= 1 if 1971
	= 0 otherwise
LNWW	logarithm of current wage of the wife
AGESP	wife's current age
AGESP2	wife's age squared
EDWIFE	wife's education
LFPHTOT	= 1 if husband is in labor force
	= 0 if husband is not in labor force
LNWHIM	imputed log of wages for husband
LNWWIM	imputed log of wages for wife
HOUSE	real housing value—net of debt
COVH	= 1 if the husband is covered by a pension
	= 0 if he is not covered by a pension
ELSSH	= 1 if husband is eligible for social security
	= 0 if husband is not eligible for social security
ELSSW	= 1 if wife is eligible for social security
	= 0 if wife is not eligible for social security
CHILD	number of children supported completely
LFPWTOT	= 1 if wife is in labor force
	= 0 if wife is not in labor force
HOURSH	current hours on job, husband
HOURSW	current hours on job, wife
WAGEH	husband's current hourly wage
WAGEW	wife's current hourly wage
HLTH	= 1 if husband's health limits his ability to work
	= 0 if husband has no health limitation
ELRETH	= 1 if husband $\geq$ 65
	= 0 if husband $<$ 65
ELRETW	= 1 if wife $\geq$ 65
	= 0 if wife $<$ 65
COVW	= 1 if wife is covered by a pension in 1971
	= 0 if wife is not covered

over 11,000 individuals aged 58 to 63 was selected to participate in a ten-year study and interviews first held in 1969.[13] The respondents were resurveyed every two years with data from 1969, 1971 and 1973 currently available.

Survey respondents consist of nonmarried men, nonmarried women, and married men. This project focuses on family retirement patterns employing the information on married men and the more limited information gathered on their spouses. This chapter is a preliminary reporting of our examination of retirement in dual-career families. In the early stages of this project, we have chosen to work with a limited sample size prior to testing specific hypotheses on the entire sample population. A random sample of 600 married men was chosen for examination. Thus, we are not contaminating the entire data set when we use sequential regressions and make changes suggested by the results. Information concerning worklives, health status, financial resources, and retirement plans for husbands and their wives has been selected from the set of data contained in the RHS files. Variables employed in the following analysis are defined in Table 1.

Empirical Results

The lack of current wage data on all nonworking respondents and spouses necessitated the imputation of wages for these individuals. The logarithm of the current wages of working respondents was regressed on current age, age squared, education, and health for 1969, 1971, and 1973. The logarithm of current wages of working spouses was regressed on age, age squared, and education for the same years. Significant differences in the values of the intercept terms were discernible when regressions were compared for each year. This suggested that the years were causing shifts in the demands for male and female labor. To estimate these shifts, regressions were run combining the time-series and cross-sectional data. Dummies for 1969 and 1971 were inserted in both male and female regressions. The results are tabulated in Tables 2 and 3. In each regression, one of the dummy variables for 1969 and 1971 was significant.[14]

The explanatory power of the male wage regression was slightly larger than the explanatory power of the female regression. In the male regression, all variables were significant except DUM69. The logarithm of wages increased at a decreasing rate with age as expected. Higher levels of education increased the logarithm of wages. Health limitations reduced the log of wages.

13. For a description of the sample, see Irelan [13].
14. The same observations are used in 1969, 1971, and 1973. Some degrees of freedom were lost in the analysis because of the lack of independence across time. The years were combined in one regression, however, to increase the sample size in the preliminary work. It was not advisable to contaminate the entire sample at this stage of the research. Later empirical work will use the entire sample, and separate regressions will be analyzed for each year.

Table 2. *Regression of the logarithm of current wages for the husband (LNWH), 1969–73*[a]

Independent variables	Coefficients
INTERCEPT	−11.865*
	(4.439)
AGEH	.399*
	(.149)
AGEH2	− .003*
	(.001)
REDUCI	.071*
	(.006)
HLTH	− .202*
	(.049)
DUM69	.073
	(.067)
DUM71	.105**
	(.059)
F ratio	28.996
R^2	.164
Sample size	892

[a] Standard errors are in the parentheses.
* Significant at the 1 percent level.
** Significant at the 10 percent level.

In the female regression, all variables were significant except education and DUM71. The logarithm of wages fell at an increasing rate with age in this case. This was not expected. Several explanations were possible for this result. First, the cross-sectional effect of age had not been completely separated from the time-series effect. Women were entering the labor force at different ages, and this variable was picking up this effect. Second, age was not a good proxy for tenure or experience in the case of women. The age variable did not pick up the discontinuity of female labor force participation. Tenure in the job market since re-entry was the desired variable, but the necessary information was unavailable on the questionnaire. Third, age was possibly picking up some of the health effects of increasing age. Again, the lack of relevant health information on spouses prevented the measurement of this effect.

The wage regressions were used to impute wages to all respondents and spouses in the sample. The only difference in the imputations for the three years—1969, 1971, and 1973—was in the size of the intercept term. To impute a wage for 1969, DUM69 was equal to one, DUM71 was equal to zero. For 1971, DUM69 was zero and DUM71 was one. For 1973, both DUM69 and DUM71 were zero.

Labor force participation of the husband was hypothesized to be a function of assets, wages, eligibility for pensions and social security, age, and personal characteristics. Imputed wages were included in the regressions as the measure

Table 3. *Regression of the logarithm of current wages for the wife (LNWW), 1969–1973*[a]

Independent variables	Coefficients
INTERCEPT	11.602*
	(3.667)
AGESP	−.394*
	(.137)
AGESP2	.003*
	(.001)
EDWIFE	.026
	(.021)
DUM69	1.048*
	(.162)
DUM71	.230
	(.160)
F ratio	14.377
R^2	.144
Sample size	433

[a] Standard errors are in the parentheses.
* Significant at the 1 percent level.

of wages. The net liquidable value of residential property was chosen as the measure of assets in all three years. This variable was selected as a proxy for assets because it was the only asset information included in the 1973 survey.[15] One problem with this variable was that it could pick up a price effect as well as an income effect. An increase in the value of a home increased the value of marginal product of the wife in the home, and she substituted home production for market production.

To simplify the estimation of pension eligibility, the variable chosen was pension coverage of the husband and the wife. The respondent or his spouse was eligible for pension benefits if he was covered by a pension on his current, past, or longest job.[16] To estimate the effect of eligibility for social security, an age criterion was chosen. If the respondent or spouse were over the age of 62, he was considered eligible for social security.[17]

Plots of the labor force participation and the age of respondent and spouse indicated a possible quadratic effect of age on retirement. Current age and age

15. The correlation between the total value of assets and the net value of residential property is 0.48 in 1969 and 0.83 in 1971.

16. This is not identical to measuring pension eligibility. This variable was used because of the difficulty in deriving the eligibility variable. A person is eligible if he was covered by a pension on his current, past, or longest job and if he could receive pension benefits. This variable is now being derived; complications in isolating skip patterns in 1969 have prevented its use in this study.

17. This is not the only criterion for social security eligibility. Matched earnings data from the Social Security Administration are currently being analyzed. From these data, we can compute how much each person had paid into the social security system since 1950 and determine his eligibility for benefits.

squared of the wife and husband were used in the regressions.[18] In addition, a large drop in labor force participation was expected after the age of 65. Dummy variables for the husband and wife were included to measure this effect.

Personal characteristics included in the regressions were health, the number of children supported completely by the household, and the number of older family members, such as parents and parents-in-law, supported by the household. The health variable was a dummy variable equal to one if the husband had a health problem that limited his ability to work. No health variable was derived for the wife because of the lack of health information on the spouse. The variables chosen to estimate the effects of children and old family members on labor force participation were the numbers of these people supported.

The first regressions estimated were separate regressions for the husband and wife in each of the three years—1969, 1971, and 1973. Ordinary least squares regression was used with a 0–1 dependent variable.[19] The coefficients were very similar across time except for the intercept terms. In addition, the ELRETH variable could not be estimated for 1969; in 1969, all respondents were under the age of 65. The three regressions were rerun together in a single regression with dummy variables for years. DUM69 was equal to one if the year was 1969, and DUM71 was equal to one if the year was 1971.[20]

The results of single-equation estimation of labor force participation using ordinary least squares regression (OLS) are presented in Table 4. The set of economic variables included in the regressions explain 30 percent of the variation in male labor force participation but only 10 percent of the variation in female labor force participation.

The estimates are generally consistent with the predictions of the model. First, the coefficient on the asset variable (HOUSE) is negative in both regressions although it is not statistically significant in the male regression. This result is supportive of the hypothesis that male and female home time are normal goods and that the income elasticity of female time is larger than the income elasticity of male time.

Second, some evidence of the complementarity of male and female home time is presented. In both regressions, the coefficient on female wages is positive and significant. An increase in the log of female wages of 1 percent encourages an increase in female labor force participation of 0.77 percent and in male labor force participation of 0.43 percent. The male wage variables are statistically insignificant in both regressions.

18. A variable designed to measure the effect of the difference in the age of the respondent and the age of his spouse (AGEHSP = AGEH − AGESP) was included in the estimation. The variable and its square were highly insignificant in both estimations. They were excluded from further analysis.

19. OLS was used for the preliminary explorations. Logit regression will be used for the final results. In this regression, the OLDFAM variable was omitted in all three years. This variable was not significant.

20. See n. 14 for explanation.

Table 4. *Regression of labor force participation of husbands and wives*[a]

	Dependent variables			
Independent variables	LFPHTOT (OLS)	LFPWTOT (OLS)	LFPHTOT (2SLS)	LFPWTOT (2SLS)
INTERCEPT	−8.868	−2.935	−8.027	2.973
	(10.445)	(12.030)	(10.661)	(14.385)
LNWHIM	−.009	−.081	.014	−.075
	(.056)	(.065)	(.071)	(.071)
LNWWIM	.434**	.774*	.212	.485
	(.178)	(.205)	(.379)	(.380)
HOUSE	−.0000004	−.00000139**	−	−.0000011
	(.0000006)	(.00000069)	−	(.0000008)
ELSSH	.09**	.052	.077	−.009
	(.045)	(.052)	(.052)	(.086)
ELSSW	−.119*	−.155*	−.075	−.076
	(.038)	(.044)	(.080)	(.094)
COVH	.015	−.066**	.034	−.077**
	(.024)	(.028)	(.040)	(.032)
AGEH	.152	−.225	.216	−.326
	(.328)	(.377)	(.350)	(.425)
AGEH2	−.002	.002	−.002	−.003
	(.003)	(.003)	(.003)	(.004)
AGESP	.213*	.356*	.111	.214
	(.071)	(.082)	(.170)	(.172)
AGESP2	−.002*	−.003*	−.0001	−.002
	(.0005)	(.0006)	(.001)	(.001)
CHILD	.029***	.019	.024	−
	(.016)	(.019)	(.019)	−
ELRETH	−.010	.041	−.022	.048
	(.069)	(.080)	(.073)	(.088)
ELRETW	−.119**	−.078	−.097	.002
	(.055)	(.064)	(.065)	(.106)
HLTH	−.343*	−.099*	−.314*	.129
	(.027)	(.031)	(.052)	(.241)
DUM69	−.344***	−.812*	−.111	−.583***
	(.187)	(.216)	(.397)	(.340)
DUM71	.080	−.098***	.108***	−.151***
	(.049)	(.057)	(.064)	(.083)
B.LFPWTOT	−	−	.286	−
	−	−	(.441)	−
B.LFPHTOT	−	−	−	.666
	−	−	−	(.697)
F ratio	37.086	9.279	−	−
*R*²	.312	.102	−	−
Sample size	1327	1327	1311	1311

[a] Standard errors are in parentheses   ** Significant at the 5 percent level.
* Significant at the 1 percent level.   *** Significant at the 10 percent level.

Third, the coefficients on the female variables in both regressions are strongly significant, whereas the coefficients on the male variables are insignificant and smaller in magnitude. This suggests that the decisions to participate in the labor force are joint decisions. With the inclusion of the female variables in the male regressions, almost all of the explanation previously attributable to changes in his own wage, age, or eligibility is now attributable to changes in his wife's wage, age, or eligibility. The husband's wage has no effect on his or his wife's labor force participation; however, an increase in the wife's wage encourages labor force participation of the husband and wife. Labor force participation of the husband and wife increases with the wife's age but reaches a

Table 5. *Logit estimation of labor force participation*[a]

Independent variables	Dependent variables			
	LFPHTOT		LFPWTOT	
	Coefficient	Derivative of probability at mean	Coefficient	Derivative of probability at mean
INTERCEPT	−1.048	–	−4.53	
	(35.628)	–	(28.604)	–
LNWHIM	−.003	−.01	−.160	−.071
	(.169)	–	(.155)	–
LNWWIM	1.189**	.594	1.792*	.861
	(.545)	–	(.500)	–
HOUSE	−.0000012	−.0000008	−.0000049**	−.0000022
	(.000002)	–	(.0000024)	–
ELSSH	.260***	.116	.095	.056
	(.142)	–	(.123)	–
ELSSW	−.307*	−.151	−.311*	−.147
	(.115)	–	(.112)	–
COVH	.070	.019	−.164**	−.070
	(1.073)	–	(.066)	–
AGEH	−.368	−.191	−.679	−.322
	(1.122)	–	(.898)	–
AGEH2	.002	.001	.006	.003
	(.009)	–	(.007)	–
AGESP	.593*	.294	.858*	.414
	(.219)	–	(.203)	–
AGESP2	−.004*	−.002	−.007*	−.003
	(.002)	–	(.002)	–
CHILD	.092***	.04	.030	.019
	(.050)	–	(.042)	–
ELRETH	−.073	−.023	.128	.054
	(.207)	–	(.199)	–
ELRETW	−.281***	−.154	−.522**	−.201
	(.170)	–	(.238)	–
HLTH	−.935*	−.405	−.134***	−.112
	(.084)	–	(.078)	–
DUM69	−.958***	−.485	−1.904*	−.634
	(.574)	–	(.524)	–
DUM71	.216	.072	−.274**	−.106
	(.147)	–	(.138)	–
LFPWTOT	−.167*	–	–	–
	(.037)	–	–	–
LFPHTOT	–	–	.167*	–
	–	–	(.037)	–

[a] Standard errors are in parentheses.
* Significant at the 1 percent level.
** Significant at the 5 percent level.
*** Significant at the 10 percent level.

maximum, declining beyond that point. Changes in the husband's age have no significant effect. The age function is not continuous. If the wife is over the age of 62 and eligible for social security, labor force participation of the husband and wife decreases. If the wife is over the age of 65 and eligible for full pension benefits, labor force participation of the husband and wife declines.

To further test the validity of the simultaneous decision-making hypothesis, the labor force participation regressions were re-estimated using two-stage least squares (2SLS) and the simultaneous logit procedure. In both estimations, labor force participation of the husband was included as a determinant of labor force participation of the wife, and labor force participation of the wife was included as a determinant of labor force participation of the husband. The 2SLS results are presented in Table 4, and the logit results are presented in Table 5.[21] Because the 2SLS results are insignificant, only the logit results are discussed.

The logit results provide additional evidence that labor force decisions are simultaneously determined. The wife's wage, age, and eligibility are more important than the husband's wage, age, and eligibility in both the husband's and wife's equations. In addition, the coefficient on LFPWTOT in the husband's equation and the coefficient on LFPHTOT in the wife's equation are highly significant and positive. Participation of the wife in the labor force raises the probability that her husband will participate, and the participation of the husband raises the wife's probability of participation.

Summary

These initial results of our project examining retirement in dual-career families illustrate the importance of considering the personal and labor market characteristics of the spouse in estimating the labor supply behavior of married individuals. The data indicate that wives of older men respond positively to increases in their own wages and that changes in the value of their market time are also positively correlated with their husband's labor force participation decision. This finding indicates that the nonmarket times of the husband and wife may be complements for couples in this age bracket. Since previous market work status is an important determinant of current wage rates, such a finding implies later retirement in the dual-career family.

The appropriateness of the use of a simultaneous decision model is supported by the high significance of the spouse's labor force participation in these equations. To the extent that current labor force participation is influenced by past market work, this positive relationship is further evidence for delayed retirement

21. Using a procedure developed by Ann Archibald McDermed of North Carolina State University, the logit coefficients are transformed into the derivative of the participation probability with respect to the independent variables evaluated at the mean of each explanatory variable. Both the coefficients and the derivatives are presented in Table 5.

in the two-worker family. This finding also supports the hypothesis of concurrent retirement in the dual-career family.

Offsetting these effects may be the response of older workers to eligibility for pension benefits by themselves and their spouses. To date, we have not incorporated female social security benefits into the husband's labor supply equation. The recently available social security earnings record will enable us to determine potential benefits for both the husband and wife. This next step of our analysis may prove to moderate the inference of later retirement discussed above. The possibility of this result is indicated by the negative influence on wife's labor force participation of the husband's pension coverage and the negative effect of the wife's becoming 62 years old—a proxy for initial eligibility for social security benefits—in both labor supply equations.

These findings confirm the importance of viewing labor force participation and retirement decisions in a household framework with simultaneous decisions being made concerning the time allocation of both the husband and the wife. Personal and labor market characteristics of each are important to the labor supply of the other. There seems to be rather strong evidence that the retirement decision of the husband will be influenced by his wife's labor market decisions. Thus, retirement patterns in dual-career families may deviate from that of the traditional male worker household. In future work, we will examine further this interaction between the market times of the spouses.

The significant increase in the labor force participation of married women over the last thirty years will produce a growth in the number of dual-career families approaching retirement during the remainder of this century. Will they exacerbate the tendency toward earlier retirement and the financial problems of supporting an aging population, or will the career orientation of these women tend to defer retirement for themselves and their husbands? Adequate answers to these questions are the primary objective of this project.

Appendix: Production of the Home Commodity

The home commodity, Z, is produced by a translog production function

$$\ln Z = \ln \gamma_0 + \gamma_1 \ln K_{1h} + \gamma_2 \ln K_{2h} + \gamma_3 \ln X + \gamma_4 \ln K_{1h} \ln K_{2h},$$

which is one of the simplest translog extensions of the Cobb-Douglas production function. Therefore the marginal productivity of the effort of spouse 1 in producing Z is

$$\frac{\partial Z}{\partial K_{1h}} = \frac{Z}{K_{1h}} [\gamma_1 + \gamma_4 \ln K_{2h}],$$

and similarly for spouse 2. The first term in brackets is the familiar Cobb-Douglas result, whereas the second term shows an additional effect of interaction of the effort by the two marriage partners.[22] This production function allows the elasticity of substitution between K_{1h} and K_{2h} to take different values. Following the suggestion of Samuelson [24] we use the "older" definition of complementarity that classifies two inputs X_k and X_1 as complements when

$$\frac{\partial MP_k}{\partial X_1} = \frac{\partial MP_1}{\partial X_k} > 0.$$

For our production function for Zeds, this says that K_{1h} and K_{2h} are complements if and only if

$$\frac{\partial^2 Z}{\partial K_{1h} \partial K_{2h}} = \frac{Z}{K_{1h} K_{2h}} [(\gamma_2 + \gamma_4 \ln K_{1h})(\gamma_1 + \gamma_4 \ln K_{2h}) + \gamma_4] > 0.$$

Since Z, K_{1h}, and K_{2h} are all nonnegative, K_{1h} and K_{2h} are complements if and only if

$$\gamma_1\gamma_2 + \gamma_4 (1 + \gamma_1 \ln K_{1h} + \gamma_2 \ln K_{2h} + \gamma_4 \ln K_{1h} \ln K_{2h}) > 0.$$

When γ_1 and γ_2 are positive, and K_{1h} and K_{2h} are greater than 1, K_{1h} and K_{2h} are complements whenever γ_4 is nonnegative. Solving the above inequality as a quadratic in γ_4 yields two negative values for γ_4, and for values of γ_4 between these two numbers, the expression is negative. Thus, there is an interval of (negative) values of γ_4 that implies that K_{1h} and K_{2h} are substitutes, whereas for values of γ_4 outside of this interval, the efforts of the two marriage partners are complements in the production of the home commodity. An exploration of the effects of different values of this parameter is one of the planned uses of the simulation algorithm.

The coefficients γ_1 and γ_2 are central in the expression of the relative productivity of the effort by the partners in producing the home commodity. It is, however, important to remember that the marginal productivity of the ith spouse also depends upon the value of other parameters and variables, but most especially upon the effort of K_{ih} of the ith spouse.

References

[1] Anderson, Kathryn H., "Economic Analysis of the Labor Supply of Married Women," mimeo, Department of Economics and Business, North Carolina State University, Raleigh, N.C., prepared for SSA Grant No. 90543, 1978.

22. Note that the marginal productivity of K_{1h}, or s_{1h} is decreasing if and only if $\gamma_1 + \gamma_4 \cdot \ln K_{2h} < 1$.

[2] Ashenfelter, Orley, and James Heckman, "The Estimation of Income and Substitution Effects in a Model of Family Labor Supply," *Econometrica*, 42 (Jan. 1974), 73–84.

[3] Bixby, L., "Retirement Patterns in the United States: Research and Policy Interactions," *Social Security Bulletin* (Aug. 1976), 3–19.

[4] Boskin, M. J., "The Economics of Labor Supply," in G. G. Cain and H. W. Watts (Eds.), *Income Maintenance and Labor Supply* (Chicago: Markham Press, 1973).

[5] Boskin, M. J., "Social Security and Retirement Decisions," *Economic Inquiry*, 15 (Jan. 1977), 1–25.

[6] Bowen, W. G., and T. A. Finegan, *The Economics of Labor Force Participation* (Princeton: Princeton University Press, 1969).

[7] Burkhauser, R., "The Early Pension Decision and Its Effect on Exit From the Labor Market," unpublished Ph.D. dissertation, University of Chicago, 1976.

[8] Cain, G. G., *Labor Force Participation of Married Women* (Chicago: University of Chicago Press, 1966).

[9] Clark, Robert, Juanita Kreps, and Joseph Spengler, "Economics of Aging: A Survey," *The Journal of Economic Literature*, 16 (Sept. 1978), 919–962.

[10] Derrick, Federick, and Thomas Johnson, "The Prudent Patron: Results from a Larger Sample," mimeo, Department of Economics and Business, North Carolina State University, Raleigh, N.C., Sept. 1978.

[11] Hall, R., "Wages, Income, and Hours of Work in the U.S. Labor Force," in G. G. Cain and H. W. Watts (Eds.), *Income Maintainence and Labor Supply* (Chicago: Markham Press, 1973).

[12] Intriligator, Michael D., *Mathematical Optimization and Economic Theory* (Englewood Cliffs: Prentice-Hall, 1971).

[13] Irelan, Lola M., "Retirement History Study: Introduction," *Social Security Bulletin* (Nov. 1972), 3–8.

[14] Johnson, Thomas, "Time in School: The Case of the Prudent Patron," *American Economic Review* (Dec. 1978), 862–872.

[15] Kalachek, E., and R. Raines, "Labor Supply of Low Income Workers," in *President's Commission of Income Maintenance, Technical Studies* (Washington, D.C.: U.S. Government Printing Office, 1970).

[16] Kniesner, T. J., "An Indirect Test of Complementarity in a Family Labor Supply Model," *Econometrica*, 44 (July 1976), 651–669.

[17] Kosters, M., *Income and Substitution Effects in a Family Labor Supply Model* (Santa Monica: Rand Corporation, 1969).

[18] McElroy, Marjorie B., and M. J. Horney, "Nash-Bargained Household Decisions: Toward a Generalization of the Theory of Demand," mimeo, Duke University, Durham, N.C., Sept. 1978.

[19] Mincer, J., "Labor Force Participation of Married Women," in H. G. Lewis (Ed.), *Aspects of Labor Economics*, National Bureau of Economic Research (Princeton: Princeton University Press, 1962), pp. 63–105.

[20] Parnes, Herbert, et al., *The Pre-Retirement Years*, Vol. 4, Manpower Research and Development Monograph No. 15, U.S. Department of Labor (Washington, D.C.: U.S. Government Printing Office, 1975).

[21] Peckman, J., H. Aaron, and M. Taussig, *Social Security: Perspectives for Reform* (Washington, D.C.: The Brookings Institution, 1968).

[22] Perrin, Richard K., and Thomas Johnson, *Linear Programming and Optimal Control: An Introduction to Optimizing Procedures in Economics*, Economics Information Report No. 54, Department of Economics and Business, North Carolina State University, Raleigh, N.C., July 1978.

[23] Quinn, Joseph F., *The Early Retirement Decision: Evidence From the 1969 Retirement History Study*, Social Security Administration, Office of Research and Statistics, HEW Publication No. 78–11855, Staff Paper No. 29 (Washington, D.C.: U.S. Government Printing Office, 1977).

[24] Samuelson, Paul, "Complementarity—An Essay on the 40th Anniversary of the Hicks-Allen Revolution in Demand Theory," *Journal of Economic Literature*, 12 (Dec. 1974), 1255–1289.

[25] Schultz, T. P., "Estimating Labor Supply Functions for Married Women," R-1265-NIH/EDA (Santa Monica: The Rand Corporation, 1975).

[26] System/360 Continuous Modeling Program III, (White Plains, N.Y.: International Business Machines Corporation, 1971).

[27] Wales, T. J., and A. D. Woodland, "Estimation of Household Utility Functions and Labor Supply Response," *International Economic Review,* 17 (June 1976), 397–410.

[28] Wentworth, Edna C., "Why Beneficiaries Retire," *Social Security Bulletin* (Jan. 1945), 16–20.

The Effects of Pension Policy Through Life   *Richard V. Burkhauser and John A. Turner*

The current pension system, both private and governmental in the form of social security, has significantly affected life-cycle behavior and especially labor supply. This chapter provides a framework in which to analyze the effects of our present pension system on the labor supply decisions of older men, and then analyzes the system's impact on the labor supply of younger men. Later, we expand the discussion to include other life-cycle responses to the pension system, and, finally, we look at recent changes in the system and suggest how it is likely to evolve.

After four decades of near-universal support, the social security system, particularly Old Age and Survivors Insurance (OASI), has become a topic of intense political debate. Given the current political turmoil over the magnitude of government spending programs, it is not too surprising that OASI, the largest single federal government program ($68 billion collected and distributed in 1977), should receive attention in both political and academic circles. There is little doubt that resistance to further tax increases is motivating much of the pressure to re-evaluate the system. This should not, however, obscure the role played by growing concern about the distribution of work across a lifetime. The increasing segmentation of life into a period of full-time work followed by one of almost total withdrawal from the workplace is a recent phenomenon whose consequences are just beginning to be questioned and whose causes have hardly been examined.

OASI is the cornerstone of this country's pension system, and in this chapter we argue that distortions contained in that system are largely responsible for a fundamental change in life-cycle work patterns. Not only have these distortions caused a decrease in work among older men, they have also increased the work effort of younger men. Too often in the debate over changes in the pension system, discussion has centered on the effect such changes have on the aged. We argue that an important, if little understood, characteristic of our present pension system is the impact it has on the behavior of the young. The young, of course, are the aged of the future and will someday directly confront the pension system. Yet they feel an impact in the present as well, because they are forced to adjust their current behavior in anticipation of such a future confrontation.

An Asset-Maximizing Approach to Pension Acceptance

The fall in labor supplied by older men over the last three decades has made the worker aged 65 or over an exception. In 1947, nearly one-half of all men this age were in the labor force; today only two men in ten over age 65 are in the labor force (see Table 1). This fall in labor supplied at older ages is particularly surprising given the continuing trend of work away from predominantly heavy toil toward more skillful and cerebral tasks. The 1978 Amendments to the Age Discrimination in Employment Act, raising to 70 the minimum age at which a worker can be discharged on the basis solely of age, are an attempt by the Congress to reverse this trend.[1]

Such antidiscrimination laws, however, do not address the economic incentives built into our present pension system that lead most men to retire well before age 70. Such retirement may appear voluntary but is, in effect, the direct result of these incentives. Older workers eligibile for private pensions or OASI must weigh the consequences of continuing work and receiving wages against those of accepting retirement benefits. Retirement will lead to benefit payments, but OASI benefits are reduced for those who earn wage and salary income, and private pensions usually require workers to leave their jobs; in some cases, they restrict earnings in other jobs.[2] In the presence of both restrictions on wage earnings and a fall in the value of a postponed pension, many workers reduce their hours of work or even completely retire. Although this choice is voluntary, its timing is influenced by the antiwork biases of the pension system.

Workers who have a pension that increases yearly benefits in an actuarially fair manner when acceptance is postponed do not have this problem and will not be induced to leave a job even if they face an earnings test.[3] Teachers Insurance and Annuity Association (TIAA) is an example of such a pension plan: for every year a worker postpones acceptance of benefits, future benefits increase, so that the lifetime value of all expected future benefits provided by the plan does not change. This type of pension removes the link between work decisions and pension acceptance. TIAA goes even further in that acceptance of benefits is not directly linked to either an earnings test or leaving a job.[4] Even if this were not the case, a worker will postpone acceptance to an age at which such work constraints do not influence his decision because benefits increase at a rate that makes him indifferent as to whether he gets them now or later. For the great majority of pension plans, however, benefits that are postponed are at least partially lost and workers are encouraged to retire voluntarily.

1. See Burkhauser and Tolley [8] for a fuller discussion of the expected ramifications of the new law.
2. The Employment Retirement Income Security Act (ERISA) now permits private pensions to restrict earnings only in jobs covered by the same plan or firm.
3. The discussion emphasizes the substitution effect caused by pension plan work constraints. Like any other asset, a pension will have a normal income effect on the labor-leisure choice, but it is important to recognize that, at least in the perfect market case, the point at which a pension is received should not have an independent income effect on labor supply. Rather, the effect should be spread across the life cycle. Only to the degree that the pension is unexpected would the income effect be confined to less than a full lifetime.
4. For income tax purposes, acceptance of TIAA is likely to coincide with reduction of full-time work.

Table 1. *Time-series changes in male labor force participation*[a]

| Year | Hours of work per week (1) | Percent males participating in labor force | | Percent eligible males receiving social security benefits | |
		Aged 65+ (2)	Aged 62–64 (3)	Aged 65–71 (4)	Aged 62–64 (5)
1900	58.5	63.1	–	–	–
1910	55.6	–	–	–	–
1920	50.6	55.6	–	–	–
1930	47.1	54.0	–	–	–
1940	42.5	41.8	–	–	–
1941	43.3	–	–	–	–
1947	42.4	47.8	–	–	–
1950	41.1	45.8	–	59[a]	–
1955	41.6	39.6	–	62[a]	–
1960	41.0	33.1	81.1	74[a]	–
1961	41.2	31.7	82.3	76	20
1965	42.0	27.9	76.8	80	32
1970	41.1	26.8	72.1	80	34
1975	40.8	21.7	59.7	90	46
1976	40.9	20.3	56.8	90	49
1977	41.3	20.1	55.7	90	51

[a] Includes all men aged 65 and older.
Sources: (1) Owen [16, p. 75], Kniesner [14, p. 5]; (2) U.S. Department of Commerce [22, pp. 131–32], U.S. Department of Labor [24, p. 30]; (3) Burkhauser [5, p. 46]; (4) U.S. Department of Health, Education, and Welfare [23, p. 85]; (5) U.S. Department of Health, Education, and Welfare [23, p. 85].

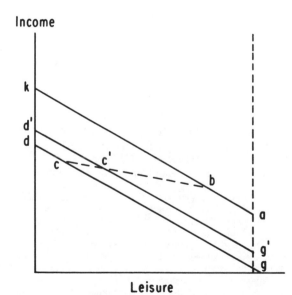

Figure 1. *Modified one-period labor-leisure choice*

The interdependence between pension acceptance and the market work decision is illustrated in the modified one-period diagram of Figure 1. Consider the case of workers aged 65 who are eligible for OASI benefits. In a one-period model these workers are seen facing the budget constraint line *abcd*. Along this line is the set of their possible choices with respect to market work and leisure. Their final choice depends on individual preferences.

Over the line segment *ab*, wage earnings are below the disregard level in the earnings test, and acceptance of benefits has no additional effect on market work. Over the line segment *bc*, the earnings test is in effect and for each dollar of wages earned, fifty cents in benefits is lost.[5] Over this range, acceptance of benefits induces less work because the earnings test reduces the net wage. Over the line segment *cd*, workers' earnings are sufficient for the earnings test to exhaust all benefits in the period.

Line segment *cd* is also part of the line *gcd*, the budget constraint line of workers who choose not to take OASI benefits in this period. As drawn, *gcd* assumes benefits are completely lost if postponed over the period. Once the asset nature of OASI is understood, it is clear that modifications in this one-period model are necessary. If future benefits are increased because acceptance in this period is postponed—and this has been the case since 1972—part of the loss is made up, and *gcd* underestimated the budget possibility set for these workers. Line *g' c' d'* reflects the net increase in the present value of future benefits caused by postponing acceptance of benefits in this period. As can be seen from the diagram, the greater the net actuarial increase in benefits in future periods (as measured by *gg'*), the higher *g' c' d'* rises, and the more attractive is the option to postpone benefits. The value *gg'* is equal to the expected present value of all additional benefits gained through delayed acceptance in the initial period.[6]

The case where the increase in future benefits is actuarially fair is represented by line *abk*. It is important to note that in this special case no point on *bc* is

---

5. The 1977 Amendments to Title II of the Social Security Act increase the amount exempted from the early earnings test to $4000 in 1978 and by $500 each year thereafter until it reaches $6000 for those 65 and older. For those under age 65, it is $3240 with yearly cost-of-living adjustments. The marginal tax rate continues to be 50 percent.

6. For a man aged 65 who delays acceptance of benefits until age 66 it would be:

$$gg' = \sum_{i=1}^{n} (p_i B_{65} d)/(1 + r)^i,$$

where

gg' = net present discounted value of additional social security benefits gained by delayed acceptance,

p_i = probability of surviving the ith period,

B_{65} = benefits at age 65 (*ea* in Figure 1),

d = rate of increase in yearly benefits in future periods due to delayed acceptance in initial period (1 percent since 1972), and

r = rate of interest.

above line *abk,* no worker will ever choose to be on line segment *bc,* and OASI has no adverse effect on work. But the greater the value of net social security benefits lost when their acceptance is postponed, the greater the range of line segment *bc,* and the more likely it is that a worker will accept OASI benefits and decrease his hours of work.[7]

The interdependence between labor supply and pension acceptance is not confined to OASI. In 1974, private pensions covered nearly 30 million workers. Although private pension coverage is not as widespread as OASI, data from the Retirement History Survey (a ten-year study, begun in 1969, of workers on the verge of retirement) shows that private pensions are important. Over all industries, 40 percent of male workers in the survey were eligible to receive a pension; in manufacturing over 60 percent were eligible. The great majority of these pensions have the same antiwork biases discussed above.

Little systematic empirical evidence on the economy-wide impacts of our current pension system exists, but recent work by Boskin [2] and Pellechio [17] finds that OASI has significantly reduced the work effort of older men. Quinn [18] finds that both private pensions and OASI affect work at older ages.

Burkhauser used the asset-maximizing approach to pension acceptance developed above to explain both the behavior of United Auto Workers eligible for a new pension [7] and the decision of men to take early OASI benefits [6]. In both these studies it was found that the greater the actuarial penalty for postponing acceptance of a pension, the more likely it was that workers would take the pension and reduce labor supply.

Changes in time-series data are consistent with a negative effect of both OASI and private pensions on the labor supply of older workers. Since 1937, the first year of OASI coverage, labor force participation rates for older workers have fallen sharply (see Table 1). For men aged 62 to 64, participation rates have fallen from 82 percent in 1961, the first year this group was eligible for OASI benefits, to 56 percent in 1977. Burkhauser [5] also used time-series data to test the effect of OASI on men aged 62 to 64. As in his studies using cross-sectional data, it was found that increases in the actuarial penalty for postponing OASI acceptance reduced labor force participation.

Changes in the labor force participation rate of older workers are not entirely due to our pension system. The secular increase in income would cause some decrease in the labor force participation rate of older workers. For instance, before the enactment of OASI, that rate for men aged 65 and older declined from 63 percent in 1900 to 54 percent in 1930. However, the acceleration in

7. This asset-maximization concept of pension acceptance is in sharp contrast to the simple, single-year, replacement-rate concept. A replacement ratio appears to show that delayed acceptance of a pension results in more lucrative benefits whenever postponement increases yearly benefits. But from asset perspective, an increase in yearly benefits is consistent with a rise, a fall, or a constant value of the pension.

the decline in the labor force participation rate of older workers as well as the studies by Boskin, Burkhauser, Pellechio, and Quinn suggest that the pension system is an important influence on labor supplied at older ages.

The Life-Cycle Effect of Pensions

A major puzzle of time-series labor supply data is the fact that although the work week for prime-age males declined continuously over the first four decades of this century, since the end of World War II it has remained relatively constant at about 42 hours. This constancy holds even after holidays and vacations are taken into account (see Table 1). The work week for all workers has declined over this period, but that decline has been due to the changing composition of the labor force with women working.

This finding about the work week is the more surprising because real income has increased considerably during this period. When data on hours of work are looked at from a life-cycle perspective, however, a possible solution to the puzzle appears. The increase in lifetime income has increased the life-time consumption of leisure, but in contrast to earlier times, the entire increase has been taken in old age. In the previous section we argued that the fall in labor supplied by men at older ages was in direct response to the antiwork biases of OASI and private pensions. In this section we will argue that the pension system is also responsible for the failure of the hours worked by prime-age males to decline.

The adjustments to the antiwork constraint of our present pension system take place not only at the age in which workers become eligible for OASI or private pensions but throughout their lifetimes. By effectively decreasing the wage rate for work performed at older ages, the OASI earnings test, in the presence of a delayed-retirement credit that is less than actuarially fair, induces workers to substitute more leisure for work at older ages. It also induces them, however, to substitute more work at younger ages for what they would have performed at older ages. It is this additional adjustment to the earnings test occurring throughout a worker's life that is captured in a life-cycle framework.

Even though the earnings test does not affect the level of net wages at younger ages, those wages are greater relative to the net wages of men at older ages; that is, wages reduced by the earnings test. Such a shift in relative wages over the life cycle has resulted in a shift in life-cycle work patterns. Instead of a gradual fall in work effort at older ages, work has become an activity performed almost solely at younger ages. This type of long-run adjustment in life-cycle behavior to age-specific taxes (e.g., the earnings test) was first suggested by Lewis [15] and more recently by Smith [19].

Up to this point, the terms "young" and "old" have been used somewhat loosely. The relevant distinction is not the age at which workers become old,

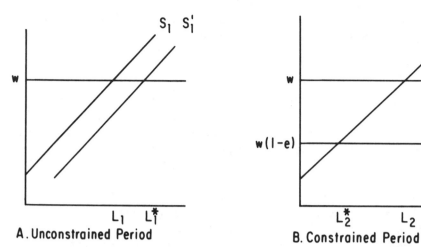

A. Unconstrained Period   B. Constrained Period

Figure 2. *Life-cycle labor supply changes*

but the age at which the earnings test places a constraint on their net market earnings. Before 1961, men aged 62–64 were not eligible for OASI benefits, and the work effort of this group was very similar to that of men aged 55–60. Today the work effort of this group is far closer to that of men 65–70. Clearly men aged 62–64 are no "older" than before, but they are subject to different economic incentives. The terms "constrained period" and "unconstrained period," though perhaps less appealing, are more accurate.[8]

The two-period labor supply model shown in Figure 2 illustrates the life-cycle changes resulting from OASI. Diagram "A" represents the unconstrained period during which the earnings test is not in effect. Diagram "B" represents the constrained period during which the earnings test is in effect. In allocating time to work and leisure activities during the two periods, individuals consider their wage in both periods as well as their lifetime nonwage income. Thus, labor supplied during one period of life is a function not only of wages in that period but also of wages during the other period of life. The higher the wage during one period of life, the less will be the labor supplied during the other period.

In Figure 2 it is assumed for simplicity that the only tax on labor earnings is the earnings test. In the absence of the earnings test, labor supplied at wage w in the unconstrained and constrained periods would be L_1 and L_2. The earnings test e reduces the net wage in the constrained period to $w(1 - e)$ and labor

8. The constrained period does not necessarily correspond to ages 62 to 71 when the earnings test is currently applicable. If a worker has retired in the absence of OASI, or if he has earned less than or the same as the earnings disregard, the earnings test will not constrain his earnings. Likewise, if the individual earns above the breakeven point where the earnings test has exhausted OASI benefits, he also would not be constrained by the earnings test.

supplied to L_2*, but the reduction in the net wage in the constrained period also causes the labor supply curve to shift to the right during the unconstrained period, and work in this period to increase to L_1*.[9]

The positive effect of OASI on labor supplied in the unconstrained period may be offset (the supply curve shifted to the left) and its negative effect on labor supplied during old age may be increased by an increase in lifetime nonwage income generated by OASI. Feldstein [12] has argued that OASI intergenerational transfers result in a net increase in the wealth of a generation. If this is the case, OASI-induced increases in wealth would increase the demand for leisure and reduce the supply of labor during all periods of life.

The wealth effect could be large. From the inception of the program, in a life-cycle sense the present value of individuals' expected benefits has greatly outweighed total contributions. The maturing of the system means that total contributions over a lifetime will more closely equal total benefits, but total OASI benefits received in 1972 by beneficiaries aged 66–67 were almost twice what they would have been in an actuarially fair system.[10]

Barro [1] has argued that despite the huge intergenerational transfer of wealth provided by OASI there is little or no net change in the wealth of the recipient generation. He argues that to the degree the older generation intends to provide positive intergenerational transfers (bequests, gifts, etc.) to their heirs, intergenerational transfers made through OASI from the younger to the older generation diminish this targeted legacy. This will then cause the older generation to react by increasing its intergenerational transfers to offset OASI. In the special case where the older generation provides positive intergenerational transfers and OASI has no intragenerational element, the original intergenerational pattern of consumption is fully restored. The final incidence of OASI on intergenerational wealth is an unsettled empirical question.

The simple diagrams of Figure 2 do not take into account the effect of the payroll tax on life-cycle labor supply. When no relationship exists between contributions into the system and benefits received, the analysis of this effect is straightforward. An increase in the payroll tax decreases the wage in the unconstrained period, having the normal income and substitution effects on labor supplied. If the substitution effect dominates, labor supplied will fall. But to the degree that contributions are related to benefits, considering the payroll contribution as a pure tax overestimates its negative labor supply effect on the young. As Browning [3] points out, in the special case where OASI benefits

---

9. Smith [19] provides a method of estimating the intertemporal substitution effect of a specific wage tax on work during both the constrained and unconstrained periods. Burkhauser and Turner [9] use a variation of his model to simulate a range of changes consistent with different values for the intertemporal elasticity of substitution in consumption, fraction of the life cycle covered by the earnings test, and share of work in the unconstrained period.

10. See Burkhauser and Warlick [11] for a fuller discussion of the life-cycle impact of OASI on income distribution.

are linked to contributions in an actuarially fair manner—that is, for every dollar paid into the system a worker expects to receive at retirement that dollar plus interest—the payroll tax has no effect on labor supply. Over the history of OASI, however, most beneficiaries have received much more than an actuarially fair return. This leaves open the possibility that for these workers the payroll tax, rather than decreasing labor supply, has in fact acted as a subsidy and induced an even greater twist of labor toward the unconstrained period of life. The actual effect of the payroll tax on labor supply is difficult to estimate since benefits are not simply a function of payroll taxes, although they are linked to lifetime contributions through the benefit calculation mechanism.[11]

Each of the above factors potentially affects the labor supply decision of the young, so the net impact of OASI on work at younger ages is ambiguous. The earnings test decreases wages at constrained older ages and through the substitution effect increases work done at unconstrained ages. The effect of the payroll tax is less clear. To the degree that it is linked to future benefits, its negative substitution effect on work at younger ages may be reduced. For current beneficiaries it may have even increased wages, further increasing the work they performed when they were younger. But labor supply at all ages falls to the degree that intergenerational increases in wealth caused by OASI are not distributed back to the younger generation by the older one.

In an earlier paper [9] we empirically tested, using time-series data, the net effect of OASI on the labor supply of prime-age men. With Feldstein's [12] data on OASI wealth we found a net increase in the work week for prime-age males. Over most of the years of our study (1937–71) the work week for prime-age males would have decreased from 2 to 3 hours in the absence of OASI.[12] A statistical estimate of the separate effect of each element of the OASI system must await further empirical testing, but our findings suggest that the system-wide effect on behavior is considerably more extensive than previously suspected.

This result should give pause to those who support the earnings test precisely because of its negative effect on work. The antiwork biases of OASI and private pension plans clearly reduce the labor supply of older men. Much of this fall

11. It is important to distinguish two aspects of the relationship between OASI payroll taxes and OASI benefits. The average rate of return to all OASI beneficiaries has been greater than the average rate of return they would have received from stocks or bonds over the period (see Burkhauser and Warlick [11]). Average benefits are related to average contributions but they also are a function of marital status, age, and the tilt in the benefit formula. It is the marginal rate of return, however, not the average rate of return that is relevant to labor supply decisions. Ideally one would like to know the marginal payroll tax for each period minus the marginal expected benefit related to that tax.

12. Time-series data were for the period 1929 through 1971. Social security wealth was used as a proxy both for OASI wealth transferred across generations and for net differences in the asset value of OASI lost by delayed acceptance of benefits. It captured both a substitution and a wealth effect. Other independent variables included the real wage, unemployment rate, family size, and price of recreation.

in work at older ages, however, is made up by increased work at younger ages. As workers have more time to adjust to the pension system, their ability to substitute labor over the life cycle increases. A major impact of the system has been to turn what might have been a smooth decline in work activity with advancing age into a sharp and often traumatic separation.

Economy-Wide Implications of Life-Cycle Responses to OASI

The empirical evidence linking an increased work effort by the young to the OASI system is far from conclusive, but to the degree that it is a factor two currently held beliefs about the economic impact of OASI must be questioned.

The first concerns the net effect of OASI on private saving. Feldstein [12] argues that OASI has depressed personal saving by 30 to 50 percent. But although Feldstein recognized that the earnings test decreases work at older ages, he failed to consider its full life-cycle effect on work. Rather than depressing saving over the past four decades, Turner [21] argues, OASI actually may have increased saving because of the trend toward increased work at younger ages.

Feldstein used a consumption measure to estimate the impact of OASI on private saving. The problem with such a specification is that it does not capture the effect on saving arising from changes in labor supplied during the unconstrained period. It is clearly possible for OASI to have a positive effect on personal saving and at the same time have a positive, negative, or insignificant effect on consumption.[13] Turner, using data on aggregate saving rather than on aggregate consumption, finds that OASI has had a positive net effect on saving.

The second belief is that the distortions caused by OASI through its payroll tax and earnings test result in huge welfare losses to society. Single-period measures of the impact of OASI on welfare unambiguously conclude that both the earnings test and the payroll tax result in welfare losses. The multiperiod labor supply effects of OASI make this type of analysis incomplete. Burkhauser and Turner [10] argue that, in the presence of an income tax, much of the welfare loss associated with the earnings test is offset by a second-best welfare gain at younger ages.

---

13. Because the earnings test does not affect the relative price of goods and time within the unconstrained period, it may be assumed that the relative use of both goods and time during that period is unchanged (though their absolute use is changed). Thus, the finding of a positive effect on labor supply in the unconstrained period implies that consumption in the unconstrained period declines. The implied positive effect on saving is due to both the increase in unconstrained-period labor supply and the decrease in unconstrained-period consumption. A consumption function does not capture the positive effect of unconstrained-period labor supply on saving. Furthermore, estimated consumption functions may be biased, owing to the inclusion of human capital investment in the aggregate consumption data and to a positive relationship between social security and human capital investment.

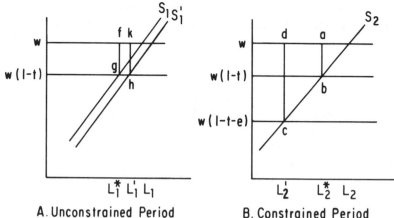

A. Unconstrained Period   B. Constrained Period

Figure 3. *Life-cycle welfare costs*

The life-cycle welfare effect of OASI is approximated by Figure 3, which drops the simplifying assumptions of Figure 2 and considers changes in life-cycle labor supply in the presence of a proportional income tax. The income tax reduces labor supplied in the unconstrained period from L_1 to L_1^*, and in the constrained period from L_2 to L_2^* as wages fall from w to $w(1 - t)$.

The introduction of an earnings test reduced wages in the constrained period to $w(1 - t - e)$ and labor to L_2'. The additional welfare loss due to this change is contained in area *abcd;* however, the increase in labor in the unconstrained period to L_1', because of the across-life substitution effect, reduces this loss by area *kfgh.*[14]

Using this simple variation of the Harberger [13] method of estimating welfare cost, we estimate that the large welfare loss caused by the OASI earnings test

14. In our analysis we follow the usual convention in assuming full employment, constant costs, and income-compensated supply curves. The actual equation used to measure the marginal effect of the earnings test in the presence of a proportional income tax is simply the two-period version of the general Harberger equation for estimating the welfare cost of a set of taxes:

$$-\Delta C = -\frac{1}{2} \epsilon_{L_2 w_2} [(e + t)^2 - t^2] w_2 L_2 - \epsilon_{L_1 w_2} et w_1 L_1 ,$$

where

$\Delta C =$ change in welfare,

$\epsilon_{L_2 w_2} =$ compensated supply elasticity of labor in the constrained period with respect to the wages in that period,

$\epsilon_{L_1 w_2} =$ compensated supply cross-elasticity of labor in the unconstrained period with respect to wages in the constrained period,

$\epsilon =$ marginal earnings test tax rate,

$t =$ marginal income tax rate,

$w_1 L_1 =$ wage income in the unconstrained period, and

$w_2 L_2 =$ wage income in the constrained period.

at older ages is offset in large measure by the welfare gain at younger ages, and that the net impact of OASI on welfare is probably small.[15]

The Future Pension System

Underlying much of the discussion of the previous three sections is the notion that the pattern of life-cycle work that has emerged over the last four decades is not an ideal one. Rather than being the result of worker choice, it is to a large extent the private and public pension system that induces workers not only to reduce their work at older ages but to increase it at younger ages.

It is always risky to predict the direction that future events may take, but a reversal of this pattern seems likely. In the debate over the 1977 Amendments to the Social Security Act, liberalization of the earnings test had strong support. At one point the House of Representatives voted to abolish the earnings test completely. The actual changes in the Social Security Act do not go so far, but they are likely to encourage a smoother life-cycle work pattern. The amount exempt from the earnings test was increased, and starting in 1982 the test itself will end at age 70 rather than at age 72. In addition, a token attempt to make the delayed retirement credit actuarially fair resulted in an increase in benefits to 3 percent (up from 1 percent) for every year they are postponed past age 65. Each of these actions will decrease the life-cycle substitution impact of the earnings test as well as increase work at older ages.

The maturing of the system has diminished the intergenerational component of OASI and will continue to do so. Thus, any subsidy component of the payroll tax will disappear for most workers, although to the degree benefits are connected to contributions, the full impact of the tax on work at younger ages will still be diminished.

Changes in the private pension system favorable to a smoother life-cycle work pattern are also emerging. In 1975 IRA (Individual Retirement Annuities) were introduced and the restrictions on Keogh plans were greatly liberalized. These pension plans allow workers to spread taxable income across their lives in much the same manner as job-related pension plans, but benefit acceptance is not tied directly to leaving a specific job. Annual contributions to Keogh plans for the self-employed are allowed up to the lesser of 15 percent of yearly salary or $7500. Contributions to IRA plans, which are for employees not covered by group pension plans, are limited to the lesser of 15 percent of yearly salary or $1500. As the contribution limits of these plans are raised to levels more consistent with those available for other pensions, a full-fledged, alternative

---

15. The actual values are a function of $\epsilon_{L_2 w_2}$, $\epsilon_{L_1 w_2}$, $w_1 L_1$, $w_2 L_2$ and the appropriate discounting factors. Over the range of values we used, the welfare loss was always less than 12 percent of the total lifetime benefits distributed through OASI.

form of pension saving is likely to develop. Even now this form of pension is popular. In 1975, the first year IRAs were available, $3 billion or 10 percent of all funded private pension saving was made in IRA and Keogh plans [20]. The increasing cost of complying with regulations imposed by ERISA (Employee Retirement Income Security Act) on firm-specific pension plans may further increase the popularity of IRA plans.

The liberalization of mandatory retirement rules contained in the 1978 Amendments to the Age Discrimination in Employment Act (ADEA) is another example of concern by Congress over the aged worker. Projected changes in the age structure of the population together with this law should make firms less willing to screen employees on simple age criteria and could lead to the possibility of more part-time work opportunities for older people. But the immediate effect of the law is unlikely to be large, since the pension system continues to discourage work at older ages. This would change dramatically if either ADEA or ERISA were interpreted to require employers to pay the actuarial equivalent of normal retirement benefits to an employee who continues to work beyond the normal retirement age.[16]

There is some concern that older workers who do not retire take jobs from younger workers. This modern-day wage-fund theory of employment is not likely to develop into a real problem now or in the future. General unemployment problems are more likely to be solved by general macroeconomic policy. Specific unemployment problems of the very young often seem mostly a problem of insufficient training and are only loosely connected to the pension system. More importantly, if the major impact of our pension system has been to shift the pattern of work across a lifetime rather than decrease work effort, then the removal of age-specific antiwork pension rules will for the most part simply reverse this process.

Conclusion

There have been two major changes in the pattern of male labor force participation since World War II. First, in sharp contrast to the secular decline in the work week preceding World War II, hours of work for prime-age males in the United States have remained relatively constant over the last three decades. Second, unlike the fall in market work during the depressed economic conditions of the 1930s, the decrease in labor force activity of older men since 1947 has continued through both slack and tight periods of general demand.

The link between the increased coverage and benefits of OASI and the rapid decline in the labor force participation rates of older men is well known. We

16. This interpretation was specifically ruled out by the Assistant Secretary of Labor for Employment Standards but remains a possible subject of judicial litigation. See Bureau of National Affairs, Inc. [4].

argue that OASI also affects the market work of younger men. It is likely that the fall in hours worked per week that has been observed in the first four decades of the century would have continued, at least to some degree, if the antiwork aspects of OASI and private pensions had not existed. The existence of this life-cycle response to OASI makes measurement of the system's effect on saving and welfare more complex and suggests that large negative effects may be overestimates.

The age-specific OASI earnings test, together with a postponed benefit credit that is less than actuarially fair, are both under strong attack by those wishing to encourage additional work by the aged. We suggest that removal of these two impediments will have a much more profound effect—the reintegration of work into full life-cycle activity.

References

[1] Barro, Robert J., "Are Government Bonds Net Wealth?" *Journal of Political Economy,* 82 (Nov. 1974), 1095–1118.

[2] Boskin, Michael, "Social Security and Retirement Decisions," *Economic Inquiry,* 15 (Jan. 1977), 1–25.

[3] Browning, Edgar, "Labor Supply Distortions of Social Security," *Southern Economic Journal,* 42 (Oct. 1975), 243–252.

[4] Bureau of National Affairs, *Explanation of the 1978 Age Discrimination Act Amendments* (Washington, D.C., 1978).

[5] Burkhauser, Richard V., "The Early Pension Decision and Its Effect on Exit from the Labor Market," Unpublished Ph.D. dissertation, University of Chicago, 1976.

[6] Burkhauser, Richard V., "The Early Acceptance of Social Security: An Asset Maximization Approach," *Industrial and Labor Relations Review* (forthcoming).

[7] Burkhauser, Richard V., "The Pension Acceptance Decision of Older Men," *Journal of Human Resources,* 14 (Winter 1979), 63–75.

[8] Burkhauser, Richard V., and George S. Tolley, "Older Americans and Market Work," *The Gerontologist,* 18 (Oct. 1978), 449–453.

[9] Burkhauser, Richard V., and John A. Turner, "A Time Series Analysis on Social Security and Its Effect on the Market Work of Men at Younger Ages," *Journal of Political Economy,* 86 (Aug. 1978), 701–715.

[10] Burkhauser, Richard V., and John A. Turner, "Life Cycle Welfare Costs of Social Security," presented at the American Economic Association meetings, Chicago, August 1978.

[11] Burkhauser, Richard V., and Jennifer Warlick, "Disentangling the Annuity from the Redistributive Aspects of Social Security," presented at Econometric Society meetings, Chicago, August 1978.

[12] Feldstein, Martin S., "Social Security, Induced Retirement, and Aggregate Capital Formation," *Journal of Political Economy,* 82 (Oct. 1974), 905–926.

[13] Harberger, Arnold C., "Taxation, Resource Allocation, and Welfare," pp. 25–80 in *The Role of Direct and Indirect Taxes in the Federal Revenue System* (Princeton: Princeton University Press, 1964).

[14] Kniesner, Thomas J., "The Full-time Workweek in the United States, 1900–1970," *Industrial and Labor Relations Review,* 30 (Oct. 1976), 3–15.

[15] Lewis, H. Gregg, "Hours of Work and Hours of Leisure," pp. 196–206 in L. Reid Tripp (ed.), *Proceedings of the Ninth Annual Meeting* (Madison, Wis.: Industrial Relations Research Association, 1957).

[16] Owen, John D., *Working Hours and Economic Analysis* (Lexington, Mass.: Lexington Books, 1979).

[17] Pellechio, Anthony J., "Social Security and Retirement Behavior," Unpublished Ph.D. dissertation, Harvard University, 1978.

[18] Quinn, Joseph, "The Micro-Economic Determinants of Early Retirement: A Cross-Sectional View of White Married Men," *Journal of Human Resources,* 12 (Summer 1977), 329–346.

[19] Smith, James P., "On the Labor Supply Effects of Age-Related Income Maintenance Programs," *Journal of Human Resources,* 10 (Winter 1975), 25–43.

[20] Turner, John A., "Saving in Different Types of Pensions," Unpublished manuscript (Washington, D.C.: Social Security Administration, 1977).

[21] Turner, John A., "Social Security, Saving and Labor Supply," Presented at Econometric Society meetings, Chicago, August 1978.

[22] U.S. Department of Commerce, Bureau of the Census, *Historical Statistics of the United States, Colonial Times to 1970* (Washington, D.C.: U.S. Government Printing Office, 1976).

[23] U.S. Department of Health, Education and Welfare, Social Security Administration, *Social Security Bulletin: Annual Statistical Supplement, 1975* (Washington, D.C.: U.S. Government Printing Office, 1977).

[24] U.S. Department of Labor, Bureau of Labor Statistics, *Handbook of Labor Statistics, 1975: Reference Edition* (Washington, D.C.: U.S. Government Printing Office, 1976).

Labor Supply: Discussion   *Cordelia W. Reimers*

For those who worry about the continuing ability of the American work force to support a growing aged population, the foregoing chapters by Polachek, Burkhauser and Turner, and Anderson, Clark, and Johnson offer hope for optimists. The assumed persistence of low fertility rates, which is after all the main reason for the aging of the population, means women will have more time to spend in market work because they won't be at home raising children. According to Polachek, women will respond by shifting their aspirations away from occupations where intermittency of work is not much penalized, toward occupations that require more on-the-job training, and so have steeper experience-earnings profiles, bigger penalties for dropping out to rear a family, higher earnings, and higher payroll tax payments. If they are successful in thus shifting the female occupational distribution, they will not only gladden the hearts of feminists, but also will swell the coffers of social security (only temporarily, however, for future benefits owed to women will also be higher).

Burkhauser and Turner argue that the social security retirement test is at once the cause and partial cure for the problem of supporting increasing numbers of retirees. The earnings test, without a complete actuarial adjustment of deferred benefits, induces people to retire at age 62, earlier than they otherwise would. However, the earnings test also induces people to work more *before* age 62 than they otherwise would. In fact, they claim, this life-cycle substitution effect has outweighed the wealth effect that stems from the excess of individual men's social security benefits over the value of their payroll taxes, plus interest. The wealth effect alone would reduce hours of work at all ages. By thus causing longer hours of work and higher earnings by younger workers, the retirement test produces higher payroll tax revenue to help pay for the early retirements it causes.

Anderson, Clark, and Johnson find that husbands whose wives are also employed tend to retire later than do sole breadwinners. If we can safely transfer this cross-section phenomenon to the long run, we would expect the increased labor force participation of wives to slow or even reverse the trend toward earlier retirement by men. At the same time, we will get fewer retirees to support and more workers, male as well as female, to support them.

The findings of these chapters would, therefore, be comforting about the potential of automatic labor force adjustments accompanying the aging of the population to mitigate the problem of supporting the dependent aged. They would be comforting, that is, if we could believe their empirical findings. But here is where I have trouble, particularly with the papers by Burkhauser and Turner and by Polachek.

Burkhauser and Turner make the usual assumptions of life-cycle modellers:

perfect foresight, perfect information, and perfect capital markets. They assume that people anticipated certain future developments in the social security system—in particular, periodic congressional actions to increase benefit levels (but not the extension of coverage). They also assume that people understood the various features of social security, especially the retirement test and the actuarial increase of deferred benefits, well enough to adjust their labor supply in a rational manner. Again, they assume the capital market would accommodate any amount of borrowing an individual might desire. Perfect information, perfect foresight, and perfect capital markets are useful heuristic assumptions, but when we are trying to determine the actual impact of a future situation on prior behavior, we need to pay close attention to the availability of information, the formation of expectations, and the constraints on borrowing.

Let's accept for now these common assumptions of life-cycle models. Burkhauser, in his previous work as well as in this paper, has contributed a great deal to clear thinking about the retirement test. He has shown that behavior is affected not by what happens to the current benefit, but by the change in asset value of the pension. Thus, the actuarial adjustment is pinpointed as the critical factor.

Burkhauser and Turner's theoretical argument about the distortions due to the retirement test is plausible, provided social security benefits are not sufficiently increased to maintain asset value when retirement is postponed beyond age 62. Not everyone agrees with them on this point. Here it is important to realize that the actuarial adjustment is based on a uniform life table for the entire population. Those who expect to live longer than average (women, for instance) gain by postponing benefits; whereas men, whose life expectancy is less than average, gain by taking benefits at 62. Since almost everyone's asset value will be reduced if he works past 65, average retirement age will be reduced to somewhere between 62 and 65 by the earnings test, even with an actuarially fair adjustment on average.

This suggests a way to eliminate or manipulate the earnings test's distorting effects: simply raise the rate at which postponed benefits are increased, even to the point of a greater-than-actuarial increase (a wage subsidy). Here we have a handy policy tool for influencing the average retirement age and thus adjusting the relative number of workers and retirees as the population continues to age.

Going along, then, with Burkhauser and Turner's contention that the earnings test does distort men's labor supply decisions, I still find their conclusion about the effect of social security on average weekly hours since World War II hard to accept. They have not convinced me that the net effect of the social security system has been to raise the average work week of prime-age men by two-to-three hours above what it otherwise would have been. I will first outline some theoretical, and then some empirical, grounds for doubting this finding.

Let us start by looking more closely at the way the social security system affected the net reward for the marginal hour worked at different ages for men now around 70, who were always below the maximum taxable earnings limit when they worked. Before age 62, the return to an extra hour's work was reduced by the payroll tax, and increased by the present value of the increment to future social security benefits. The latter was determined by the impact of an additional hour's earnings on the Average Monthly Wage (AMW), together with the concave function linking the Primary Insurance Amount (PIA) to the AMW. The payroll tax on the marginal hour worked rose over a man's lifetime due to both rate increases and wage growth. The present value of the increment to future benefits also rose over a man's lifetime, due to several factors: increases in his wage, nonindexing of earnings records, the limited averaging period, and shorter discounting periods as old age drew nearer. The difference, present value of benefit increment minus payroll tax, was probably negative at early ages because of the short averaging period, but became positive and grew throughout the entire working life, even beyond age 62 or 65, if the man continued to work full time. This growth occurred because he could substitute high current earnings for low early earnings in calculating his AMW.[1] With rapid rates of growth of money wages, this was not a trivial effect. Thus the impact of social security on the net marginal wage over the life cycle of these men served to steepen the age-wage profile, inducing a shift of labor supply from *younger* to *older* ages. (This assumes, of course, that the men were aware of the impact of earnings on future benefits, as well as of the payroll tax, and an accommodating capital market.)

The retirement test, with a less-than-fair actuarial increase of postponed benefits, does, of course, "tax" earnings after age 62. For those whose marginal wage was affected, this feature of the social security system caused a drop in the net marginal wage at age 62. The other features of social security discussed above continued to affect the net marginal wage, with the likely outcome that the total effect of the system on the marginal reward to working after age 62 was virtually nil. But since the system increased the net marginal wage before age 62, it did distort the relative wage between these periods.

The point of all this is that the intertemporal substitution effect of social security theoretically would have induced a shift of labor supply toward the years between, perhaps, 45 or 50 and 62, from *both* younger and older ages, for men who were always below the maximum taxable earnings.

We must also consider the ordinary (leisure-goods) substitution effect and the income effect of social security on labor supply. The difference between the present value of the benefit increment and the payroll tax in each year, discounted and summed, is the individual's net social security wealth. Therefore, net social security wealth measures the system's effect, on average, over a lifetime, on the average (as distinct from the marginal) wage in each period. If the

---

1. I owe this point to Roger Gordon.

social security system increased the net wealth of men who are now around 70, it raised their average wage, on average, over their life cycle; i.e., the periods in which it decreased the net wage were outweighed by those when the net wage was raised.[2]

The backward-bending labor supply curve of prime-age men indicates that the income effect outweighs the substitution effect of a permanent wage change, when the average and marginal wage rates are the same. Moreover, social security raises the average wage more than the marginal wage, due to the concavity of the function linking the AMW to the PIA. Therefore, the income effect of social security must have far outweighed its leisure-goods substitution effect (which is determined by the impact on the marginal wage), and these two effects combined would have reduced hours, on average, over the life cycle. When we look at the total impact of social security on labor supply averaged across *all* ages, the increase in hours worked by those in late middle age due to the intertemporal substitution effect is countered both by the intertemporal decrease in hours of younger men, and by the decrease on average, due to the income and goods-leisure substitution effects. The net result is hardly likely to be much of an increase in average hours worked for men who were always below the taxable maximum.[3]

Think too, of the implications of Burkhauser and Turner's finding for labor supply elasticities. For a marginal tax rate of less than 50 percent (there is some increase in deferred benefits, after all), operating during a ten-year period of life, to increase labor supply during the other 40 years by two-to-three hours a week out of 40, or about 6 percent, even after a rather large offset from the combined wealth and goods-leisure substitution effects, the intertemporal wage elasticity must be much greater than 0.5. This is over four times the size of our best estimates of the *compensated* current wage elasticity of labor supply for adult men. It is hard to believe that leisure can be substituted across periods so much more easily than leisure can be substituted for goods.

2. Robert J. Barro [1, p.1106], and more recently [2, pp. 2–4], contends that people have neutralized any tendency of social security to affect their net wealth by making offsetting adjustments in private intergenerational transfers. If a man did view any change in his net social security wealth from an additional hour's work as automatically causing an offsetting adjustment in transfers to or from his children, then there would be no effective impact on his net reward for working and no distortion of labor supply behavior due to the social security system. My argument rests on an assumption that adjustments in private intergenerational transfers have been incomplete, so that social security has had a positive effect on the net wealth of men now around 70.

3. This conclusion is reinforced when we add in those men who always earned above the taxable maximum and were unaffected by the earnings test. Their marginal wage rates were not altered by the payroll tax or the benefit increment, so the social security system had only a wealth effect, reducing their labor supply at all ages. The many men who earned below the taxable maximum when young and then went above it as they acquired experience and promotions, and who were affected by the earnings test after age 62, had an age pattern of social security impacts on their net wage similar to those who were always below the taxable maximum. When we combine all types in the population, the increase in labor supply for certain age-earnings groups would have to have been very great indeed to offset the decrease for the others and produce an increase of two-to-three hours in the average work week of all prime-age men.

How, then, can we explain Burkhauser and Turner's empirical results? I believe we may have here a case of correlation by construction. The social security wealth variable they use—Feldstein's gross figure—is essentially proportional to a time trend multiplied by real per capita disposable income, which is the real disposable wage times hours worked.[4] With the real (gross) wage also in the equation, it should surprise no one that this variable is significantly positively related to the dependent variable, hours worked. It is as if we were to regress hours worked on both earnings and the wage rate—we would "discover" that earnings are positively related to hours!

As long as we believe the available time-series data on annual hours worked, I suppose economists will keep trying to explain the apparent failure of men's hours to decline in the United States since World War II. I, personally, do not believe the data. No one—not even Owen—has adequately accounted for increases in vacations and holidays, not to mention personal days, "sick" leave, longer lunch hours and coffee breaks, and other "on the job leisure."[5] All of our casual observation tells us these have been increasing. It is interesting in this regard that the Canadian data, starting from almost the same number of hours as in the United States in 1947 (43.0), show a drop of 6.5 hours a week by 1972 [3]. I'm afraid we may be wasting a lot of effort trying to explain a spurious "fact" about the trend of men's annual hours in the United States, produced by the way we collect our data and not by workers' actual behavior.

To turn, now, to Polachek's paper. Many people will find it hard to accept his view of the occupational distribution resulting from a rational choice process, especially where women are concerned. Between the not-so-subtle socialization of girls and outright discrimination against women in many fields, it is tempting to view the occupations of women as imposed on them, with their own decisions playing no part. However, the story is more complicated. Here Polachek's insights can help us understand how women's own rational responses to the terms and conditions offered by the world have served to help keep them in their "place." His basic idea, that the rate of wage loss per year out of the labor force should influence occupational choices for those contemplating intermittent labor force participation, makes a lot of sense to me. Similarly, his prediction that occupational aspirations will shift along with increasing labor force participation of women seems reasonable. We already see a surge of young women into law, medicine, and business.

---

4. For a description of this variable, see Martin Feldstein [4].

5. The Current Population Survey (CPS) deliberately avoids using survey weeks containing holidays, and those when most vacations occur, by conducting its interviews in the middle of each month. Owen claims to adjust for the resulting undercount of vacations and holidays by applying a correction factor of 1.2 used by Henle in 1972. Henle's correction factor, however, applies only to the period in the 1950s from which it was derived. Surely if the average worker's holiday and vacation days have been increasing faster than the CPS would reveal, applying a constant correction factor to all years since World War II is inappropriate. Rather, the correction factor itself should increase over time, producing a decline in estimated annual hours. For a description of Owen's and Henle's adjustments, see the Appendix to Owen [8], and Henle [6].

Polachek's paper thus makes a valuable contribution to our understanding of developments in the occupational distribution of women. The reservations I am about to express concerning his numerical estimates and forecasts do not detract from the importance of his main points. Polachek himself is aware of many problems with the empirical work and claims for it no more than a suggestive character. Nevertheless, I think some of his *caveats* bear repeating, lest the unwary take the numbers at face value.

First, cross-sectional findings can be applied to predicting future trends only under a set of heroic assumptions, which cannot be maintained in the case at hand. As Polachek emphasizes, changing the occupational distribution depends not just on women's desires, but on the availability of jobs. We cannot assume infinite elasticity of demand for each occupation. There simply isn't room for all women to enter the high-training occupations that "career women" now occupy—not without a dramatic decline in the relative wage!

Too, the past and present occupational choices of women have been heavily conditioned by their socialization and by discrimination, as well as by considerations of "atrophy rates" and time out of the labor force. The first two factors are shifting rapidly, so that the very structure of the relationship between occupation and such explanatory variables as time out of the labor force will no doubt be different in the future from that found in current cross-sectional studies.

In any case, as Polachek recognizes, his cross-section estimates are subject to several sources of bias. The amount of home time is assumed to be exogenous. This may have been plausible for the generation of the 1950s, but it doesn't fit the young women of today. Surely occupational aspirations and labor force participation are jointly determined. If so, his estimates of the impact of home time on the likelihood of being a clerical worker rather than a manager are upwardly biased, and he would overpredict the occupational shift as women's labor force participation grows, even if the true structure were not changing.

Polachek's specification of the within-occupation "atrophy rate" equation,

$$\ln W = a_0 + a_1 S + a_2 \frac{T - N}{T} + e,$$ also bothers me. By entering the percentage

of time spent at home without controlling for total potential time, he is saying that staying home for 15 years out of 30 has the same percentage impact on one's wage as staying home one year out of two. The coefficient a_2 does not give the rate of wage loss per year out of work, which we naturally think of as an "atrophy rate," but rather the rate of wage loss per percentage point increase in time out of work. I find this awkward. In light of Polachek's own previous work,[6] it is hard to see why he did not use such a specification as $\ln W = a_0 + a_1 S + a_2 T + a_3 (T - N) + e$. This equation, unlike the one he used, has a theoretical justification and gives meaningful coefficients. Here, a_3 would be the percentage wage loss per year out of work, because of the combined effects of skill deterioration and foregone experience.

---

6. In particular, Jacob Mincer and Solomon Polachek [7].

Even without this difficulty, however, Polachek would not really be measuring an occupation's "atrophy rate." He observes *current* occupation (usually after a spell out of the labor force). His "atrophy rates" do not tell us how much a woman manager and a secretary each stands to lose for spending 50 percent of her time at home. Rather, they tell us how much less one woman who is *now* a manager, and who spent half her time at home, earns than another woman who is *now* a manager and who has worked without interruption. But the fruits of experience in wage gains often occur via occupational mobility from clerical or sales to manager, and re-entrants may not have access to the same occupations they left, even at lower wages. This aspect of the penalty imposed on intermittency cannot be captured by Polachek's procedure. Although, as he points out, the use of very broad, one-digit occupational categories minimizes biases due to occupational mobility, I think there is still a problem with movements into and out of the managerial classification.

The various difficulties Polachek and I have mentioned must be kept in mind when we consider his numerical estimates of the effect of women's increasing labor force participation on their occupations. As he says, the estimates are not intended to be exact forecasts, but rather to illustrate his method of analysis.

Anderson, Clark, and Johnson's paper demonstrates the need to consider a husband's and wife's joint determination of their labor supplies. The complementarity of older couples' leisure time is revealed. It seems that the wife's characteristics are more important in determining the husband's labor supply, as well as her own, than are his own characteristics—shades of Dagwood and Blondie! Health is the only characteristic of the husband that has much effect on his labor force participation. I have found a similar result in my own work on men's propensities to retire, using data from the National Longitudinal Survey of Mature Men [9]. In my single-equation model of a man's probability of retiring, his health was the only variable that consistently had a strong effect. His wage, assets, pension and social security availability failed to show the expected effects, just as in Anderson, Clark, and Johnson's paper.

One puzzle in their results is the apparent failure of the husband's age to affect his labor force participation. Multicollinearity may be obscuring the age effect, with the ages of both spouses, as well as the difference in their ages, all with quadratic terms, included in the logit equations.

The measures of pension and social security availability are too crude to tell us much about these presumably important influences on labor supply. Also, the wage equations they use to impute wage rates are subject to sample selection bias. These wage equations were estimated using the labor force participants in the sample. If very low wage earners are more likely to be out of the labor force, the estimated coefficients will be biased toward zero. The imputed wage will then be too high for low-wage people and too low for high-wage people. Heckman's [5] technique for correcting for selectivity bias might be used.

All three of these papers have tackled important issues and broken new ground. That they have not satisfactorily answered the questions they raise attests to the complexity of these problems. The variety of topics addressed by these papers dramatically demonstrates the range of side effects we must anticipate when any major change occurs within our economic system.

References

[1] Barro, Robert J., "Are Government Bonds Net Wealth?" *Journal of Political Economy,* 82 (Nov./Dec. 1974), 1095–1117.

[2] Barro, Robert J., *The Impact of Social Security on Private Saving* (Washington, D.C.: American Enterprise Institute for Public Policy Research, 1978).

[3] Canada Department of Labor, Economics and Research Branch, Wages Research Division, "Trends in Working Time," unpublished manuscript, June 1974.

[4] Feldstein, Martin, "Social Security, Induced Retirement, and Aggregate Capital Accumulation," *Journal of Political Economy,* 82 (Sept./Oct. 1974), 911–912.

[5] Heckman, James J., "Sample Selection Bias as a Specification Error," *Econometrica,* 47 (Jan. 1979), 153–161.

[6] Henle, Peter, "Recent Growth of Paid Leisure for U.S. Workers," *Monthly Labor Review,* 84 (March 1962), 254.

[7] Mincer, Jacob, and Solomon Polachek, "Family Investments in Human Capital: Earnings of Women," *Journal of Political Economy* 82 (March/April 1974), S76–S108.

[8] Owen, John D., "The Demand for Leisure," *Journal of Political Economy,* 79 (Jan./Feb. 1971), 70–71.

[9] Reimers, Cordelia, "The Timing of Retirement of American Men," unpublished Ph.D. dissertation, Columbia University, 1977.

Rejoinder   *Richard V. Burkhauser and John A. Turner*

In her comments on our paper "The Effects of Pension Policy Through Life" Reimers criticizes our findings that Old Age and Survivors Insurance has offset the secular decline in hours worked by men at younger (unconstrained) ages. She considers five possible ways in which the OASI system can affect labor supply in the unconstrained period. First, the earnings test may change the life-cycle pattern of net wages, causing a shift of labor supply to the unconstrained period. Reimers apparently accepts that argument. Second, the payroll tax may affect directly labor supplied during the unconstrained period. Third, marginal payroll tax contributions may be related to future benefits. Fourth, there may be intertemporal substitution within the constrained period. Fifth, social security may have a wealth effect that would reduce labor supplied at all ages.

In our paper we concentrate on the first of these potential effects. In a previous paper [3], we empirically tested the effect of OASI on hours worked per week by prime-age males. During the period of our empirical study (1937–71) we considered the earnings test to have the most important impact on intertemporal relative wages. Throughout the period 1939 to 1971 the earnings test reached a maximum tax rate of 100 percent, and even though the earnings disregard was liberalized several times, in 1971 the 100 percent rate still began at the relatively low level of $2880 per year.[1]

Reimers stresses the impact of the payroll tax on relative wages. If payroll tax payments are not positively related to future benefits, the payroll tax can be treated as a pure tax. In this case net wages fall in the unconstrained period and hours worked would fall (assuming the substitution effect is greater than the income effect). But during the period of our empirical analysis the combined employee-employer payroll tax began at 2 percent and had increased to only 9.2 percent by 1971.

Reimers correctly argues that if future benefits are related to OASI payroll taxes this will mitigate the change in labor supply due to the tax and might even act as a subsidy. To the degree that this is important, it further induces substitution from the constrained to the unconstrained periods.[2] We might point out, however, that there are no marginal effects of the payroll tax, either as a tax or a subsidy, for workers above the taxable maximum. In 13 of the 22 years between 1950 and 1971 over one-half of male workers earning four quarters of coverage had taxable earnings above the taxable maximum, and in all years in that period except one, 40 percent or more were above the taxable maximum (U.S. Department of Health, Education and Welfare [7, p.73]). This makes the marginal effect of the payroll tax less important than might be the case today.

Given both the increase in the taxable maximum and the payroll tax rate over the history of the system together with the increasing earnings of workers over their lifetime, the net impact of the tax has affected workers differentially at different ages within the unconstrained period. The relationship between payroll taxes and benefits is more complicated than the one sketched by Reimers, however. For instance, the rate of return on payroll taxes paid during an unconstrained year depends on work done in the constrained period. In the extreme case of the full-time worker whose wages are sufficiently high so that he never accepts OASI benefits, the payroll tax to him is always a pure tax.[3] We do agree with Reimers that an expansion of the two-period model used in our paper to one that will capture the multiperiod effects of OASI is needed.

Finally, OASI may have a positive wealth effect that would reduce work

---

1. In fact, for many workers the true tax on wages during this period was greater than 100 percent since OASI benefits were tax free, whereas wages were subject to federal and state income tax.

2. This point is discussed in Burkhauser and Turner [3].

3. In 1972 the earnings test was removed for a worker aged 72 so that at this point he would receive some return on his contributions regardless of his wage earnings.

across all periods of life. It is important to note that it is the final incidence of the OASI system rather than the initial incidence that is relevant in determining the net change in wealth due to OASI. For instance, Barro [1] argues that intergenerational transfers caused by OASI could be exactly off-set by private intergenerational transfers. In our opinion the size of the wealth effect is far from certain and recent empirical evidence suggests it may be quite small [2,4].

The net effect of these five possible influences on labor supplied at unconstrained ages is ambiguous. But clearly the net increase of two to three hours a week or about 6 percent found in our study cannot be ruled out. It is important to note that the impact of OASI on labor supplied over the entire life cycle is not addressed in our paper and any rise in work in the unconstrained period must be considered in the light of the very large fall in work at older (constrained) ages. We simply point out that in addition to the substitution of work for leisure at older ages, some of the fall in work at older ages is a result of across-life substitution of work to younger ages.

Reimers states that our findings imply an implausibly large uncompensated intertemporal labor supply elasticity of at least 0.5. Since she does not present the elasticity formula she uses, we cannot be sure how this value was derived. In our original paper we present calculations that indicate that a compensated intertemporal elasticity of substitution between labor supply in the unconstrained period and wages in the constrained period of about 0.09 or less would be consistent with our empirical findings given a small positive wealth effect [3, p. 709].

The empirical evidence linking increased work effort by the young to the OASI system is far from conclusive. Reimers has two specific problems with the data we used. First, she believes the positive relationship between hours worked per week and OASI wealth is due to construction of the latter variable. This variable originally was constructed by Feldstein [5] and in addition to disposable personal income is also a function of coverage, demographic changes, and changes in mortality. In addition to its wage component, personal income also includes a return from nonwage sources. The partial correlation between social security wealth and hours worked, holding the time trend and the wage rate constant, is 0.47 (years 1937–71). This modest partial correlation that holds constant the linear effect of the other variables is not evidence of correlation by construction.

Second, Reimers claims that our data on hours worked by prime-age males are contaminated by measurement error due to insufficient adjustment for vacations and holidays. Two corrections for vacations and holidays have been applied to the Census Bureau household survey data on male hours of work that we used in our analysis. First, because persons who are employed but who were absent from work during the entire survey week were not included in the computation of weekly average hours, average hours are deflated to account for men on vacation during survey weeks. Second, because the survey week was chosen to avoid most holidays, and vacations are more likely to occur in a week with a holiday, the data are further deflated. This second deflation is based on a constant (1.2) multiplied by the previously estimated annual hours of vacation and holiday. Reimers argues that all casual observations tell us that vacations, holidays, personal days, sick leave, etc. have been increasing at a rate that makes use of these hours data a wasted effort. Her criticism is valid to the extent that this ratio has changed over time.

A closer look at the small amount of systematic data currently available provides a somewhat less clear picture. For instance, paid holidays for office workers in metropolitan areas increased, on average, only from 7.8 per year in 1959–60 to 8.9 in 1973–74. For the same group, 76 percent had two weeks or more vacation after one year of service in 1959–60, whereas in 1973–74 that figure had risen to 80 percent.[4] For federal employees, there have been no changes in the leave schedule since the enactment of the Annual and Sick Leave Act of 1951. When considering the effect of changes in vacation time on the average work week it should be noted that fairly large increases in vacation time have little effect on the length of the work week. For instance, a 50 percent increase in vacation time from two to three weeks, given a 42-hour work week, would lower the average work week less than an hour.

Reimers cites Canadian data including both women and men workers that show a drop since 1974 in average hours worked. A similar decline is indicated by United States data that include women workers, and it is likely that in both cases the explanation is the same. The increase in women workers has lowered the average work week for all workers, but there has been little change in the work week for prime-age men. It is possible that currently used data on hours of work overestimate hours actually worked. In a recent article, Stafford and Duncan [6] compare time use studies in 1965 and 1975 and conclude that actual work time was lower in 1975. Their findings, however, are far from conclusive and may be due to cyclical rather than to secular changes in hours worked.

What is needed in addition to careful analysis of current time-series data is an analysis of micro data sets that will permit a more detailed study of the multiperiod labor supply effects of OASI. The potential importance of life-cycle considerations of the effects of current pension policy makes further analysis of this type worthwhile.

---

4. See Department of Labor [8, pp. 301–302]. For plant workers, paid holidays increased from 6.9 to 8.4 and the percent of plant workers with two or more weeks vacation after one year increased from 21 to 31 percent. There were greater increases for higher tenured employees. In 1959–60, 38 percent of office workers had three or more weeks vacation after ten years, whereas in 1972–74 that figure had risen to 87 percent.

References

[1] Barro, Robert J., "Are Government Bonds Net Wealth?" *Journal of Political Economy,* 82 (Nov. 1974), 1095–1118.

[2] Barro, Robert J. *The Impact of Social Security on Private Saving* (Washington, D.C.: American Enterprise Institute, 1978).

[3] Burkhauser, Richard V., and John A. Turner, "A Time Series Analysis on Social Security and Its Effect on the Market Work of Men at Younger Ages," *Journal of Political Economy* 86 (Aug. 1978), 701–715.

[4] Darby, Michael R., *The Effect of Social Security on Income and the Capital Stock* (Washington, D.C.: American Enterprise Institute, 1978).

[5] Feldstein, Martin S., "Social Security, Induced Retirement, and Aggregate Capital Formation," *Journal of Political Economy,* 82 (Sept. 1974), 905–926.

[6] Stafford, Frank P., and Greg J. Duncan, "Market Hours, Real Hours, and Labor Productivity," *Economic Outlook USA,* 5 (Autumn 1978), 74–76.

[7] U.S. Department of Health, Education, and Welfare, Social Security Administration, *Social Security Bulletin: Annual Statistical Supplement 1975* (Washington, D.C.: U.S. Government Printing Office, 1977).

[8] U.S. Department of Labor, Bureau of Labor Statistics, *Handbook of Labor Statistics, 1975: Reference Edition* (Washington, D.C.: U.S. Government Printing Office, 1976).

Retirement Policy

Economic Responses to Population Aging With Special Emphasis on Retirement Policy   *Robert L. Clark and Joseph Spengler*

Examination of economic responses to changes in the age structure of the population must include a consideration of individual life-cycle decisions as well as the macroeconomic influences of age-specific rates of labor supply, savings, and consumption. In recent works, we have attempted to identify many of these important relationships and to assess current economic knowledge in the area [4, 6]. Growth in the size of the aged population and fluctuations in the size of cohorts entering the labor force have stimulated a renewed interest in the influences of demographic variables on economic institutions and relationships. Public policies aimed at ensuring retirement income have been the topic of considerable public debate and are the primary focus of this volume, but considerable attention also has been placed on the problems of relatively large young cohorts and their impact on aggregate unemployment rates.

The economic role of population age structure is complex and cannot be captured adequately by a single measure such as the total dependency rate. We have argued that age composition of dependent groups is highly important and must be considered in the assessment of alternative dependency rates on potential economic well being [7]. Several important points should be noted. First, dependency ratios do not allow for individual choice but instead depend on arbitrary age limits. Differences between dependency ratios associated with high and low rates of fertility are quite sensitive to the selection of the age of entry into and exit from the labor force.

Of considerable importance is the need to account for the relative cost of supporting the young and the old. We have estimated that public costs of transfer benefits per old dependent are three times greater than are those for youths. Recognition of differences in expenditures per dependent is necessary to weight dependency ratios appropriately [5, 7]. Age structure changes within each dependent group are also important since fertility declines increase the relative number of older young dependents and older old dependents. The level of expenditures on children and the elderly is a function of public policy decisions and intrafamily resource allocation decisions. Spending per dependent therefore is an endogenous variable and may be related to the size of the dependent cohort. This quality-quantity relationship diminishes the usefulness of a dependency ratio.

This chapter concentrates on the relationships between age structure changes, retirement policy, and income security of the elderly. In the next section, we illustrate the effect of projected population aging on the relative size of key demographic groups. The importance of delayed retirement is illustrated and factors that will ease this transition are examined. The subsequent section will address the problem of financing retirement income and the effect of inflation on the sources of income in late life.

Population Aging and Retirement Age

Projected changes in the age structure of U.S. population will be somewhat unfavorable to overall labor force participation unless conditions currently conducive to relatively early withdrawal from the labor force are modified. Table 1 illustrates that with replacement-level fertility, the proportion of the population aged 18–64 increases from its present 59 percent until about 2015 and then returns to approximately its 1976 rate. In general, slow rates of population growth produce a relatively high proportion of the population in the primary working age groups; however, declines in labor force participation by older workers may offset this effect.

The proportion of the population aged 65 years and over will increase steadily during the next half century. The ratio of this group to those aged 18–64 climbs slowly from .18 in 1976 to .20 in 2010 and rises sharply to approximately .30 in 2025. This significant increase in the old age dependency ratio will place considerable financial pressure on the nation's retirement programs.

The tax burden on those in the labor force is further exacerbated by declines in the labor supply of the elderly. The labor force participation rate of men 65 years old and over dropped from 47.8 percent in 1947 to 20.1 percent in 1977. During that same period, the labor force participation rate of men aged 55 to 64 fell from 89.6 percent to 74 percent. This latter decline is even more significant when we note from Table 1 that the relative importance of this cohort to the population aged 18–64 increases sharply after the year 2000. Thus, the tendency toward early withdrawal from the labor force further aug-

Table 1. *Age structure ratios with economic implications, 1976–2050, with replacement-level fertility*

Age	1976	1985	2000	2010	2015	2025	2050
0–17/18–64	.5133	.4348	.4324	.3920	.3980	.4206	.4168
18–64/total	.5903	.6153	.6129	.6275	.6155	.5827	.5817
65 and over/ 18–64	.1806	.1906	.2000	.2016	.2268	.2955	.3022
18–24/55–64	1.4038	1.2814	1.0600	.8614	.7546	.7804	.8076
18–24/18–64	.2218	.1944	.1545	.1642	.1565	.1565	.1586
55–64/18–64	.1580	.1517	.1457	.1906	.2074	.2006	.1964
20–39/40–64	1.1590	1.3319	.8968	.8009	.8388	.8835	.8811
75 and over/ 65 and over	.3811	.3941	.4521	.4323	.3888	.3923	.4420

ments the cost of supporting an aging population incident upon those enrolled and employed in the labor force.

Although disability and illness may deny employment to some persons, this source of unemployment of persons over 55 has not increased in recent decades. Mainly but not quite wholly responsible for the decline in employment of older persons in recent years has been the availability of pecuniary incentives (e.g., pensions, social security, and other financial support for older persons).[1] Discrimination against the employment of older workers, especially those who have "lost their jobs," may also explain part of the decline in market work by the elderly.[2] Of course, if only a limited number of older persons lost their jobs owing to compulsory retirement provisions, the employment-denying power of mandatory retirement provisions may have been quite limited. Moreover, it has been reduced in recent years by the Age Discrimination Act and its 1978 amendments outlawing most mandatory retirement prior to age 70.[3] Also, somewhat responsible for recent declines in the employment of older workers may have been such factors as continuing increases in hiring and other costs of employing representative workers as well as the growing pressure of the increased number of new job-seekers in the "labor markets."[4]

The same demographic forces that increase the relative number of older persons decrease the size of younger cohorts. For example, in 1976 the group aged 18–24 represented 22 percent of the population aged 18–64; however, this ratio declines to less than 16 percent in 2000 and, with replacement-level fertility, remains in that range. The Bureau of Labor Statistics moderate growth assumption indicates a more pronounced fall in the relative importance to the labor force of the cohort aged 16–24 for the remainder of this century. As noted in Table 2, youths accounted for 24 percent of the labor force in 1977, but are expected to represent 16 percent in 2000.

With the continuation of low fertility rates, there will be less pressure of young job-seekers upon the labor market than there has been during the past decade when those born during the post-1948 baby boom attained working age.[5]

Another important indicator of demographic influence on the labor market is the ratio of new entrants to those nearing normal retirement age. As shown in Table 1, population aging has a favorable effect on the ratio of youths aged 18–24 to older workers aged 55–64 as it declines from 1.4 in 1976 to .75 in

1. See Clark, Kreps, and Spengler [4] for a review of the recent evidence concerning the determinants of labor supply of the elderly.
2. See MacDonald [14, pp. 1–3].
3. Ibid., pp. 1–5, 22–26.
4. For example, see Ginzberg [13].
5. For the causes and consequences of such pressure, see Easterlin, Wachter, and Wachter [10].

Table 2. *Labor force projections (in thousands), 1977–2000*

Labor force	1977	1985	1990	2000
Total	97,401	112,953	119,366	125,209
16–24	23,685	24,399	22,381	20,429
Percent 16–24	24	21	18	16

Source: [19], and unpublished BLS data.

2015 before rising slightly. Wachter [20] finds that population aging should reduce the noninflationary rate of unemployment during the next decade.

Reduction in the size of young cohorts should enhance employment opportunities for older job seekers. Shifts in the relative supply of young and old workers should encourage firms to continue to use their older workers.[6] Political emphasis should be shifted away from the plight of younger workers as their employment status improves. Thus, public policy can be shifted toward improving labor market opportunities for the elderly.

As we have noted earlier, an assortment of present governmental policies tends to encourage early retirement. Social security benefits and the earnings test, preferential tax treatment for the elderly, mandatory retirement, and other transfer programs to the elderly provide incentives for retirement. The obvious rationale for these programs has been to improve the economic status of the elderly. Some persons have argued that the initiation and improvements of these policies have been timed so as to improve job prospects for youths by inducing early retirement. This motive should decline in importance in the future, and thus, it should be easier to examine retirement age policy on the merits of benefits to the elderly and costs to the employed.

The growing tax burden on the employed will serve as a constant reminder to policymakers of the cost of alternative retirement age policies. We may indicate roughly the "burden" and changes therein by comparing the population 18–64 with that aged 65 and over. In 1977 there were 5.5 persons in the age group 18–64 for each one in the 65-and-over age group. By 2000, this ratio could fall to about 5 to 1, and by 2050 to between 2.6 and 3.3 to 1. Hence, there will be increasing pressure on the part of those in the labor force to delay exit from the labor force of potential pensioners, particularly if they seek to withdraw before age 65.

Should half of those aged 65–74 remain in the labor force, the ratio of those in the labor force to the older persons not in it would approximate 7 to 1 in 2000 and 4–5 to 1 in 2050. Thus, with deferred retirement, the dependency

---

6. We are presently attempting to specify more clearly this relationship and hope to estimate the importance of this effect.

ratio in 2050 would be similar to present dependency rates. There will be increasing pressure for the postponement of retirement given that social security and other costs of incomes flowing to retirees will be found less and less tolerable by the employed, either in the form of taxes or of limitations upon payments to active members of the labor force.

Despite our recognition of the shortcomings of dependency ratios, it is helpful to visualize a population as consisting of (a) *nonproducing* receivers of goods and services, and (b) *producers* of all goods and services including those commanded by virtue of their initial receipt and subsequent expenditure of pension, annuity, social security, welfare, charity, and similar monetary payments. The magnitude of the *output* and the share of this output available to dependents depends mainly on the comparative numbers of producers and nonproducers and on the amount of output that the employed produce and surrender in recognition of the monetary claims of the dependent groups. It is evident, therefore, that both the *output* that can be provided and the share of this output to be transferred are limited. The economic state of the dependent group thus depends ultimately and essentially upon the relative size of the producing group.[7]

The importance of maintaining the labor force participation of the elderly at relatively high rates can be shown in a simple framework that extends equal retirement benefits to all those above the designated retirement age and assumes that everyone aged 18 to retirement age is in the labor force. The sensitivity of tax rates to alternative retirement ages is clearly indicated in Tables 3 and 4. The cost per worker of providing a dollar of benefit per retiree in 1977 ranges from $.40 for a retirement age of 55 to $.11 for an age of 70 (see Table 3). For each retirement age, Table 4 indicates that tax rates must rise over time assuming replacement fertility and a constant benefit to income ratio *(B/Y)*. The importance of a relatively late retirement age is vividly depicted. Of considerable significance in these models is the result that a gradual rise in the retirement age to 70 could virtually completely offset the increased tax required by changing population age structure. Thus, the removal of incentives for earlier withdrawal from the labor force increases in importance when combined with population aging. Therefore, public policy should be revised so as to diminish the economic and other incentives to early retirement, redesign job tasks and reduce the physical demands made by jobs. These tax reductions resulting from higher retirement ages are biased upward due to the fact that not all those 65–70 years of age would remain in the labor force even if the present incentives for withdrawal were removed [3, 6].

7. See Spengler [18]. Spengler notes the costliness of early retirement to a community whose population is stationary. Given retirement at age 65, 57.5 percent of the population is of working age and the ratio of those aged 18–64 to those aged 65 and over approximates 3 to 1. Should retirement age be raised to 75, this ratio would be raised to nearly 7 to 1. If retirement age were reduced to 55, the corresponding ratio would be reduced to about 1.5 to 1. Moreover, given a labor force aged 18–54 instead of one aged 18–64, total output would only be about eight-tenths as large.

Table 3. *Tax per worker required to finance benefits with various retirement ages, 1977*

Retirement age	Population (thousands)		Tax in cents per worker for $1 of benefits per retiree
	Retired[a]	Workers[b]	
55	43,837	108,717	40
60	32,793	119,761	27
62	28,976	123,578	23
65	23,431	129,123	18
70	14,991	137,563	11

[a] Everyone above the retirement age is assumed to be a nonworking beneficiary.
[b] Everyone between 18 and the retirement age is assumed to be a wage earner subject to the uniform payroll tax.

Continued labor force participation is compatible with the significant increases in life expectancy at older ages that have occurred during this century. Decreases in mortality for those above 65 work in conjunction with low fertility to increase the relative size of the aged population. And, even though future improvements in life-supporting systems increase the resources necessary to support the elderly, the elderly's improving health status should make continued labor force activity more feasible and promote later retirement.

Deferment of retirement to a later age may be viewed as a substitute for maintaining fertility at a relatively high level and for withdrawing earlier from the labor force, for instance at age 55–64 instead of at 65–74. Moreover, increased female labor force participation may be viewed as a kind of substitute for growth in the population of labor force ages. Were human fertility not subject to biospheric and other physical constraints, a higher rate of population growth might be preferable since it produces a relatively high ratio of persons of productive age relative to those in the older retired population. However, insofar as the resulting high population growth rate tends finally to produce output-limiting

Table 4. *Tax rates with constant benefit-earnings ratio and replacement level fertility*[a]

Retirement age	1976	1985	1990	1995	2000	2005	2010	2015	2025	2050
55		2.22 T	2.18 T	2.18 T	2.23 T	2.41 T	2.67 T	3.02 T	3.42 T	3.42 T
62		1.35 T	1.39 T	1.39 T	1.35 T	1.36 T	1.46 T	1.65 T	2.11 T	2.10 T
65	T	1.05 T	1.10 T	1.13 T	1.10 T	1.07 T	1.11 T	1.25 T	1.63 T	1.67 T
70		.65 T	.69 T	.73 T	.74 T	.73 T	.69 T	.73 T	.97 T	1.08 T

[a] Tax rates are generated from the following model derived from equation (1): $t = (B/Y)(R/L)$. L is composed of the population between 18 and the retirement age, whereas R denotes everyone over the retirement age. (B/Y) is assumed constant over the entire period.

constraints, a lower fertility rate and longer participation in the labor force are preferable.[8]

Inflation, Population Aging, and Retirement Policy

The aging of a population intensifies problems associated with the impact of inflation on older dependents, whose level of support depends largely on the purchasing power of their money incomes. This purchasing power is subject to erosion by inflation, whereas the support of young dependents rests upon the purchasing power of the expanding incomes of their parents. The primary sources of income for the elderly are social security, private pensions, continued earnings, asset income and dissaving, and governmental poverty programs. The ability of these alternative income sources to maintain the real purchasing power of the aged is critically important in establishing a national retirement policy.

Market wage rates typically reflect real productivity gains as well as price changes. In periods of high rates of inflation, older workers will have increased incentives to remain in the labor force as a means of protecting their real income from current and future price erosion. To the extent that pension benefits are keyed to final years' earnings, the value of continued labor force participation is enhanced by price and wage inflation. This same characteristic may reduce the attractiveness of part-time work unless alternative arrangements are made for the worker seeking gradually to reduce his hours of work.

Social security benefits of retirees are automatically adjusted for inflation and therefore remain constant in real value over the life of the beneficiary. Although a majority of public employee pensions provide for inflation adjustments, virtually no private pensions automatically increase benefits fully with changes in consumer prices; however, some ad hoc benefit increases are made to reduce the decline in real benefits. Table 5 illustrates the devastating effect of inflation on the real value of pension income. Even relatively low rates of inflation will dramatically reduce the real value of benefits over the life of the retiree. The indexing of social security benefits and the lack of this adjustment in private pension benefits alters the relative desirability of these two forms of retirement income and may induce an increased dependency on social security in the future.

The ability of the social security system to guarantee benefits in real terms is in part a function of its method of financing. Although a pay-as-you-go system such as social security does not reflect an investment yield similar to that of a pension or an annuity, it can be made relatively secure against inflation and

---

8. On the issues involved see Samuelson [16] and [17], Deardorff [8] and Arthur and McNicholl [1]. Arthur and McNicholl state that "Life cycle assumptions therefore tend to reenforce the neoclassical argument rather than offset it" (p. 242). Here neoclassical refers to the argument that population growth encounters limits.

Table 5. *Real replacement rates after 5, 10, 15, and 20 years of retirement with alternative rates of inflation*

		Real value of retirement income based on initial replacement rate of 100 percent		
Years in retirement	No inflation	3 percent annual rate of inflation	5 percent annual rate of inflation	10 percent annual rate of inflation
0	100	100	100	100
5	100	86	78	62
10	100	74	61	39
15	100	64	48	24
20	100	55	38	15

Source: [2, p. 42].

subject to increase in keeping with the rate of output per member of the labor force. Let r denote average income or benefit per retiree from social security; R, the number of retirees in a society; P, the number of productively employed persons who support the social security system; y, the average income per member of P; and t, the tax on y that supports the social security system. Then

$$r = \frac{tyP}{R}.$$

In the event of inflation, the money value of y will tend to keep pace with the price level. Moreover, y may increase over time, rising with the increase in the productivity of the members of P. The pool, tyP, divided among dependents, R, thus tends to keep pace with the money and the real value of y.

In contrast to this system, the money return on an annuity being drawn on by a retiree cannot easily be made to increase adequately to offset a rising price level and assure the initial real return contracted for. Thus, a funded system would have to rely on current contributions to provide a full, automatic inflation adjustment. The cost of such current payments will probably preclude the adoption of automatic adjustment provisions in the private sector.

Two potential disadvantages of the reliance on pay-as-you-go financing are the possible retarding effects on capital accumulation and fluctuations in the size of successive cohorts. Feldstein [12] and Munnell [15] present evidence that the growth in the social security system has decreased national savings. This result has been criticized on theoretical and statistical grounds.[9] Additional, more conclusive evidence is needed to justify major innovations in social security funding.

Variations in the rate of fertility from year to year are quite likely. These fluctuations produce short-term changes in the age structure that may create

9. See Esposito [11, p. 17].

special economic problems that are masked by assumptions of constant fertility. Oscillations around a particular fertility rate, perhaps in response to economic conditions, will generate bulges in the age structure [9]. In this type of pseudo-stable population, the economy must continually adjust to varying sizes of important cohorts. The implications for pay-as-you-go retirement financing should be clear. A relatively small cohort while in the labor force may be faced with providing retirement income for a large cohort and subsequently in retirement the small cohort may be supported by a larger one. Thus, intergenerational equity issues may be raised because the relatively small cohort will be required to pay a higher per capita tax rate while in the working years and yet necessitate a lower tax on the subsequent larger cohort to finance a similar level of benefits. The current transition from the high fertility of the post–World War II decade to the present subreplacement levels is in part responsible for the required future increases in the social security tax.

If inflation is not significantly reduced, it may prove necessary for the federal government to guarantee the purchasing power not only of social security and federal pension benefits but also of private pensions and annuities purchased by the elderly. This could be done through the sale of cost-of-living bonds or annuities to pension funds or directly to retirees. The principle of this protection has been accepted for federal workers—it need only be applied to all retirees. Government guaranteed purchasing power for pension benefits would eliminate their current disadvantage relative to social security and would promote the continued viability of private pensions. Additionally, it would insure the retirement income of millions of pensioners against inflation.

Conclusion

The importance of continued population aging for the development of a national retirement policy has been the primary topic of analysis of this chapter. We have illustrated how the future cost of financing retirement income depends significantly on the age of retirement. Early retirement (prior to age 65), financed by government transfers, is probably incompatible with population aging, whereas deferred retirement is one method of significantly moderating future costs.

Demographic factors will be conducive to later retirement. The relative size of young cohorts seeking to enter the labor force will decline, thus reducing pressure on older cohorts to retire. Continued improvements in the health status of the elderly and increased life expectancy should also encourage continued labor force participation. Government policy should be reevaluated to encourage the labor supply of older workers. Present policies that induce workers into retirement should be closely examined and probably altered.

High rates of inflation will also encourage market work by the elderly since wages typically rise with price changes. Inflation also increases the desirability of pay-as-you-go financing and, in general, tends to induce retirees to favor social security benefits that are automatically adjusted with price changes. To maintain the viability of private pensions, the federal government should explore methods of guaranteeing the real value of pension benefits.

Our examination of the implications of population aging for retirement policy generates the following policy recommendations. First, an immediate review should be made of policies and programs that affect retirement decisions. Consideration should be given to planning a gradual rise in the age of eligibility for most of the age-related retirement benefit programs. Retirement income needs additional protection against price erosion and continued labor force participation is one method of accomplishing this goal. In addition, the government should explore the concept of providing cost-of-living bonds or annuities to retirees.

References

[1] Arthur, W. B., and Geoffrey McNicholl, "Samuelson, Population and Intergenerational Transfers," *International Economic Review,* 19 (Feb. 1978), 241–246.

[2] Clark, Robert, *The Role of Private Pensions in Maintaining Living Standards in Retirement* (Washington, D.C.: National Planning Association, 1977).

[3] Clark, Robert, "Impact of Retirement Age on the Social Security System," Testimony Before the House Select Committee on Population, June 1, 1978.

[4] Clark, Robert, Juanita Kreps, and Joseph Spengler, "Economics of Aging: A Survey," *Journal of Economic Literature,* 16 (Sept. 1978), 919–962.

[5] Clark, Robert, and Joseph Spengler, "Changing Demography and Dependency Costs: The Implications of New Dependency Ratios and Their Composition," in Barbara Herzog (Ed.), *Income and Aging: Essays on Policy Prospects* (New York: Human Sciences Press), 1978.

[6] Clark, Robert, and Joseph Spengler, "Economic Implications of Population Aging," presented to American Economic Association meeting, Aug. 1978.

[7] Clark, Robert, and Joseph Spengler, "Dependency Ratios: Their Use in Economic Analysis," in Julian L. Simon and Julie daVanzo (Eds.), *Research in Population Economics,* Vol. 2 (Greenwich, Conn.: JAI Press, 1980).

[8] Deardoroff, A. V., "The Growth Rate for Population: Comment," *International Economic Review,* 17 (June 1976), pp. 510–515.

[9] Easterlin, Richard, Michael Wachter, and Susan Wachter, "Demographic Influences on Economic Stability: The United States Experience," *Population and Development Review* (Mar. 1978), 1–22.

[10] Easterlin, Richard, Michael Wachter, and Susan Wachter, "Demography and Full Employment: The Changing Impact of Population Swings on the American Economy," *Proceedings of the American Philosophical Society,* 122 (June 1978), 119–130.

[11] Esposito, Louis, "Effect of Social Security on Savings: Review of Studies Using U.S. Time-Series Data," *Social Security Bulletin* (May 1978), pp. 9–17.

[12] Feldstein, Martin, "Social Security, Induced Retirement, and Aggregate Capital Accumulation," *Journal of Political Economy* (Sept./Oct. 1974), 905–926.

[13] Ginzberg, Eli, "The Politics of Employment," *Proceedings of the American Philosophical Society,* 112 (June 1978), 131–134.

[14] MacDonald, Robert M., *Mandatory Retirement and the Law* (Washington, D.C.: American Enterprise Institute), 1978, pp. 1–3.

[15] Munnell, Alicia, *The Effect of Social Security on Personal Savings* (Cambridge, Mass.: Ballinger Publishing Company, 1974).
[16] Samuelson, Paul A., "The Optimum Growth Rate for Population," *International Economic Review*, 16 (Oct. 1975), 531–538.
[17] Samuelson, Paul A., "The Optimum Growth Rate for Population: Agreement and Evaluations," *International Economic Review*, 17 (June 1976), 516–525.
[18] Spengler, J. J., "Population Aging and Security of the Aged," *Atlantic Economic Journal*, 6 (Mar. 1978), 1–7.
[19] U.S. Department of Labor, "New Labor Force Projections to 1990: Three Possible Paths," *News*, Aug. 16 (Washington, D.C.: Bureau of Labor Statistics, 1978).
[20] Wachter, Michael, "The Demographic Impact on Unemployment," in *Demographic Trends and Full Employment*, Special Report No. 12 (Washington, D.C.: National Commission for Manpower Policy, 1976), 27–99.

The Impact of Inflation on Private Pensions   *Alicia H. Munnell*

Private pensions and social security clearly represent alternative mechanisms for accomplishing the same goal—namely, the provision of an adequate retirement income. Despite the expansion of social security during the 1970s, ample room still exists for private pensions to supplement the retirement income of workers with earnings above the median. However, for private plans to fulfill this role successfully, they must be able to preserve the real value of the employee's benefits as they accumulate during his working years as well as after his retirement. This chapter will focus on the relative ability of private pensions and social security to preserve the value of pension benefits in an inflationary environment.

For private plans, the preservation of the value of benefits over the employee's worklife depends on how the plans are structured. Vesting, portability, and the nature of the compensation base determine whether the worker's initial benefit reflects inflation-induced wage increases. After retirement, protection hinges on whether pensioners are provided annual cost-of-living adjustments. Although the institutional arrangements are quite different, the underlying economic requirement for the provision of benefits that keep pace with inflation is the same—namely, the pension plan must be able to earn a return on assets that fully reflects the increase in prices. Therefore, pension funds must have access to investments where the real rate of return is not affected by the rate of inflation. As a result, real profits net of the corporate income tax decrease as the rate of inflation increases.

Reform of the corporate income tax so that the prices of capital goods and inventories are adjusted to reflect the increase in the price level would eliminate the rise in the corporate tax rate on real profits during inflation and avoid the decline in the real rate of return. This would permit pension funds to invest in a security (corporate stock) that would be protected against inflation. Alternatively, pension funds could be permitted to invest in index bonds—bonds that guarantee real rates of return adequate for providing real benefits. However, it seems clear that under the current tax laws, private firms will never be willing to issue this type of security as their real rates of return fall when inflation rises. Hence, the only alternative source for these securities is the federal government. The key question is whether the government could issue a sufficient volume of these securities to enable pensions to provide indexed benefits without disrupting capital markets.

The author would like to thank Jennifer Katz for excellent research assistance and Richard Kopcke for endless discussions and for working out the equations. Janice Halpern and Peter Mieszkowski also provided useful comments.

This chapter first explores the provisions for preretirement cost-of-living adjustments in the United States. Although final earnings plans have become increasingly prevalent, the lack of portability of pension benefits among plans results in loss of the real value of the benefits over the worker's career. The second section focuses on the provisions for cost-of-living adjustments after retirement. Private pension plans have initiated some ad hoc adjustments to compensate for rising prices but these increases generally have provided only partial offsets. In the third section, a model is presented that summarizes the investment performance required to provide full cost-of-living adjustments both before and after retirement. Since the model indicates that full indexing requires nominal interest rates to reflect fully the rate of inflation, the final sections explore the potential for pension funds to find assets that satisfy this criterion.

Preserving the Value of Preretirement Benefits

The preservation of the value of preretirement benefits depends on the nature of the pension plan and its vulnerability to inflation. Employee-sponsored private plans are divided into two main categories: defined contribution and defined benefit. In defined contribution plans, the employee's benefit is determined by the accumulated value of contributions made on his behalf and on the investment earnings. Defined contribution plans account for only a minor proportion of total benefit payments.

In defined benefit plans, benefits are based on a specified formula that relates the pension to salaries and/or length of service. Defined benefit plans can have either flat or unit benefit formulas. Flat benefit formulas, those in which the benefit varies with years of service but not with the compensation of the employee, are characteristic of "pattern" type plans. Pattern plans have been adopted by some international unions and negotiated with minor variations by individual companies or groups of companies.

The most common benefit formula, characteristic of most salaried worker plans and some collectively bargained plans, relates benefits to compensation and length of service [16, p. 11]. This type of formula allocates benefit units, expressed as percentage points, for each year of creditable service. The product of these benefit units and years of service determine the percentage of the compensation base to which the employee is entitled at retirement. For example, an employee may earn 2 percent a year for thirty years and receive a pension benefit of 60 percent of his final salary.

Benefits may be calculated with a compensation base of earnings averaged over the worker's entire career, part of his career, or only his final year of employment. For any given benefit formula, the use of final pay as the compensation base will yield higher benefits than those based on career average earnings. Averaging over the person's entire working life means including his early earnings, which are usually lower than those of later years, thereby depressing the base to which replacement percentages are applied.

Since wages tend to rise with inflation, only final earnings plans effectively preserve the real value of workers' benefits. Unless the benefit formula is liberalized periodically, the real purchasing power of benefits calculated on the basis of career average will be diminished by rising prices. In response to the high level of inflation during the 1970s, the number of final earnings plans has increased substantially. According to the 1975 Bankers Trust study (which does not include the collectively bargained multiemployer plans), only 22 percent of conventional plans in the 1970–75 period utilized a career average formula exclusively, whereas more than half of those plans based full benefits on final pay (see Table 1). Most final earnings plans are based on average compensation in the last five years of employment.[1] With 6 percent inflation, even the five-year average is about 11 percent below the salary in the final year. Nevertheless, final earnings plans are the only form of pension that preserves on a contractual basis the value of pension benefits as they accrue.

However, the ability of even final earnings plans to offset the effects of inflation is limited by the lack of portability between plans for even vested benefits. Consider the case of a worker who enters the labor force at age 25 and changes jobs every ten years until he retires. Because of his job changes, even if each of his employers sponsors a final earnings plan and his benefits are fully vested, his final pension will resemble that of a career average plan. Table 2 provides an example of the ratio of benefits under continuous and discontinuous employment with different rates of inflation. As expected, the higher the rate of inflation, the more discontinuous employment lowers the value of benefits. The erosion of benefits occurs because there are no provisions for indexing benefits between termination of employment and retirement or for portability among plans.

Alternative measures to protect the value of a worker's pension during his career have obvious disadvantages and fail to prevent the erosion of workers' benefits by inflation. For example, simple schemes that would allow workers to transfer credit between defined benefit plans when they changed jobs are virtually unworkable in view of the almost infinite variety of retirement ages, forms and amounts of annuities. Furthermore, even if all retirement plans were identical, a simple transfer of credits would not solve the problem of maintaining the value of benefits in an inflationary environment. A complex contribution schedule would be required to protect the worker's final employer from being forced to pay almost the entire cost of the inflated benefits. Moreover, proposals to promote portability through the creation of a central pension fund to which

---

1. There has been a consistent trend toward shortening the number of years over which earnings are averaged in final pay plans. In 1959, 41 percent of final pay plans used a ten-year average and 53 percent used five-year averages. In 1975, only 4 percent employed ten-year averages, whereas 93 percent based benefits on earnings in the last five years.

Table 1. *Compensation basis of conventional pension plans*

	1970–75	1965–70	1960–65	1956–59	1953–55	1950–52
Type of plans	(percent of plans)					
All benefits based on career average compensation	22	35	45	56	62	72
All benefits based on final average compensation	54	39	31	27	26	18
Regular benefits based on career average compensation, minimum benefits based on final average compensation	16	20	16	12	6	4
Benefits based in part on career average compensation and in part on final average compensation	8	6	5	2	1	–
Other	0	0	3	3	5	6
Total	100	100	100	100	100	100
Length of compensation base for plans using final average 3-year average compensation	2	1	–	–	–	–
5-year average compensation	93	77	57	53	–	–
10-year average compensation	4	15	37	41	–	–
Other	1	7	6	6	–	–
Total	100	100	100	100	–	–

Source: [1, 2, 3].

workers could transfer vested benefits when they changed jobs are aimed primarily at the preservation of benefits for retirement that might otherwise be cashed out and do not address the inflation issue [10].

The most promising approach appears to be replacing defined benefit plans with defined contribution plans so that each worker has a readily identifiable account that he could transfer from one employer to another. Workers would gain portability, but would be exposed to the risks of inflation if the rate of return on accumulated assets failed to keep pace with rising prices.

The preservation of the value of pension benefits between termination and retirement is not a problem that can be solved merely by increasing vesting. The erosion of benefits for workers who change jobs is significant as shown in Table 3. A pension of $100 vested at age 30 would have the purchasing power of only $36 by age 65 if annual inflation were 3 percent. With an inflation rate of 9 percent, purchasing power would be reduced to $5. Because of this,

Table 2. *Comparison of benefits for a single-job worker and a four-job worker over forty years of employment during different rates of inflation*

Rate of inflation[a]	Compensation base final pay[c]	Compensation rule (percent of salary)	Benefits	Total benefits	Ratio of benefits (single-job worker/ four-job worker)
0% Single-job worker	$ 10,000	40	$ 4,000	$ 4,000	1
Four-job worker[b]					
	10,000	10	1,000		
	10,000	10	1,000	4,000	
	10,000	10	1,000		
	10,000	10	1,000		
2% Single-job worker	22,080	40	8,832	8,832	1.31
Four-job worker					
	12,189	10	1,218		
	14,859	10	1,485	6,724	
	18,113	10	1,811		
	22,080	10	2,208		
4% Single-job worker	48,010	40	19,204	19,204	1.64
Four-job worker					
	14,802	10	1,480		
	21,911	10	2,191	11,715	
	32,433	10	3,243		
	48,010	10	4,801		
6% Single-job worker	102,851	40	41,140	41,140	1.96
Four-job worker					
	17,908	10	1,790		
	32,071	10	3,207	21,027	
	57,434	10	5,743		
	102,851	10	10,285		

[a] Assumes a consistent annual increase.
[b] Assumes worker stays at each job for ten years.
[c] Base salary is $10,000.
[d] Assumes annual benefit accrual of 1 percent per year.
Source: Author's calculations.

Table 3. *Effect of inflation and age of vesting on purchasing power at age 65 of $100 vested benefit*

Age at vesting	Rate of inflation		
	3%	6%	9%
30	$36	$13	$5
40	48	23	12
50	64	42	27

Source [11, p. 8].

countries with persistently high rates of inflation have recognized the importance of indexing benefits between termination and retirement. In England, the universal earnings-related pension, which supplements the basic pension, is based on either final pay or the best 20 years of earnings revalued according to the nationwide average earnings between that year and the year of retirement. This indexing of previous earnings in order to provide an inflation-adjusted base for benefit computation is required whether the firm "contracts in" to the new state pension scheme or "contracts out" to provide pensions under the traditional occupational scheme [5].

In the United States, all workers covered by social security are now institutionally protected against an erosion of benefits over their lifetime. Social security coverage is almost universal so that workers continue to build up benefits in all types of employment. Therefore, extensive portability protects the worker against any erosion of benefits as a result of changing jobs. However, since social security benefits are based on career averages rather than final earnings, either periodic liberalization of the benefit formula or indexation of earnings histories is required for benefits to keep pace with inflation. Prior to the 1972 Amendments, adjustments for inflation and wage growth were made by ad hoc increases in the benefit formula. In an effort to introduce automatic adjustments for inflation, the 1972 legislation overindexed the benefit structure that more than compensated retiring workers for increases in prices. The 1977 Amendments finally corrected the overindexing through a procedure that maintains the ratio of benefits to preretirement earnings. This procedure explicitly adjusts both the worker's prior earnings and the social security benefit formula for increases in average wages.[2] By calculating benefits on the basis of past earnings that have been revalued to reflect increases in prices and productivity, the social security program now protects the worker against any erosion of benefits over his worklife.

Providing similar protection under private plans would require indexing benefits between the time a worker terminated his employment and his retirement from the labor market. Although final earnings plans provide implicit indexation for people who work until retirement, employers may resist indexing vested benefits for terminated employees. Rapidly rising wages together with declining real yields on pension assets would significantly raise the required level of pension contribution. With active employees, firms can shift part of this additional cost to the employee by slowing the rate of wage growth, but with terminated employees a firm would be forced to bear the full burden. Furthermore, providing lower benefits to mobile employees may be one of the ways that firms attempt to reduce employee turnover and retain skilled workers.

If firms are to provide adequate retirement income in an inflationary environ-

---

2. Without annual adjustments, the progressivity of the benefit formula would result in declining replacement rates as the level of wages increased.

ment, indexation is essential. Vesting alone does not protect workers from benefit erosion in periods of rising prices.

Preserving the Value of Benefits After Retirement

Maintaining the value of pension benefits prior to retirement is only half the issue. Without postretirement cost-of-living adjustments, the retiree's living standard will decline as inflation erodes the purchasing power of his benefits. Since the future pattern of price increases cannot be predicted accurately, no amount of preplanning can ensure total protection from inflation. The only way to insulate retirees from the erosion of their pension benefits is to provide cost-of-living adjustments that compensate for the full amount of price increases. In the absence of such adjustments, a retiree's economic welfare is entirely dependent on the vagaries of the economy—a situation that completely undermines the establishment of a rational retirement system.

Automatic cost-of-living adjustments during retirement maintain the worker's standard of living by preserving his command of goods and services. Nevertheless, the retiree's economic position will decline relative to that of current workers because those still in the workforce receive increases for productivity improvements as well as inflation adjustments. Adjusting pension benefits for improvements in the average wage rather than tying increases to the consumer price index (CPI) would permit retirees to share in the growth of the economy as well as insulating them from price increases. Such an arrangement would prevent a deterioration in their position relative to that of employed workers.

Although most people recognize the need for inflation adjustments, the desirability of increases that allow for productivity growth is not as generally accepted. Resistance centers on two points: the desirability of extending rewards for productivity gains to those who did not earn them and the ability of society to afford such increases. The philosophical debate over whether standards of living should be measured in real or relative terms is as yet unsettled. However, the fact that social security ties postretirement increases to CPI movements makes adjustments for prices the relevant criterion against which to evaluate the performance of private plans.

The key difference between OASI and private pension benefits is that the former are indexed for inflation after retirement, whereas the latter generally are not. With an inflation rate of 6 percent, the real purchasing power of a $2,101 private pension benefit (the average in 1975) would be reduced to $1,173 in ten years.

Private plans, however, have been cognizant of the erosive power of inflation and generally have provided some adjustments to beneficiaries. The Bankers Trust study estimated that 71 percent of conventional plans in their sample extended increases to retired employees. The average increase between 1969 and 1975 for a person who had retired in the mid-60s was 16 percent [3]. Although the 16 percent increase in benefits obviously relieved some of the pressure on retirees, clearly it is only partial compensation in the face of the 47 percent increase in the CPI during the same period.

In contrast, the 1972 Amendments to the Social Security Act introduced automatic cost-of-living adjustments so social security benefits are increased annually to reflect the full rise in prices. This procedure prevents erosion of purchasing power over the beneficiary's retirement years and makes social security benefits considerably more valuable than an equivalent initial benefit from a private pension plan. Since social security is financed on a pay-as-you-go basis, these automatic postretirement adjustments require no increase in the payroll tax rate.[3]

Can Private Pensions Provide Indexed Benefits and Remain Actuarially Sound?

Although private pension plans currently do not provide fully indexed benefits, their future depends, at least partially, on their ability to protect workers from the erosive effects of inflation. An important issue, therefore, is the ability of private pensions to provide fully indexed benefits and remain actuarially sound in an inflationary environment. A simple model reveals that full indexation with current contribution rates is possible only if the real rate of return on the plan assets is not affected adversely by inflation.

Consider the most general case where an employee's benefit (Bj) is a function of his past salary, S_i, and the contribution rate β, is set at a level so that the present discounted value of benefits (PVB) between retirement, e, and death, d, equals the present discounted value of contributions (PVC). That is,

$$Bj = \sum_{i=1}^{e} \alpha_i S_i \qquad j = e+1, \ldots, d, \tag{1}$$

$$C_i = \beta S_i, \tag{2}$$

$$PVB = \sum_{j=e+1}^{d} (1+r)^{-j} \sum_{i=1}^{e} \alpha_i S_i$$

$$= \sum_{i=1}^{e} S_i \{\alpha_i (1+r)^{-e}[1-(1+r)^{-d}]/r\}, \tag{3}$$

$$PVC = \sum_{i=1}^{e} S_i \{\beta (1+r)^{-i}\}. \tag{4}$$

3. Payroll tax rates will be forced to increase if the ratio of elderly to working population increases, but once this ratio stabilizes, inflation alone will have no impact on the tax rate. The fact that the taxable earnings base is increased in line with the growth in annual wages means that the tax base rises with inflation.

Thus, setting *PVB* equal to *PVC* and rearranging,

$$\beta = \frac{\sum\limits_{i=1}^{e} S_i\{\alpha_i(1+r)^{-e}[1-(1+r)^{-d}]/r\}}{\sum\limits_{i=1}^{e} S_i\{\beta(1+r)^{-i}\}}. \tag{5}$$

If the pension is a unit benefit plan based on average earnings, then α_i in Equation (5) is equal to $\frac{a}{e}$, where a is the product of the benefit accrual rate and years of service, e. For instance, if the employee earns 1 percent of salary and works forty years, then $a = 40$. On the other hand, if benefits are based on final earnings, then $\alpha_i = 0$ for all except the final year *(i + e)*, and the value of α in the final year, α_e, is equal to the accrual rate multiplied by years of service or a.

With a constant inflation rate, Π, the benefit and contribution equations become:

$$Bj = \sum_{i=1}^{e} \alpha_i S_i (1+\Pi)^i \qquad j = e+1, \ldots, d, \tag{1'}$$

$$C_i = \tilde{\beta} S_i (1+\Pi)^i, \tag{2'}$$

$$P\tilde{V}B = \sum_{j=e+1}^{d} (1+r')^{-j} \sum_{i=1}^{e} \alpha_i S_i (1+\Pi)^i$$

$$= \sum_{i=1}^{e} S_i\{\alpha_i (1+\Pi)^i (1+r')^{-e}[1-(1+r')^{-d}]/r'\}, \tag{3'}$$

$$P\tilde{V}C = \sum_{i=1}^{e} \{S_i\tilde{\beta}(1+\Pi)^i (1+r')^{-i}\}, \tag{4'}$$

$$\tilde{\beta} = \frac{\sum\limits_{i=1}^{e} S_i\{\alpha_i (1+\Pi)^i (1+r')^{-e}[1-(1+r')^{-d}]/r'\}}{\sum\limits_{i=1}^{e} S_i[(1+\Pi)^i (1+r')^{-i}]}. \tag{5'}$$

For the contribution rate to remain unchanged, $\tilde{\beta} = \beta$, the following equality must hold

$$\frac{(1+r')^{-e}[1-(1+r')^{-d}]/r'}{(1+r')^{-i}} = \frac{(1+r)^{-e}[1-(1+r)^{-d}]/r}{(1+r)^{-i}} \text{ for all } i. \tag{6}$$

With this framework, it is possible to determine for four separate cases the interest rate required for the contribution rate, β, set in the noninflationary period to yield sufficient revenues to cover benefits in the inflationary period.

Case 1. Career Average Plan with No Postretirement Indexing

If benefits are tied to average earnings, then a constant nominal rate $(r' = r)$ satisfies Equation 6 and the contribution rate can remain unchanged. A constant nominal rate generates sufficient revenues because higher nominal benefits are matched exactly by increased contributions from the inflated wage base. Similarly, if interest rates were to rise in response to inflation, contribution rates could be lowered in career average plans with no postretirement indexing.

Case 2. Final Earnings Plan with No Postretirement Indexing

For a final earnings plan in an inflationary environment, the benefit and contribution equations become

$$P\tilde{V}B = S_e\{a(1 + \Pi)^e(1 + r')^{-e}[1 - (1 + r')^{-d}]/r'\}, \tag{7}$$

$$P\tilde{V}C = \sum_{i=1}^{e} S_i\{\tilde{\beta}(1 + \Pi)^i(1 + r')^{-i}\}, \tag{8}$$

$$\tilde{\beta} = \frac{S_e(1 + \Pi)^e\{a(1 + r')^{-e}[1 - (1 + r')^{-d}]/r'\}}{\sum_{i=1}^{e} S_i\{(1 + \Pi)^i(1 + r')^{-i}\}}. \tag{9}$$

In this case, the required change in interest rates can be determined by comparing $\tilde{\beta}$ with the contribution rate for a similar plan during a period without inflation.

$$\beta = \frac{S_e\{a(1 + r)^{-e}[1 - (1 + r)^{-d}]/r\}}{\sum_{i=1}^{e} S_i(1 + r)^{-i}}. \tag{10}$$

If the interest rate remained unchanged $(r' = r)$, then the contribution rate would have to increase $(\tilde{\beta} > \beta)$. On the other hand, if the new interest rate fully incorporated the inflation premium $[r' = r + \Pi$, or more precisely $(1 + r') = (1 + r)(1 + \Pi)]$, then the contribution rate could be lowered $(\tilde{\beta} < \beta)$. Therefore, to maintain the preinflation contribution rate, β, some inflation premium must be reflected in after-tax discount rates and yields. Nominal yields need not rise by the full increase in prices, however, since with no postretirement indexing the inflated yields on fund assets after the employee retires represent a gain to the pension fund that compensates for the inadequate financing of the final earnings plan over the employee's worklife.

Case 3. Career Average Plan with Postretirement Indexing

In pension plans with benefits based on career average earnings, but with provision of postretirement cost-of-living adjustments, the present values of benefits and contributions are

$$P\tilde{V}B = \sum_{i=1}^{e} S_i \left\{ \frac{a}{e}(1 + \Pi)^i (1 + r')^{-e} \right.$$

$$[1 - (1 + r')^{-d}(1 + \Pi)^d]/[(1 + r')(1 + \Pi)^{-1} - 1]\}, \quad (11)$$

$$P\tilde{V}C = \sum_{i=1}^{e} S_i \{\tilde{\beta}(1 + \Pi)^i (1 + r')^{-i}\}, \quad (12)$$

$$\tilde{\beta} = \frac{\sum\limits_{i=1}^{e} S_i \left\{ \dfrac{a}{e}(1 + \Pi)^i (1 + r')^{-e}[1 - (1 + r')^{-d}(1 + \Pi)^d]/ \atop [(1 + r')(1 + \Pi)^{-1} - 1]] \right\}}{\sum\limits_{i=1}^{e} S_i \{(1 + \Pi)^i (1 + r')^{-i}\}}. \quad (13)$$

For contribution rates to remain unchanged, the following equality must hold:

$$\frac{(1 + r')^{-e}[1 - (1 + r')^{-d}(1 + \Pi)^d]/[(1 + r')(1 + \Pi)^{-1} - 1]}{(1 + r')^{-i}}$$

$$= \frac{(1 + r)^{-e}[1 - (1 + r)^{-d}]/r}{(1 + r)^{-i}}. \quad (14)$$

If the nominal interest rate remains constant, that is $r' = r$, then the left side of Equation (14) would be greater than the right side and the contribution rate would have to increase ($\tilde{\beta} > \beta$). On the other hand, if the nominal interest rate increased to reflect the inflation fully, that is $(1 + r') = (1 + r)(1 + \Pi)$, then the contribution rate could be reduced from the preinflation level ($\tilde{\beta} < \beta$). Therefore, cost-of-living adjustments after retirement in a career average plan require nominal rates to rise in order to maintain the preinflation contribution rate; however, nominal rates need not rise by the full rate of inflation.

Case 4. Final Earnings Plan With Postretirement Indexing

The most relevant case for comparing social security and private pensions is a plan in which the initial benefit is based on final earnings and benefits are adjusted for cost-of-living increases after retirement. In this case, the present values of benefits and contributions become

$$P\tilde{V}B = S_e\{a(1 + \Pi)^e(1 + r')^{-e}[1 - (1 + r')^{-d}(1 + \Pi)^{d}]/$$
$$[(1 + r')(1 + \Pi)^{-1} - 1]\}, \quad (15)$$

$$P\tilde{V}C = \sum_{i=1}^{e} S_i\{\beta(1 + \Pi)^i(1 + r')^{-i}\}, \quad (16)$$

$$\tilde{\beta} = \frac{S_e\{a(1 + \Pi)^e(1 + r')^{-e}[1 - (1 + r')^{-d}(1 + \Pi)^{d}]/}{\sum_{i=1}^{e} S_i(1 + r')^{-i}(1 + \Pi)^i} , \quad (17)$$

whereas the contribution rate in the absence of inflation is

$$\beta = \frac{S_e\{a(1 + r)^{-e}[1 - (1 + r)^{-d}]/r\}}{\sum_{i=1}^{e} S_i(1 + r)^{-i}} . \quad (18)$$

Therefore, if $(1 + r') = (1 + \Pi)(1 + r)$, then $\tilde{\beta} = \beta$. In other words, for the pension plan to remain actuarially sound without increasing the contribution rate while providing benefits based on final earnings and postretirement cost-of-living adjustments, the nominal interest rate must rise by the full inflation premium.

This analysis clearly abstracts from the difficulties of preserving pension benefits of mobile employees. Instead, it addresses the more basic question assuming that the private pension system is a giant, universal uniform pension plan covering all workers. Even with this ideal hypothetical system, the goal of providing benefits that keep pace with inflation may be unattainable unless pension funds have access to investments that fully incorporate the inflation premium in nominal rates of return.

Impact of Inflation on Pension Assets

For the nominal yield on pension assets to rise by the full amount of inflation, the real return on plan assets must be unaffected by inflation. Unfortunately, most of the recent evidence in the economics literature suggests that real returns on corporate equities and fixed income securities decline in response to an increase in the rate of inflation.

In the case of corporate equities, the decline in the real rate of return reflects the increase in the effective corporate income tax rate [9, 12, 18]. In periods of rising prices, conventional rules for calculating business expenses understate both depreciation allowances and the material costs of products sold. Consequently, corporate income tax liabilities increase considerably faster than do realistic assessments of operating profits. On the other hand, corporations benefit somewhat from inflation since the decline in the real value of outstanding liabili-

Table 4. *Assets of private noninsured pension funds in 1965, 1970, and 1975*

Assets	Book value, $ millions, end of year		
	1965	1970	1975
Cash and deposits	$ 940	$ 1,804	$ 2,962
U.S. government securities	2,990	3,029	10,764
Corporate and other			
bonds	23,130	29,666	37,809
Preferred stock	750	1,736	1,188
Common stock	25,120	51,744	83,654
Own company	1,830	3,330	5,075
Other companies	23,290	48,414	78,579
Mortgages	3,380	4,172	2,383
Other assets	2,870	4,860	6,406
Total assets	$59,180	$ 97,011	$145,166
	Market value, $ millions, end of year		
Cash and deposits	$ 900	$ 1,804	$ 2,962
U.S. government securities	2,900	2,998	11,097
Corporate and other			
bonds	21,900	24,919	34,519
Preferred stock	800	1,631	892
Common stock	40,000	65,456	87,669
Own company	4,400	6,038	6,958
Other companies	35,600	59,418	80,711
Mortgages	3,400	3,604	2,139
Other assets	3,000	4,422	6,341
Total assets	$72,900	$104,737	$145,622

Note.—Includes deferred profit-sharing funds and pension funds of corporations, unions, multi-employer groups, and nonprofit organizations.
Source: [14, p. 457; 15, pp. 6–7].

ties (such as bank loans, bonds, and accounts payable) is not included in taxable income. If inflation persists, however, corporation tax liabilities tend to be higher under the current procedure than they would be if taxes were assessed on inflation-adjusted income.[4] This increase in the effective tax rate reduces the real return on corporate assets, which causes equity prices to decline.

The return on corporate bonds also will be affected adversely by inflation. Holders of outstanding corporate liabilities will suffer a capital loss as inflation increases since they are locked into the preinflation nominal yields. Some ambiguity exists about the yields on new issues, but most likely with the decline in corporate profitability, firms will not be able to offer yields that fully compensate for inflation.

Table 4 presents the book and market value of the assets for noninsured pension funds. In 1975, noninsured pensions accounted for 83 percent of total pension benefits. Table 5 compares the rate of return on noninsured pension

4. See Kopcke [12] and Tideman and Tucker [18].

Table 5. *Rate of return for noninsured[a] pension assets and rate of inflation from 1964–75*

Year	Rate of return[b]		Rate of inflation[c]	
1964	11.3		1.6	
1965	8.6		2.2	
1966	−5.1	4.5[d]	3.3	3.2
1967	11.9		2.9	
1968	7.6		4.4	
1969	−5.8		5.0	
1970	5.6		5.3	
1971	16.1		5.1	
1972	17.2	2.0[d]	4.1	6.6
1973	−18.4		5.8	
1974	−21.3		9.7	
1975	22.2		9.6	

[a] Life insurance companies do not retain separate pension funds, rather reserve a portion of their general revenues to pay pension liabilities. As a result, there is no information available to calculate insured pension assets' rates of return. Since noninsured pensions represent 83 percent of all benefits paid in 1975, the rates of return calculated above do describe the trend of most pension funds.

[b] Rate of return $= \dfrac{(\text{Assets}_t - \text{Assets}_{t-1}) - (\text{Contributions}_t - \text{Benefits}_t)}{\text{Assets}_{t-1}}$ where assets are valued at market value.

[c] Inflation is based on the annual increase in the GNP deflator.

[d] The average annual growth rate for the six-year period is calculated as follows:

$$\text{Annual rate of return over 6 years} = \left(\left[\prod_{t=1}^{6} \left(1 + \frac{\text{rate of return}_t}{100}\right) \right]^{1/6} - 1 \right) 100.$$

This average annual growth rate obviously differs from the average of the annual growth rates.
Source: [7, p. 260; 15, p. 7; 17, p. 4.

fund assets with the inflation rate from 1964 to 1975. During the 1960s the annual return amounted to 4.5 percent and inflation averaged 3.2 percent; between 1970 and 1975 the return on the assets of noninsured funds declined to 2.0 percent per year and the average increase in the price level over this period rose to 6.6 percent. Although these numbers should be interpreted cautiously since the later period encompassed the severe 1974–75 recession, the data appear consistent with the contention that pension funds do not have access to assets with returns that fully reflect the inflation premium.

One could argue, however, that declining real rates of return are a short-run phenomenon and that eventually, in response to these lower yields, the capital stock will decline relative to the labor force until the previous real rate of return is restored. Two problems exist with this sanguine view. First, with a smaller capital stock, total compensation (including pensions) will be lower than it otherwise would have been without the decline in corporate profitability. Second, even if the pension fund manager were interested only in the returns to the plan's portfolio, the transition period during which the capital stock adjusts to restore former yields can be quite long. It is not clear that workers will tolerate inadequate pensions or that companies can afford the rising benefit costs while this adjustment process takes place.

Without the availability of financial assets whose real rate of return is unaffected by inflation and which fully incorporate an inflation premium in nominal yields, private pension plans are not in a position to offer fully indexed benefits. Although the required financial instruments currently are not available, many have suggested that the issuance of index bonds would solve the problem.

Index Bonds for Private Pensions

The availability of index bonds—bonds that guarantee a real rate of return plus an inflation premium—would enable plan sponsors to commit themselves to fully indexed benefits. The key question is whether either private firms or the federal government can issue this type of security.

Despite the apparent demand for index bonds and the likelihood that they could be issued at a lower *ex ante* cost than that of traditional bonds, firms have made no effort to initiate this form of financing.[5] The lack of innovation in this area by the private sector is not surprising, however, in light of the negative impact of inflation on corporate profitability. With index bonds, this inverse relationship would worsen since corporations would forfeit the mitigating effect of the decline in the value of outstanding liabilities as inflation increased. It would seem that index bonds would become an attractive alternative to private firms only if the corporate income tax were levied on inflation-adjusted income.

If the private sector is unable to issue index bonds, then the only alternative source of these securities would be the federal government. This approach, however, seems to have serious limitations unless similar securities are issued concurrently by the private sector.

If the Treasury were to substitute index bonds for long-term securities in its annual financing, it could issue about $10 billion in index securities each year.[6] Even if the purchase of these securities were limited to private pensions, plan sponsors would only gradually be able to acquire a sufficient volume of these securities to provide fully indexed pensions and remain actuarially sound. If no restrictions were imposed on the purchase of these securities, the period over which pension plans acquired these securities would be considerably longer.

On the other hand, the existence of index bonds might result in a shift in

5. See Pesando [13, pp. 40–46]. This article provides an excellent discussion of the limited experience with index bonds in other countries and also summarizes the academic literature on index bonds.

6. The $10 billion figure was derived by adding the $6.4 billion of increase in net long-term borrowing between 1976 and 1977 and an estimated $4 billion for refinancing existing long-term debt, based on the assumption of an average maturity of five years [8, Table 1.42, p. A32].

the maturity mix of Treasury offerings toward long-term securities, since index bonds would eliminate the risk of capital losses due to inflation. If the government issued index bonds to meet all its financing needs, the annual increase would be substantial[7] and private pensions could rapidly accumulate an adequate amount to finance indexed pensions. Such a large volume of federal index bonds, however, would seriously disrupt markets for existing assets.

A substantial volume of index bonds can be achieved without serious disruption of the credit markets only if the private sector also issues index securities. For this to occur, the corporate tax must be reformed to avoid increases in tax liabilities in periods of inflation.

Conclusion

Although the increase in the proportion of private pensions that base benefits on final earnings represents a step toward preserving the value of benefits over the employees' preretirement years, postretirement cost-of-living adjustments under private plans are still rare and generally fail to compensate fully for the rise in prices. The lack of portability between plans exposes workers to serious losses in the value of their benefits. Moreover, no workable scheme exists for transferring pension credits between defined benefit plans. Only widespread adoption of defined contribution plans so that each worker has a readily identifiable account would enable workers to transfer their accrued pension credits between plans. However, unless employees or plan sponsors have access to assets that incorporate a full inflation premium, workers will not be provided with the real benefits they have earned. One solution that would help members of defined contribution plans to earn an adequate rate of return or permit sponsors of defined benefit plans to provide fully indexed benefits is the issuance of index bonds. With the current corporate income tax structure, however, these securities are not likely to be issued by the private sector. If the federal government were to take the initiative, a sufficient volume of indexed securities might disrupt the capital markets, whereas anything less would involve a long period before private plans could accumulate enough index securities to finance fully indexed pensions. Therefore, it is tempting to conclude that the role of social security in providing retirement income should be expanded and that of private plans reduced. Social security has the obvious advantage of providing universal coverage, portability, and benefits that keep pace with inflation.

On the other hand, expanding social security would necessitate increasing payroll taxes that add to business costs and may create inflationary pressures.

---

7. The net annual increase in total public debt between 1974 and 1977 averaged about $70 billion. In addition, short-term securities are constantly maturing and could be reissued in the form of index securities.

Social security also may have a negative impact on saving, although recent evidence suggests that the early allegations that social security has reduced the capital stock by 38 percent are completely unfounded [4, 6]. A further expansion of the social security program also raises the philosophical issue of the right of government to infringe upon individual freedom beyond assuring a basic retirement benefit. The most compelling institutional argument against replacing private pensions by expanding social security for high wage workers, however, is that their welfare cannot be well served by a program that is heavily weighted with redistribution toward the lower end.

Private pensions play an important role in our economy since they offer variety and flexibility. However, the inability to provide fully indexed benefits is a serious limitation in an inflationary environment. Moreover, ensuring benefits that keep pace with prices both over the employee's worklife and after retirement is impossible within the existing system. To achieve this goal, pensions must take the form of defined contribution plans so that the employee has a readily identifiable account to move from employer to employer and employees and plan sponsors must have access to an asset that does not now exist—namely, an index bond.

References

[1] Banker's Trust Company, *1956 Study of Industrial Retirement Plans* (New York, 1956).

[2] Banker's Trust Company, *1965 Study of Industrial Retirement Plans* (New York, 1965).

[3] Banker's Trust Company, *1975 Study of Corporate Pension Plans* (New York, 1975).

[4] Barro, Robert J., *The Impact of Social Security on Private Saving: Evidence from U.S. Time Series* (Washington, D.C.: American Enterprise Institute, 1978).

[5] "Britain's New Pensions," *The Economist* (Dec. 18, 1976), 84–85.

[6] Darby, Michael R., "The Effects of Social Security on Income and the Capital Stock," Discussion Paper No. 95, Mimeo (Washington, D.C.: American Enterprise Institute, 1977).

[7] *Economic Report of the President* (Washington, D.C.: U.S. Government Printing Office, Jan. 1978).

[8] Federal Reserve Bulletin (June 1978), A32.

[9] Feldstein, Martin S., "Inflation and the Stock Market," Mimeo (National Bureau of Economic Research, 1978).

[10] Grubbs, Donald S., "Pension Portability," presented to Subcommittee on Retirement Income and Employment Select Committee on Aging, U.S. House of Representatives, Mimeo (Washington, D.C.: U.S. Government Printing Office, April 6, 1978).

[11] *Inflation and Pension Planning—Europe* (Marsh & McLennan Benefit Services, 1975).

[12] Kopcke, Richard, W., "The Decline in Corporate Profitability," *New England Economic Review* (May/June 1978), 36–60.

[13] Pesando, James, "Private Pensions in an Inflationary Climate: Limitations and Policy Alternatives," Discussion Paper No. 114 (Economic Council of Canada, 1978).

[14] Securities and Exchange Commission, *Statistical Bulletin* (Apr. 1974), 457.

[15] Securities and Exchange Commission, *Statistical Bulletin* (May 1978), 6–7.

[16] Skolnik, Alfred M., "Private Pension Plans, 1950–1974," *Social Security Bulletin* (June 1976).

[17] Social Security Administration, *Social Security Bulletin* (June 1976).

[18] Tideman, T. Nicholaus, and Donald P. Tucker, "The Tax Treatment of Business Profits Under Inflationary Conditions" in Henry J. Aaron (Ed.), *Inflation and the Income Tax*, (Washington, D.C.: The Brookings Institution, 1976), 33–80.

The Future of Employer Pensions *William C. Greenough*

In discussing the role of employer pensions, I have been asked to deal with the ability of private pension plans to respond to fluctuating economic conditions, with special emphasis on the impact of inflation. It seems to me that this raises exactly the right issues because institutions set up to assure employees that they will have economic security in retirement must be appropriate not only to economic conditions when the individual begins his or her working career but also to those prevailing when retirement income is being received forty or fifty years later, though at best these can be perceived only dimly.

The economic changes that have taken place in the United States during the past twenty years have been enormous: the energy price revolution; the burgeoning of social programs in the late 1960s; the surge from very low inflation in the 1960s to double-digit inflation in the early 1970s; the uninterrupted economic growth in the 1960s giving way to the instability of the 1970s. The list could go on. How wrong we would have been in the mid-1960s to predict the shape of the 1970s by using the early 1960s as a model. And if the past is any guide, we will be wrong if we predict the shape of the late 1980s by using the 1970s as a model. Once we go beyond what the demographers and actuaries can tell us about population trends and life spans, the uncertainty surrounding any long-term forecast of the future rises rapidly. If our system of institutions is to meet the challenge of providing adequate retirement income for the aged, it must have the vitality, the flexibility, the resourcefulness to be able to generate huge amounts of savings and huge income transfers in all sorts of changing cyclical conditions in an environment subject to major structural changes.

My assignment is to concentrate on employer pension plans. But they are only one of the four mechanisms we have developed to meet the challenge: private savings, employer pensions, old-age, survivors and disability benefits through social security, and welfare programs, protection for those who have, in a sense, fallen through the net of the other three. None of the four mechanisms can be discussed properly without reference to the others, for they work together, and must work together in order to maintain the economic viability of the support systems as a whole.

Why all four mechanisms? Do we still need them all in our current society? Yes, I believe we do. Although their relative importance has changed over the decades, the systems complement each other. Let me sketch the role of each in support of this view.

Private Savings

As retirement income, private savings and investment unquestionably will play less and less of a part, as is already happening. Currently, income from savings and investments amounts to only about 15 percent of the total income being received by persons age 65 and over [2, p. 11]. Earnings on individual investments tend to be taxed away, either by legislated taxes or by that superthief, inflation. Since World War II, net earnings on savings accounts after taxes and inflation have generally been negative. Heavy taxation of capital gains discourages equity investment and, in effect, confiscates capital in times of inflation. Partly as a result of these factors, the stock market is viewed by many as unrewarding speculation. The old National Bureau of Economic Research study of *Consumers Report* subscribers showing that private pensions and social security encouraged private savings is now outdated and deserves to be forgotten.

The amounts of retirement income provided through social security transfers and employer pension plans give far more security in old age than private savings were ever able to do. But these programs by no means eliminate the need for private savings as an important source of additional income, and of capital for the economy. The flows of savings to thrift institutions currently are at a high level, but this may well reflect concern that future inflation will not permit individuals to maintain living standards or meet debt repayment obligations. And, to be realistic, private savings at best are somewhat uncertain to depend upon in old age, since the emergencies and hazards of the prior years, not to mention inflation, can erode or even eliminate this extra financial cushion.

Welfare

Welfare used to be a last charge on the public purse, or no charge at all— left to private philanthropy. Now it is, and should be, a first charge. We will and we must have some kind of welfare benefits for those aged whose situations, for one reason or another, have not provided them with social security income of sufficient amounts or with an adequate combination of social security and employer-sponsored pension benefits. Our society sponsors hundreds of plans for the alleviation of suffering and the meeting of basic human needs through lifting a burden from the unduly burdened. One of the largest of all programs is rather new—Supplemental Security Income (SSI)—provided through general revenue appropriations supported by progressive taxation. The federal government and the states are heavily committed in these areas of economic security and only governments can, in fact, meet these needs adequately.

Social Security

Social insurance systems seek to meet social objectives through intergenerational and intragenerational transfers. Social security is no exception. Its initial passage in 1935 was motivated in large part by a need to address huge problems: unemployment and poverty in old age, both of which were so seriously aggravated by the Great Depression. From this beginning it has developed into a vast transfer system that helps beneficiaries meet the problem of inflation while itself exacerbating the inflation rate.

From its beginnings, social security has been presented to the public as an "earnings-related" program. The widespread public support of the program has been based at least in part on that premise. But it has become more and more a program of regressively designed benefits that result in progressive taxes to support it. When you consider the vast transfers from young to old, from higher paid to lower paid through the design of the benefit formula, from the family benefit provisions, the minimum benefit, and the benefit escalators, what we have is a social transfer system involving only limited elements of individual equity. *This,* I believe, *is as it should be*—but let us say so frankly and openly.

The new social security benefit formula starting in 1979 well illustrates this point. The formula is nonlinear and can effect substantial income redistribution as well as intergenerational transfer.

The benefit formula redistributes employer and employee social security taxes to retired or other beneficiaries who were at the lower end of the wage scales (or—as an unintended windfall—to high earners outside of the social security system who have a second job covered minimally by social security). The skewed formula appropriately incorporates a social recognition that lower paid workers and their families have less margin for reduction in income in retirement than do workers with average or above average earnings. There are other reasonable "presumed needs" that define other redistributions in the system. The new benefit formula for the computation of the primary insurance amount is the following (AIME refers to the average indexed monthly earnings of the covered worker):

90 percent of the first $180 of AIME, plus
32 percent of the next $905 of AIME, plus
15 percent of AIME over $1,085.

Thus, under the new formula only a token benefit is paid above the second "breakpoint." Benefits based on indexed monthly earnings above $1,085 are one-sixth of the benefits from the first $180 of such earnings, and less than one-half of those based on the $905 between the two points. Since OASDI taxes are the same on all covered salaries, the result is a heavily *progressive* tax rate when related to benefits on covered salary.

What does this mean for employer pensions? The attenuation of social security benefits on the upper part of the taxable earnings base is a challenge to employer pensions to fill out the upper levels through proper methods of "plan integration." Recognizing the high level of transfers in social security, integration has one main goal, to provide benefits that, when combined with social security, will add up to a percentage of final salary (replacement rate) that is reasonably uniform for all salary levels from low to high. It is generally considered acceptable to provide combined social insurance and employer benefits of 80 to 90 percent of final wages for retirees with a history of low or average wages, and for high-earning retirees, including those whose earnings exceed the social security earnings base, of some 50 to 60 percent of final salary. Integration is the means through which social security and employer pensions work together for a balanced result.

Between 1978 and 1981, the maximum taxable OASDI earnings base is scheduled to increase 67 percent (from $17,700 to $29,700). At the same time, the second "breakpoint" will rise only 25 percent. In other words, the part of AIME with the lowest benefit purchasing power is going to expand rapidly. This means that wage earners above the median will soon be paying a higher price for their social security benefits or, perhaps I should say, a higher price for the benefits of others, for it is here that the redistribution factor is at its strongest. This limited illustration shows how vulnerable the social security program is to demographic and political shifts, and how sensitive those of us who are considering the role of social security must be to the viability of the support system as a whole. As extraordinary a social mechanism as social security is, and it has been an effective and essential one, it has reached a point in cost that must bring to an end its "growth" phase. The force of demographic changes and attitudinal responses of those "transferred from" will increasingly determine the provisions of social security. The noted Nobel award economist Paul Samuelson once described social security as a gigantic Ponzi scheme, a scheme from which participants could all take more than they gave. But Ponzi schemes do not spiral upward forever!

Employer Pensions

The most exciting and challenging role of employer pensions today is in their move toward fulfillment of their complementary relationship to social insurance.

You notice that I have been referring to *employer* pensions. Usually the term *private* pensions is used in discussions of retirement income support, but reference only to private pensions omits systematic consideration of the pension plans that are provided by public employers. Whenever we are really speaking of public and private employer plans we should use the full term or shorten it to employer plans. I suggest this because I think that it will be helpful in discussing the four tiers of income replacement mechanisms and because it helps to distinguish all employer plans from social security. Thus, the title of this paper is "The Future of Employer Pensions" rather than "The Future of Private Pensions." Public employee and private employee retirement systems do not and should not differ in fundamental ways.[1]

Certain characteristics of employer pension plans distinguish them from social insurance: (1) employer pension plans are established unilaterally by the employer or are the product of labor negotiations, or are a combination of the two; (2) they provide for contributions by the employer only or jointly by employer and employees; (3) plan benefits are related to the salary and service history of plan members; (4) benefits become vested after a specified period of plan membership (comparable to the forty quarters of coverage required for social security retirement benefits but, unlike social security, not cumulative under successive employers); (5) retirement income options are offered to provide actuarially equivalent benefits to employees who elect an income option for a surviving spouse; (6) the plans are based either on the defined benefit or the defined contribution approach to retirement plan funding, or sometimes (particularly in public plans) a combination of the two; (7) the plans are based on the principle of reserve funding, although they vary in the degree of funding of vested liabilities; (8) the earnings on invested assets help pay for the costs of the benefits or increase the benefits payable; (9) assets are invested in securities, mortgages, and equity investments by professional staff, either in-house or through outside investment advisory services, or both; and (10) employer contributions and the investment earnings on the funds accumulated currently are not taxable as income to the plan participants and taxation is deferred until the benefits are received. This tax treatment recognizes the significant social and economic function of institutionalized retirement plans, and that they would be severely handicapped in meeting their purpose if employer contributions and investment yield were treated as currently taxable income to the employees. For private employers, plan contributions are treated as a business expense as are wages and other expenses of production and therefore are deductible as ordinary business expense; parallel treatment is provided for the contributions of public employers.

Participants in employer pensions also make their contributions to the social security transfer system, with the exception of about 30 percent of state and local government employees and, as previously mentioned, federal civil service employees.

---

1. I include in the category "employer" the nation's private pension plans—insured and noninsured—and the six thousand or so public employee retirement systems of state and local governments. I exclude the Federal Civil Service Retirement System because, although it is an employer pension plan and bears some characteristics in common with other plans, it does not contribute to capital formation and it is so heavily underfunded that it approaches a pay-after-you-go plan. It therefore includes significant amounts of *inter* generational tax transfers from U.S. taxpayers to federal government employees.

I suggest six principal issues that are involved in shaping the future of employer pension plans and their ability to respond to changing economic conditions: (1) coverage, (2) regulation, (3) funding levels, (4) efficiency of retirement savings, (5) inflation, and (6) investment, capital formation.

Coverage

At present, about 90 percent of state and local government employees are covered by employer retirement programs and approximately half of the employees in private, nonfarm business establishments are employed by employers with pension plans. There are plans with tens of thousands of participants, and plans with only a handful. There are plans established by units of government, and plans established by the business, industrial, commercial and service firms that provide the goods and services—not to mention the tax revenue—upon which our economy depends. There are defined contribution plans and defined benefit plans, multiemployer plans and single-employer plans, insured plans and noninsured plans, plans governed by ERISA and plans exempt from ERISA, plans qualified under Section 401(a) of the Internal Revenue Code and plans qualified under Section 403(b), plans that are fully funded and plans that are underfunded, negotiated plans and nonnegotiated plans, conventional plans and pattern plans, plans for salaried personnel and plans for hourly personnel, plans for the self-employed and for the employer-employed. Further distinctions can be made according to plan funding methods, investment approaches, and investment policies.

What I want to emphasize by this list is the diversity, the adaptability, the flexibility, and the responsiveness of employer pension plans to the wants and needs of employed workers. These plans represent positive and agreed upon values for employees, labor organizations, governmental units, and private employers, large and small. And I want to make a crucial point. I think some of these plans, methods, provisions, and approaches are better than others. But I would leave it to the competitive and private forces to sort out which is best for which employment sector, under federal fiduciary supervision and minimum standards. Some people would go much farther than this; they know in detail just what ought to be done and how it ought to be done, across the board, one design. Let us remember, however, the possibility that arrogance sometimes exceeds wisdom.

Most of the growth in the pension coverage of the public sector occurred after the depression of the 1930s and as government functions began to expand. Most of the growth of pension coverage of private employers has taken place since the end of World War II. In 1940, 12 percent of private nonagricultural employees were employed by firms with pension plans; in 1973, the number had increased more than eightfold (from 4.1 million to 33.1 million employees), about 49 percent of private nonagricultural employees. In 1950, private insured and noninsured pension plans paid $370 million in retirement benefits to 450,000 annuitants; in 1973, benefits totaling more than $11 billion were paid to 6 million annuitants. Employer and employee contributions to private plans in 1973 were $22 billion, over ten times the 1950 total.[2]

In 1975, about 10.4 million state and local government employees were covered under public employee retirement systems and another 2.3 million persons were receiving benefits or were eligible for deferred benefits under such plans. In 1975, benefit payments amounted to $7.25 billion, paid to nearly 2 million persons. Public employer and employee contributions in 1975 amounted to $15.5 billion, about 17 times the 1950 total.[3]

Underlying the development of institutionalized systems of savings for retirement are fundamental changes in the composition of economic activity and output that have occurred since the early years of this century. In particular, the rapid rate of industrialization and the increase in manufacturing output and employment are judged to have been essential preconditions for the growth of employer pensions [7, p. 5]. Equally important, perhaps, is the fact that basic economic changes were associated with substantial increases in the size of the typical work force of the firm in the industrial sector (or in governmental units) compared with that of the firms in those sectors, such as agriculture, which supplied the growing work force for increasingly large firms. The changes in the scale of the work force made it possible for a firm to avail itself of the economies provided by group approaches to the coverage of workers under insurance and pension plans.

That the size of the employing unit was partially responsible for the growth of the pension plans is further suggested by the figures on current coverage that indicate that gaps in coverage are found mainly among smaller employers. This, in turn, suggests the kinds of measures that might be taken in the future to encourage pension plan development in the lagging sectors. To the extent that scale economies can be made available to smaller firms for the protection of smaller groups of employees, further development of group insurance and pension plan coverage may be expected.

Despite the rapid growth of coverage under employer pension plans in the United States, a growth that has taken place over a remarkably short period of thirty years or so, a few observers, noting that not all the nonagricultural work force in the private sector is covered by employer pension plans, conclude that employer pension plans are a failure and that they should be absorbed by the social security system. Their view is that we shall pour out the water in the glass rather than fill the glass fuller. It makes little sense to substitute an unfunded system for partially and wholly funded systems, or to conclude

2. See [5, Tables C-24 and C-29] and [1 pp. 31–32, 36].
3. See U.S. House of Representatives [10, p. 51, and Table G-12, pp. 173–74].

that since all workers are not covered under employer pension plans, no workers should have further opportunities to enter employer plans. On the contrary, the appropriate course is to examine the steps necessary to stimulate new retirement plan formation.

Our public policy goal should be to continue to encourage and develop employer pension plans as a part of the nation's structure for institutionalized means of deferring consumption for retirement. Perhaps constructive proposals could be added to the legislation recently introduced by Senators Javits and Williams (S. 3017), which already includes provisions to encourage and facilitate pension programs for smaller employers.

Regulation

The diversity of employer pension plans is important because it reflects diverse needs of employers and employees. We are not a homogenized society and government should not attempt to homogenize employer pension plans. Nor should regulation of employer plans be carried out in such a way as to achieve redistributions of one kind or another. Where social transfers are to be made, social security and public welfare programs are the proper arenas. And regulation should not attempt to invade every small subcell of employer pensions. Employer pension plans are sensitive economic instruments, vulnerable to overzealous or stultifying regulations, to oppressive inundations of government-inspired paperwork, and to costly bureaucratic layerings of rules, rulings, and guidelines.

Employer pension plans will serve well or poorly depending on whether government will leave room for experiment and diversity—room to breathe. ERISA embodied excellent objectives, but as is now recognized, it overreached in its mechanism, forms, and paperwork. It led to increased costs, especially for medium- and smaller-sized employers, and thereby reduced incentive for establishment of pension plans.

For future pension legislation, we need a spirit of encouragement, a positive approach to the values represented by employer pension plans.

Funding Levels

Although employer pension plans are based on reserve funding, not all private or state and local pension plans are fully funded. A handful of the public employee plans are still on an unfunded "pay-after-you-go" basis. The unfunded pension obligations of the other public plans vary all the way from very little to essentially fully funded. In the private sector, unfunded pension obligations have come under scrutiny as never before because of the passage of ERISA, with its requirements for certification of actuarial cost methods and for the amortization of unfunded prior service liabilities. The majority of pension plans in the private sector, however, are of the defined benefit type, and the extent of their unfunded pension liabilities has been affected by recent rates of inflation and by generous labor settlements. A recent survey by *Business Week* [9, pp. 60–64], covering one hundred major U.S. companies, showed that during 1977 unfunded vested benefits increased among the companies by 19 percent over 1976, to $18.5 billion. Another measure of pension obligations, unfunded prior service costs, rose by just over 8 percent. Total corporate profits grew by 10 percent.

We should also note that many companies have well funded pension plans. More than 25 percent of the large companies in the *Business Week* survey reported that they had no significant unfunded vested benefits. Among large corporations outside the survey, it is believed that a majority—particularly those in the insurance, banking, petroleum, and retailing industries—have no significant unfunded pension liabilities. Defined contribution plans like TIAA-CREF have no unfunded liabilities.

Among companies that have experienced difficulties with their pension liabilities are those that have been under recent profit pressures and those with older, highly unionized labor forces. For the Lockheed Corporation, unfunded vested liabilities amount to 185 percent of corporate net worth, and at LTV Corporation, 121 percent. Bethlehem Steel, National Steel, and Republic Steel report high levels of unfunded vested benefit liabilities (more than 40 percent). The $3.5 billion obligation of General Motors amounts to 22 percent of the company's net worth. AT&T, in contrast, with a $560 million liability representing only 1.4 percent of net balance-sheet value, is an example on the opposite side. For the average company in the *Business Week* survey, the unfunded vested benefit obligation came to a rather manageable 7.2 percent of corporate net worth. A 1977 study showed that the average company could pay off its unfunded liability with three months of pretax earnings. A 1978 study of leading companies showed some 30 percent had no vested unfunded liabilities at all. Another 1978 study [6, p. 2] showed only 5 percent of the firms examined had a potential pension liability of 30 percent of net worth.

Turning to funding levels in the public sector, the recent Pension Task Force Report on Public Employee Retirement Systems [10, p. 4] has this to say:

> In the vast majority of public employee retirement systems, plan partici-
> pants, plan sponsors, and the general public are kept in the dark with
> regard to a realistic assessment of true pension costs. . . . Approximately
> 17% of governmental plans continue to use the discredited pay-as-you-go
> financing approach to satisfy business obligations. Efforts should be made
> to eliminate any incentives which may exist for public plans to continue
> using such inappropriate financing methods. Efforts should also be made
> to encourage the accumulation of pension reserves through the use of actuar-
> ial funding methods.

The Pension Task Force has offered a comparison of the funding status of public plans compared with private plans. It concluded that for the period ending in 1975, just before the effective date of ERISA, "The status of private pension plan funding for the system as a whole had progressed considerably beyond the funded status of the public employee retirement system. Generally it can be expected that the vast majority of the private plans failing to meet a (recognized) funding standard do so because of their more recent adoption, usually being within the past 15 or 20 years. For public plans the opposite holds—i.e., the older plans are more likely to be underfunded. The percentage of public plans that fail any given funding test can be expected to be significantly greater than the corresponding percentage of private plans that fail. On the other end of the funding distribution it can be expected that a near majority of private pension plans are 'fully funded' using the BSR[4] as a measurement, whereas less than 25 percent of all public systems are as adequately funded [10, pp. 177–78]."

Many employer pension plans are well funded, others are becoming more so, and all of these funds represent a vital flow of investment capital. ERISA affirms the importance of proper current cost methods and has provided for strict amortization schedules for unfunded liabilities. Until we have a PERISA, however, we will have a double standard for employer pension plans, with public plans free of the constraints and requirements of sound funding methods. Vested benefits in employer pension plans represent promises to people. I am sure that no one will disagree when I say that these promises must be kept. Our efforts should be, as they were under the ERISA legislation, to take the necessary steps to ensure that unfunded vested liabilities are diminished in an orderly manner that is consistent with maintaining the economic health of the employing organization itself.

Savings Efficiency of Retirement Plans

Our present tax structure makes personal savings—the fourth tier of retirement protection—an inefficient way of trying to accumulate funds currently for later use. Personal savers have at their disposal only after-tax dollars. Savers retain these after-tax dollars with increasing difficulty because marginal tax rates increase when an unchanging tax table is applied to a more inflation-responsive current income. Yields from invested savings are also taxed at highest marginal rates, with consequent discouragement of savings and investment. Under certain circumstances, investment yield is taxed at an even higher rate than income earned from employment. In addition, capital gains are taxed in the

---

4. BSR = Benefit Security Ratio, the ratio of the value of plan assets to the actuarial present value of all accrued pension benefits.

United States, and by methods that do not distinguish between real gain and inflation. As a result, capital gains taxes can and do confiscate capital by their failure to distinguish between the inflation component of a price difference between purchase and sale (whether a home, securities, or common stocks) and real profit for the risk-taking investor. Thus, about the only chance of most workers to save enough for their old age is through employer pension plans supplementing social security.

Employer pension plans represent savings discipline that is difficult or impossible for many, if not most, workers to impose on themselves. The increasing costs of housing, food, and other necessities, high property taxes, rising education costs, and so on, leave most workers in a poor position to save enough for their own for retirement. As already mentioned, income from savings and investments amounts to only about 15 percent of the total income being received by persons aged 65 and over. The institutionalized savings discipline of employer pension plans is an important part of their economic and social value.

In addition, employer pensions offer important efficiency gains in savings that workers on their own cannot match. These efficiency gains are of two kinds: those derived from appropriately favorable tax provisions and those derived from the information, transaction, management, and diversification economies that large-scale pension plans make possible.

The tax-deferral provisions are an important source of the efficiency gains of employer pension plans. Additional wage payments in lieu of pension participation would be incremental to both the employee's adjusted gross and taxable income, and currently taxed at the employee's highest marginal rate. Were the employee to save this incremental wage, less the tax, the investment return would also be taxable as it was earned, again at a marginal rate. In contrast, the amount saved by the employee in the form of the employer's contribution to the pension plan is not included in current adjusted gross or taxable income. The earnings of the pension fund are also excluded from the employee's tax base. Pension plan benefits are fully taxable to the employee when the benefits are received (except for any part of the pension benefit that is attributable to prior employee contributions from after-tax earnings). Generally the employee's marginal tax rate during retirement is expected to be lower than during the working years; pension benefits thus are taxed at a lower rate than they would have been had they been received as additional wages or salary during the working years.

The other main source of efficiency gain of employer pension plans over individual savings derives from scale advantages in investment costs and portfolio diversification. The average worker's annual savings, even including an employer's pension contribution, is so limited as to preclude effective diversification. In addition, the information and transaction costs per dollar of savings that a worker would incur in an attempt at sophisticated investment results would be far greater than those available to him or her through a pension plan.

Ture and Fields [8], in their study published by the American Enterprise Institute, have given a rough measure of the overall efficiency gains associated with pension fund savings by comparing (1) the average annual contribution per covered employee over the period 1953–72 in noninsured pension funds with (2) the amount of saving the average worker would have had to invest in a passbook savings account each year in order to achieve the same accumulation as the pension funds. The latter type of investment may be viewed as one that minimizes the worker's own information, transaction, and management costs. Assuming a level annual pension fund contribution and savings account deposit, the average annual accumulation rate in the pension fund was about 7.09 percent compared with 1.0 percent on the worker's fully taxed saving in a savings account. The combined efficiency gains from the favorable tax treatment and portfolio diversification were found by the study to be approximately 85.9 percent as of the end of the period [8, p. 4].

The tax provisions that make possible these efficiency gains have been a part of the U.S. law for more than fifty years, dating back to 1922 and the earliest attention to the public policy needs of institutionalized mechanisms of deferring compensation for retirement. This public policy has been confirmed on many occasions subsequently—in the Revenue Reform Act of 1942, in ERISA, and in tax provisions for income deferral for self-employed persons.

Inflation

Inflation poses the most serious problem for our system of providing income security for the aged. We must meet this challenge in ways that help reduce inflation or at least do not worsen it.

Under social security it is easy enough for Congress to raise benefits to keep pace with inflation. Measured by this narrow criterion it has been admirably successful. The problem is that the rapid extension of social programs, including social security, since the late 1960s, was itself one of the important ingredients in the rise in inflation that has plagued our economy ever since.

In 1965, transfer payments to persons by all layers of government amounted to 20 percent of total government spending. In 1977 they amounted to 32 percent. Between 1960 and 1965, government transfers to persons averaged 7 percent of personal income. By 1975, somewhat swelled by unemployment insurance, the ratio had reached 13.5 percent. In 1977 it was 12.9 percent. The transfer payment share probably will not decline much further even if current policy is simply extended. Data Resources Incorporated, an influential economic consulting firm, estimates that by 1990 government transfers as a percent of personal income will be just over 14 percent unless measures are taken such as a reduction in welfare costs, containment of the health cost explosion, and a comprehensive revision of social security benefits [4, pp. 1.29–1.30].

The transfer payment explosion has helped increase inflation in two major ways. It has raised employer hourly compensation costs, and it has increased the federal government deficit and consequently the rate of money supply growth.

Looking at the issue from the cost side, wages and salaries plus payroll taxes averaged 68 percent of national income between 1960 and 1965. Beginning in 1966 there was a sharp four-year increase in the share of wages and salaries alone in national income from 64 percent to 68 percent of the national income in 1970. Since then, however, the wage and salary share has drifted back down to 65 percent in 1977. Employer payroll taxes have risen sharply throughout the entire period since the early 1960s so that they now represent 5.2 percent of national income compared with a 3 percent average from 1960 to 1965. It seems clear to me that although any success we have in holding down wage costs in the fight against inflation is all to the good, a much more fundamental need is to hold down the expansion of programs that require funding that raises employers' costs of putting people to work. Let me emphasize the Congress *should* have acted as it did last year to raise social security taxes, an action that clearly gave a boost to prices early this year and will do so again next year. The problem is in the rate of extension of benefits, not in the facing up to the necessity of financing them. To the extent that underfinancing of social programs contributes to the growth in the federal government deficit and therefore to the money supply, inflationary pressures are being generated that can extend well into the future. So do we want (1) current inflation in the cost of hiring people, accompanied by lower employment rates, substitution of machines for people, pricing our U.S. goods out of international markets; or (2) deficit financing and still more inflation; or (3) less elaborate and costly social security and other income transfer systems?

In the past, we have been too willing to expand the broad complex of government transfer payment programs, which range from food stamp benefits to old-age insurance, without considering their impact on inflation in the present and in the near and the more distant future. If we were to take the extreme position that all of these transfer payment programs should have been paid for by employer and personal contributions, then the cumulative shortfall of receipts between 1965 and 1977 would have exceeded the cumulative federal government deficit during this period. Looking more narrowly at current receipts and expenditures under OASDHI, there were deficits of $12 billion in 1977, nearly $9 billion in 1976 and $5.4 billion in 1975 compared with near balance between 1960 and 1965.

Inflation adversely affects employer pension plans and the beneficiaries in several ways. The accelerating dollar wage gains with inflation increase prior-service benefit liabilities and escalate unfunded liabilities. Rising interest rates reduce the market value of securities. Nominal rates of return on pension assets may rise but real rates of return generally do not. Once a retiree has started retirement income, inflation can steadily erode the purchasing power of that income. Inflation does much damage to income deferral systems and their participants.

Attempts to Ameliorate Inflation.   A number of devices may soften the impact of inflation on the individual in some plans. In TIAA-CREF plans individuals participate in both a traditional "fixed-dollar" annuity (TIAA) and a variable annuity (CREF). In CREF, contributions are invested regularly in common stocks throughout the individual's working career. The participant shares fully in the fund's investment experience during the entire period spanning working and retired years.

Historically, the long-term return on common stock investment has substantially exceeded the return on high-grade corporate bonds. It should, because of the greater variability in common stock returns. The CREF compound annual rate of return from the beginning of 1953 through the end of 1977 was 8.2 percent. The CPI rose at a 3.5 percent annual rate during the same period. For shorter periods of time the CREF return has considerably exceeded or fallen short of the 1953–77 average experience. For example, from 1953 to the end of 1968, at which latter point the market was overvalued by historical standards, the CREF annual rate of return was 12.5 percent. Measured from the high market prices at the end of 1968 to the end of 1977, the CREF return was only 1 percent per year, but it has averaged 14.5 percent per year since the low of 1974.

A variable annuity like CREF is intended for individuals who will be participating for a very long time in a program that includes participation in a fixed-dollar annuity. This participation may span as many as 40 years of making contributions and 15 or more of receiving income. For long-term participants, even a fairly long period of low common stock returns, as during the six years preceding the market low of 1974, will tend to be averaged out by the higher average returns during the other years of participation. For those still making contributions, periods of low market prices offer an opportunity to participate in the purchase of stocks at which may turn out to be bargain prices.

Too often we lose sight of the importance of high returns that are being earned by funds like TIAA that are predominantly invested in fixed-dollar securities, returns that were particularly helpful to employer pension funds during those years of poor common stock performance in the late 1960s and early 1970s. In 1968 TIAA's net return on total invested assets was 5.4 percent, up from 4.35 percent in 1960. By 1977 it had reached 8.39 percent.

Those investors who were caught up in the enthusiasm of common stocks in the "go-go" days of the mid-1960s and failed to perceive opportunities in other forms of investments have had reason to regret it. And those who, with the same keen hindsight, are now staying out of the market because of deep disappointment with market behavior as the economic and political realities of the early 1970s changed euphoria to gloom may well live to regret this too. If investment history has any lesson to give us it is that the fluctuations and structural changes that are inherent in the life of any economy and particularly in the life of an open society and predominantly market economy provide the necessity as well as the opportunity for very broad diversification of the funds of employer pension plans.

Indexing Benefits.   Employers generally have been reluctant to add inflation-indexed pension benefits to plans already facing increasing unfunded liabilities, increases in which inflation has played a key role. Extra costs are high for the funding of benefits related to final average salaries compared with career average salaries. The addition of postretirement indexing in employer pension plans would greatly increase the unfunded liabilities of the plans. At times, private sector employers have been able to provide ad hoc benefit increases, within the constraints of the profitability of the firm and the price of the product. Government employers in the past have freely committed taxpayers to open-ended pension costs, but there is some question now as to whether it is prudent to assume that there are no limits. There is no slick answer, either before or after retirement. Our greatest efforts should be to address ourselves to underlying causes, not to the symptoms, to inflation, not to the dismantling of pension plans because they are among the many institutions victimized by inflation.

What we need, and what we all ought to be working for, is a more stable and healthier economy that will minimize the need for cost-of-living adjustments on pensions, indexing techniques, and other devices to cover over a failure to control inflation.

Investment and Capital Formation.   Employer pension plans play a vital role in the supply of investment capital for the nation's economy. In 1977, for example, private pension funds supplied $21 billion to the credit markets; state and local retirement funds supplied $13 billion; and insurance companies increased pension fund reserves by $14.9 billion, for a total of $48.9 billion. These institutions bought government securities amounting to $11.4 billion. The balance—$37.5 billion—was equal to 35 percent of the amount of funds raised in the credit markets in the United States by nonfinancial business in 1977 [3, pp. 3, 25].

In any society, whether its economy is market oriented or state controlled, capital formation is essential for future growth. It is of particular importance to us now if we are to succeed in lowering inflation. Earlier I said that I believed that the surge in government transfer payment programs had played an important part in the inflation of the late 1960s and early 1970s. Another of the keys to inflation is the very poor productivity experience of the economy during this period. Between 1950 and 1965 the trend rate of growth of output per hour in the nonfarm private business sector of the economy was 2.5 percent per year. Between 1965 and 1977 it was 1.4 percent. Many factors have helped produce this deceleration in productivity growth. Among them are the OPEC energy price revolution and environmental and safety provisions, which have made some of our capital stock either uneconomic or illegal. At the same time, business capital spending measured in constant dollars fell further and longer than in any previous cycle in the past twenty years. By the second quarter of 1978, real business fixed investment was only 6 percent above the cycle peak eighteen quarters earlier. This compares with a 16 percent increase in sixteen quarters following the 1969 peak and a 26 percent increase during the eighteen quarters following the 1960 cyclical peak.

Employer pension plans are a powerful source of capital for use by business in expanding and modernizing the country's productive plant and equipment, and thus in helping increase productivity. This investment is helping to put people to work today and it is making possible higher living standards in the future through potentially greater output of goods and services. In effect, current pension contributions are providing physical and technological resources that will help permit benefits to be paid during retirement without burdening future generations through taxes or inflation. In this way employer pension systems not only are responding to economic change but are helping to shape it constructively.

Policy Recommendations

The coming generation of retired people can easily be the most secure, and by a large margin, in America's history. Population dynamics support this possibility, as do pension advances already made. Only the plague of inflation really stands in the way.

In summary, let us start with the four-tier system: (1) needs-tested welfare programs, (2) the social security program (OASDHI), (3) employer pensions, and (4) private retirement savings. In approaching a national policy for income support systems for the elderly, it will be helpful to base policies and actions on this four-tier structure.

Welfare

Our welfare system is composed of numerous components, SSI, AFDC, food stamps, and many other elements. Coordination of these programs is desirable, and SSI in particular has helped effect such coordination. In addition, but briefly, we need programs that do not thrust heavy burdens on urban areas, burdens that exacerbate already serious financial difficulties. Poverty is a national problem and it requires national solutions with the burden shared by the nation's citizens as a whole. Job training programs, employment services, and other related programs are important for all persons no matter what their age. We must be certain that we do have the means of supporting in old age those persons (or their dependents) who have not been associated with the productive part of the economy long enough to gain livable benefits under social security and employer pensions.

Social Security

The second level of income support in old age is the old age and survivor's part of the social security system, as well as the Medicare program. Only the most unrealistic of proponents can now fail to recognize that the system has developed, matured, and must now be accepted as an established system whose days of expansion are largely completed. Specifically, I would suggest the following policies regarding social security:

1. Recognition of the maturity of the program.
2. Recognition that a social insurance system requires broad public support and therefore must be reasonable in terms of both benefits and costs. Social insurance transfer costs are best controlled when such programs are specifically supported by earmarked employer and employee taxes, as is now the case with social security (with the exception of the medical portion). Social insurance is not the kind of program under which general revenue contributions would be appropriate; it is stronger when both benefits and costs are clearly visible and are at least somewhat associated with one another.
3. Maintenance of the "retirement test." This controversial measure recently has been changed (effective in 1982) by the Congress—too far, I believe. But I hope that it is still generally recognized that the retirement test helps control costs of the program. Furthermore, this test supports a very important social insurance concept: the transfer of funds from workers to nonworkers, not from some workers to other workers. Maintaining this philosophy, I believe, is vital if we are to limit properly the role of social insurance to that of provider of benefits for those who are not currently part of the labor force.
4. Reassessment of the retirement age provisions of the social security program so that we may recognize and take into account the future effects of demographic change. We must plan for the proper management of the increasing burden that will affect the social security transfer system as the proportion of workers declines in relation to social security beneficiaries, and as longevity increases. We should gradually increase the earliest age for social security benefits to age 67, the normal age to 70, and the age for benefits without regard to earnings to at least 75 by the year

2010. This change should be phased in slowly over the next thirty years, but it must be done.

Employer Plans

Public policy should encourage the continued growth of employer-sponsored pension plans. ERISA has recognized the importance of sound financing, reporting and disclosure, and the proper exercise of fiduciary responsibilities. ERISA is a good start. But we need more in some areas, less in others.

1. We need a tax philosophy that frees employer-employee funds for investment in the national economy, ultimately available as the source of future consumption for retired employees. This means that we must specifically recognize that siphoning employer and employee funds to government is no substitute for the role these funds can and must play in pension security and capital formation. Negative public tax policies could be disastrously counterproductive to the third tier of old-age income protection.
2. There should be a great reduction in the reporting paperwork required by the Departments of Labor and Treasury under ERISA. ERISA was experimental; there are several places where burdens can be eliminated with concurrent *improvement* in meeting objectives.
3. We should simplify and encourage the process of starting new pension plans for smaller employers. Insured pension plans can and should play a greater role through their ability to diversify investment risks, spread mortality fluctuations, and minimize overhead unit costs.
4. There should be further strengthening of the vesting requirements of ERISA. Specifically, I suggest consideration of a minimum five-year vesting rule, to be introduced gradually in the future. At the same time, it would be appropriate to modify ERISA's pension plan participation rules. Thus, a new five-year vesting requirement might be accompanied by a corresponding five-year upward change in the present ERISA participation requirement. Now employees cannot be excluded from the plan after attainment of age 25 and completion of one year of service. This could well be changed to attainment of age 30 and completion of one year of service. This later entry age would help offset the added cost of earlier vesting and would also be responsive to the potentially increased length of working life represented by greater human longevity and by the recommended future upward change in the normal social security retirement age.
5. I don't favor a requirement that every employer establish a pension plan for his employees. I believe that Congress, through its provisions for the individual retirement accounts (first established by ERISA), has estab-

lished a method of pension protection for persons not participating in an employer pension plan. But I do believe that the IRA limits are too low and recommend consideration of an enlargement of the IRA deferred consumption allowances to correspond with the existing Keogh plan allowances; that is, a change of the amount that may be allocated to IRAs before taxes to 15 percent of earnings or $7,500, whichever is less, instead of the 15 percent or $1,500 currently applicable to IRAs.

Finally, as I have indicated, it is the responsibility of all levels of government to pursue policies that control inflationary trends. All economic institutions, including pension plans—public and private—have a stake in sound economic policies. Our economy now faces perhaps some of the greatest challenges in its history. Public policies designed to eliminate inflationary forces and to introduce basic corrections in every economic sector will be essential to the achievement of objectives in all of our public and private enterprises.

Inflation is taxation without representation, and as such richly deserves to be dumped in Boston Harbor as the start of a new economic revolution.

References

[1] American Council of Life Insurance, *Pension Facts,* 1977.
[2] Bixby, Lenore E., "Income of People Age 65 and Older: Overview from 1968 Survey of the Aged," *Social Security Bulletin,* 33 (Apr. 1970).
[3] Board of Governors of the Federal Reserve System, *Flow of Funds Accounts* (Washington, D.C., Aug. 1978).
[4] Data Resources, Inc., *U.S. Long-Term Review* (Lexington, Mass., Spring 1978).
[5] Economic Reports of the President and Annual Report of the Council of Economic Advisers (Washington, D.C.: U.S. Government Printing Office, 1975).
[6] "The Future of Private Pension Plans," *Mercer Bulletin* (July 1978).
[7] Murray, Roger F., *Economic Aspects of Pensions* (New York: National Bureau of Economic Research, 1968).
[8] Ture, Norman B., and Barbara A. Fields, *The Future of Private Pensions* (Washington, D.C.: American Enterprise Institute for Public Policy Research, 1976).
[9] "Unfunded Pension Liabilities: A Continuing Burden," *Business Week* (Aug. 14, 1978), 60–64.
[10] U.S. House of Representatives, Committee on Education and Labor, *Pension Task Force Report on Public Employee Retirement Systems,* 95th Cong., 2nd Sess., Committee Print, March 15 (Washington, D.C.: U.S. Government Printing Office, 1978).

Retirement Policy: Discussion   *John J. Carroll*

These three interesting chapters range over a wide subject area. Each focuses on significant public policy issues that flow from the growing significance of the aged population and the sharing of dependency burdens that it implies. Each is concerned with the role of private versus government pensions. Either explicitly or by implication, each questions the present mix. Also, considerable attention is paid to inflation and the threat it poses for the effectiveness of retirement programs.

Dr. Munnell does not urge consideration of ways to induce later retirement but the others do. I'm assuming that this view is not seriously contested.[1] Almost surely the Social Security Advisory Council and commissions being set up by the president and the Congress will be studying it. Two of the chapters (Munnell's and the joint paper by Professors Clark and Spengler) discuss government efforts to make retirement income inflation-proof by indexing bonds, and some of the most interesting parts of these papers deal with difficulties the government may have in doing this via the private pension route. On the other hand, Dr. Greenough dismisses indexed bonds with a hope that we will eliminate inflation rather than design ways to paper over its existence.

Professors Clark and Spengler, in addition to giving detailed breakdowns of the importance of the changing percentage of the population over 65 that is considerably older than 65, illustrate how even low rates of inflation deteriorate fixed incomes for groups that will experience long retirements. They point out that social security benefits and most public employee pensions are protected against inflation, whereas virtually no private pensions are. They follow up with a cursory observation that since the federal government has in these cases accepted the principle of protecting the retired against inflation, it should apply the principle to all retirees by the sale to pension funds or directly to retirees of cost-of-living bonds or annuities.

Dr. Munnell's chapter shows that this proposed solution is anything but simple. In fact, she indicates that it is highly unlikely that either private firms or the government is apt to make available the massive supply of indexed bonds that would be required. I have only one comment to add to her careful analysis of the difficulties inherent in implementation of this notion. She stresses the difficulties that prevent the private sector from issuing indexed bonds as long as the corporate income tax is not indexed. No one should conclude that a

---

The views expressed in this chapter are the author's own and not necessarily those of the Social Security Administration.

1. Foreign experience, however, is discouraging—policies have not been very effective. Nonetheless, we probably should keep our eye on the Swedish partial pension innovation.

fairly simple resolution of the difficulties is available. Henry Aaron, in summarizing discussions of a conference on *Inflation and the Income Tax* sponsored by the Fund for Public Policy Research and the Brookings Institution, points out that "indexing the tax base involves massive redistribution of tax liabilities among businesses and individuals" [1, p. 28]. He indicated that despite the discussion of numerous proposals for cushioning or spreading out the effects, it became clear that "problems of transitional equity although possibly serious were only vaguely understood" [1].

Clark-Spengler and Munnell find it tempting to conclude that it might be simpler to explore greater reliance on social security. Although they do not dwell upon it, they may be conscious of the social policy problem implicit in the fact that half of the work force does not have private pensions. However, a shift to more reliance on social security would leave us with problems of how to provide the kinds of diversity, adaptability, and flexibility Greenough correctly stresses have been important values in our multitiered system of retirement protection. In addition, all the authors express concern that a shift away from funded private plans might decrease savings and capital formation.

Clark-Spengler and Munnell believe that more study of capital impact is needed before innovations in the private pension-social security mix should be undertaken. Society may have to wait a long time for the answer to that question. How long will it take, for example, to reconcile existing estimates of the reduction in savings caused by social security? Martin Feldstein defends his $38 billion estimate against assertions by Munnell that her estimate is only a tenth as big. Add the views of Robert J. Barro, who says the reduction in savings is zero, of Michael Darby, who agrees, and of Louis Esposito, who says that "the empirical results [of the studies made by the above authors] do not support the hypothesis that the social security program decreases private savings" [2, p. 17], and we have some appreciation of the reconciliation problem that lies ahead. In the drive for a rational national retirement policy, political decisions may be taken before there is a final resolution.

I want to turn now to a brief comment about Dr. Greenough's concerns that the transfer sector is causing inflation. Clark-Spengler and Munnell reference the obvious advantage of social security vis à vis private pension protection in coping with inflation, but Greenough points out that while social security is adjusting for inflation it is at the same time causing the inflation. I find it difficult to understand his claim that old-age insurance, among other transfers, has been increased without considering the impact on inflation. The fact is that the system annually publishes Trustees Reports with detailed analyses of estimated benefits and outlays—currently for 75 years into the future. In addition, the Office of the Actuary regularly supplies the Congress with detailed estimates on every proposal that is considered by Ways and Means and Senate Finance Committees.

Dr. Greenough should reexamine the facts about social security financing.

He tells us that the system played an important part in the inflation of the late 1960s. However, during that period the social security system was running surpluses. In analyzing the implications of the trust funds for budget policy, I think we need to make two distinctions. From the point of view of the trust funds balances, as reflected in the analysis done by the Trustees Reports, the appropriate definition should include income from whatever source including, for example, interest income and general revenue contributions to match SMI premiums. (Interest earnings of the trust funds are a return for holding part of the debt just as TIAA has interest returns because it holds government securities.) From the point of view of unified budget policy, we appropriately start with some bottom-line deficit figure. How this deficit (surplus) is distributed between general funds and the trust funds will obviously depend on how the government decides to finance these programs. If, for example, it wants to have the trust funds balanced roughly on a year-to-year basis, and if it wants to make a general revenue contribution as it would to finance defense expenditures for example, then by definition the trust funds would receive less money from the public than it pays out. If the government wants the bottom-line deficit to be zero, then again by definition it must run a surplus for the rest of the budget. Where I differ with Greenough is that I would not say that the trust funds caused the deficit. Rather the size of deficit was determined by decisions on overall economic stabilization policy.

Now I would like to turn to some things that are largely ignored in the three foregoing chapters but that I think should be given some consideration. Greenough briefly mentions the noncoverage issue when complaining that some few critics call the system a failure because private plan coverage is not more complete. As mentioned earlier, the thrust of the common concern is different: Why has the growth of percentage of workers covered virtually halted? And how can social policy cope with the implications of the coverage gap?

I would also like to see more emphasis on the special problems of the very old. As our population ages, society is going to have to wrestle with these problems.

Perhaps I have made it clear earlier (but maybe it needs to be said again) that no complete private protection against inflation is feasible on an actuarial basis because of the inherent uncertainties. Only the government can give a flat assurance of offsetting inflation for any particular group. If it wishes to do so, the government can insulate any group it desires to insulate. Surprisingly, there is very little discussion in these papers of the point of view of those (for example, Browning) who believe that it is dangerous to increase the proportion of the population that has no incentive to use its political strength to resist inflation.

However plausible it seems that the society may be unwilling to keep up the present level of protection for the aged as that group grows substantially vis à vis the working population, it should not be accepted as a foregone conclusion. Society can afford to take care of its dependents if it wishes, especially a rich society such as our own. The *way* the burden is borne may influence the willingness of society to bear it. I would have expected more emphasis on the way in which the costs are shared in both private and public plans. As Greenough points out, the government has for over fifty years given favorable tax treatment to encourage private plans. Both Greenough and Munnell ignore the possibility of general revenue financing of social security. Munnell says expansion of social security would "necessitate increasing payroll taxes" and Greenough adds that use of general revenues is completely "inappropriate" in a social insurance program. Either partial or complete substitution of general revenue financing for payroll taxes implies underlying assumptions about the nature of support for the elderly and the consequent role of welfare expenditures. However, general revenues are used in the social security systems of many other developed countries around the world.

Our office recently has published a summary of the principal legislative proposals made over the last five years to introduce general revenues into the U.S. social security system [3]. It shows how the burden of social security taxation for illustrative earners would be altered by these proposals. We have used illustrative earners in this publication but we are actively pursuing efforts to measure the changes in overall tax incidence by income class on an empirical basis. We have already published in our *Studies in Income Distribution* series an estimation of social security taxes based on the Current Population Survey [4] and are able to make similar estimates for personal income taxes. We hope very soon to have the capacity to show the incidence significance of various mixes of payroll and income taxes projected through 1979 for different financing proposals. We have been doing this work in full expectation that the issue of how social security will be financed will be the subject of major debate and that more information on the implications of changes is sorely needed. It is for similar reasons that we are actively trying to introduce into our data systems survey information about consumption in an effort to supply researchers a more useful data base.

References

[1] Aaron, Henry J. (Ed.), *Inflation and the Income Tax* (Washington, D.C.: The Brookings Institution, 1976).

[2] Esposito, Louis, "Effect of Social Security on Saving: Review of Studies Using U.S. Time-Series Data," *Social Security Bulletin* (May 1978).

[3] Esposito, Louis, and David Podoff, *General Revenue Financing of the Social Security System,* Staff Paper No. 33 (Washington, D.C.: Social Security Administration, 1978).

[4] Johnston, Mary P., and Bernard Wixon, "Payroll Tax Liability and Its Relation to Family Unit Income, 1971, 1973, and 1974," *Studies in Income Distribution,* No. 8 (Washington, D.C.: Social Security Administration, 1978).

Retirement Policy: Discussion *Peter Henle*

The job of any expert is, of course, a difficult one, fraught with much uncertainty, but the job of being an expert on aging does offer at least two built-in attractions. First, with each passing day, the expert on aging gains first-hand experience with his special field of interest. What other aspect of economics allows the expert such a costless addition to his stock of human capital? And, second, experts on aging seldom can be brought to book for their crimes within their own lifetimes. Age structure changes so gradually that its force and effect become evident only after an extended time period. Thus, most of the experts on aging will long since have departed the scene before their projections can turn sour. Young people just entering the field, of course, must assume greater risks.

The chapters by Clark and Spengler, Munnell, and Greenough provide useful insights into possible public policy reactions to changing age structure and to other major retirement issues. My remarks will be directed primarily at those aspects of the three chapters that deal primarily with private pension plans.

The private pension system is going through a critical phase in its history. The early growth has slackened. In fact, during the past five years, there has been little change in the proportion of the workforce covered by private pensions. This is not the result of ERISA but had been evident several years earlier. Incidentally, the official statistics for several years were misleading because faulty methodology obscured the slowdown in growth.

The slowdown in growth is one of the two most critical issues facing the private pension system. The second is the problem of inflation. Let me look at the way these three chapters have discussed these two questions.

The first problem dealing with coverage is addressed directly in the chapter by Greenough. He expertly highlights the advantages of the diversity of private plans. There is genuine value to a system that allows employers and employees to tailor their plans to their needs. It encourages innovation, it allows the system to sort out the good from the bad, and it allows the labor force and work characteristics of the job to help shape individual pension plans. These advantages, however, have not encouraged much recent growth in private plans. Greenough's suggestion is to add some additional tax benefits to encourage small employers to establish new plans. His suggestion is couched in general terms, but he comments favorably on the Javits-Williams Bill (S-3017 Section 304) that allows a tax credit in addition to the present tax deduction to small employers establishing a tax-qualified pension plan (beginning at 5 percent of the employer's annual contribution to the plan).

It certainly is true that an additional tax credit could lead to additional pension plans. I am not at all convinced, however, that this would be a wise expenditure of federal funds. In recent years tax expenditures for private pension plans total over $10 billion. An additional tax credit for small businesses might create windfall credits in many different types of situations. It is very easy to start (or stop) a small business.

Another proposal that Greenough advances is liberalization of the present IRA (Individual Retirement Account). By making the IRA more attractive, of course, Greenough is making the private pension plans appear somewhat less attractive, which is contrary to his interest in expanding the private pension system. Here again, I have some doubts about his approach. Table 1 shows the current use of IRAs in 1976 tax returns. It is true that a total of 1.6 million tax returns (out of 84.5 million) have utilized the IRA deduction. But 73 percent of these are in returns with $15,000 or more annual adjusted gross income, and 54 percent of these are in the 20 percent of returns with annual adjusted gross incomes of $20,000 or more. It is significant that the highest degree of participation occurs in the income class groups of $50,000 to $100,000 and $100,000 to $200,000. The IRA system may be quite useful for managerial and professional types whose employment, for one reason or another, does not include a private pension plan, but I doubt that as it is currently operating, it really meets the needs of the vast majority of those without private plan coverage.

I think we have to consider some alternative options to provide broader

Table 1. *Use of IRA accounts by adjusted gross income, 1976*

| Size of adjusted gross income (1) | Number of returns | | Percent using IRAs |
	Total (2)	With IRA deduction (3)	
Under $2,000	9,990,404	3,585	(-)[a]
$2,000–3,999	9,532,054	15,865	(-)
$4,000–5,999	8,972,753	43,352	(-)
$6,000–7,999	8,208,262	51,009	(-)
$8,000–9,999	7,039,340	96,589	1.4
$10,000–11,999	6,130,880	85,155	1.4
$12,000–14,999	8,402,915	178,974	2.1
$15,000–19,999	11,182,362	283,666	2.5
$20,000–24,999	6,662,024	243,662	3.7
$25,000–29,999	3,610,979	208,866	5.8
$30,000–49,999	3,632,248	272,445	7.5
$50,000–99,999	945,253	117,944	12.5
$100,000–199,999	184,284	18,664	10.1
$200,000–499,999	36,495	3,087	8.5
$500,000–999,999	4,179	270	6.5
$1,000,000 and over	1,370	71	5.2
Total	84,536,143	1,623,104	1.9

[a] (-) indicates less than 1.0 percent.
Source: Internal Revenue Service.

coverage. To begin with, we should look at the sectors of the economy where coverage is low. Data are available on this point showing that coverage is particularly limited in the service and trade industries, but the key variables seem to be the size of establishment and level of compensation. Table 2 shows that in 1974, 82 percent of all employees without private pension plans were in establishments with under 100 workers. But for employees covered by a pension plan, only 31 percent were in such small establishments. Similarly, for employees without pension plans, 70 percent were in establishments where compensation was less than $5 an hour compared with 28 percent of employees covered by pension plans.

These are establishments where employer motivation to establish a pension plan is low because turnover is relatively high among much of the workforce. Similarly, in such establishments employee motivation for a private pension plan is relatively low because these low- and moderate-wage employees usually prefer to increase their basic wage rather than fringe benefits. Some of these workers, it is true, may qualify for a private pension plan later in their work

Table 2. *Percent of private sector nonfarm workers employed by establishments with and without expenditures for retirement plans, 1974*

Characteristic of establishment	Share of all private nonfarm employment	Percentage of workers in firms with retirement expenditures	Share of covered workers[a]	Share of noncovered workers
Type of employee				
Office	41	73	41	27
Nonoffice	59	59	59	73
Total	100	64	100	100
Average compensation				
Under $3	13	12	2	32
$3–4.99	30	55	26	38
$5–6.99	23	72	26	18
$7–8.99	18	83	23	6
$9–10.99	10	87	14	4
$11 and over	7	89	10	2
Total	100	64	100	100
Employee organization				
Union	26	91	37	6
Nonunion	74	54	63	94
Total	100	64	100	100
Number of employees in establishments				
Under 100	49	40	31	82
100–499	20	77	24	13
500 and over	31	94	46	5
Total	100	64	100	100

[a] "Covered Workers" are employees in covered *groups*. Actual participation was lower due to age or service requirements, contributory character of some plans, etc.
Source: Bureau of Labor Statistics.

lives, but many millions will not, and improving tax incentives for employers or raising the legal limit on IRAs are unlikely to improve the situation.

The Greenough paper dismisses Robert Paul's proposal that private employers should be required to establish a pension plan. Although I think this proposal deserves more consideration than it has received, I am not one of its admirers. There are, however, some variations on this proposal that I think would be more realistic. For example, can we devise a simple way for employers and employees to add to their social security contribution to yield a higher retirement benefit? The add-on could be treated as a defined contribution to yield an actuarially correct additional retirement benefit. Advantages of such an arrangement over an individual's IRA would be: (1) the employer's contribution with before-tax dollars, and (2) cost savings from using the social security administrative machinery. Perhaps the add-on could be made available in several different size packages that individuals could elect once a year—much as many current employees have the option annually of changing their health plan. Obviously such a proposal needs more extensive study, but it offers one way for the economy to supplement inadequate social security retirement benefits.

A more limited but somewhat similar approach is included in the recently passed tax legislation that greatly expands the freedom of employers to contribute to individual employee IRA accounts. Under this legislation: (1) employer contributions to an account can be up to 15 percent of compensation with a maximum of $7,500; (2) employers choosing this type of plan must sponsor an account for each employee over age 25 with three or more years service; and (3) contributions must be nondiscriminatory and bear a uniform relationship to each employee's total compensation. An offset is permitted, however, for the employer-paid share of the employee's FICA tax. It will be instructive to learn the extent to which this new arrangement is utilized.

Now let us look briefly at this miserable business of inflation and particularly how it hurts private pension plans. Clark and Spengler address this problem and recommend that the government explore the concept of providing cost-of-living bonds or annuities to retirees.

Greenough emphasizes a tough policy on inflation, including a tightening up on social security liberalization. He points out quite correctly the increasing role of transfer payments in the government budget and feels that this expansion has helped foster the present degree of inflation. All of us can applaud his call for "a more stable and healthier economy that will minimize the need for cost-of-living adjustments on pensions, indexing techniques, and other devices to cover over a failure to control inflation," but a certain degree of skepticism in my bones suggests that a strong element of inflation is likely to persist and that those affected by it will want to protect themselves as much as possible. Thus, the question of purchasing power bonds, or indexation of private pension benefits comes very much to the fore. Greenough does not endorse any special protective arrangement for private pension beneficiaries.

Alicia Munnell really attacks this problem. First, she tackles the question of protection against inflation while the employee is still working. Here she finds quite logically that the final average payment formula provides much greater protection than any formula based on career average. Formulas specifying a dollar amount per year of service also are deficient unless periodically updated.

But, as she says, the big problem is not pre- but postretirement adjustment of benefits. She shows that a private pension plan would need to maintain continuing real rates of return on its funds in order to finance indexation. Her methodology is a model based on the present value formula. Pension benefits are equated to pension contributions and inflation is incorporated. Cases are developed for pension funds that base benefits on both career average and final earnings. The funding implications of introducing postretirement indexing are explored for both cases. Financing an indexed pension based on final earnings (the one that provides full protection against inflation) would require a constant real rate of return or increased contributions. She feels that only a pension fund based on securities yielding a constant return in terms of purchasing power would be able to afford indexation of benefits. In her view, the private sector could not afford to issue such bonds, and although the federal government could do so, such a step could lead to some serious complications.

In the end she leaves some questions unanswered. How seriously would private capital markets be disrupted by U.S. Treasury-indexed bonds? Would private firms issue such bonds if changes were made in the corporate income tax? To what extent would purchasing power bonds erode the will to fight inflation?

My major quarrel, however, is not with what is included in her analysis but with what is omitted. Her paper assumes the only way private plans can offset the effects of inflation on postretirement benefits is through purchase of indexed bonds. Perhaps this would be the most effective way, but in view of inherent difficulties there are other possibilities that should be explored.

For example, what we have now is a private pension system with a schedule of benefits whose real replacement rate to participants is at a peak at retirement time and declines steadily thereafter. But this system was not ordained by the heavens—it is man-made and can be unmade by man. It can even be changed without altering the cost to employers, although admittedly an employer's willingness to increase his pension costs would make a modification in benefit structure much easier.

Certainly, for any given schedule of benefits, it is possible to devise at no increase in cost a somewhat reduced schedule of benefits plus some type of limited postretirement increase in nominal benefits. Such an increase in benefits could be fixed or indeterminant. An indeterminant increase based on open-ended changes in the cost of living probably would be financially too risky, but other alternatives are available. One might be fixed increases of perhaps 3 to 4 percent a year, or increases determined by changes in the CPI up to a cap of 3 to 4 percent a year. Almost half the workers in state and local retirement systems currently benefit from such arrangements. A prominent actuary recently testified that an initial benefit reduction of 14 percent would be consistent with a 2 percent annual postretirement increase in benefits; a 26 percent reduction would be equivalent to an annual 4 percent postretirement increase in benefits.

I suggest that many, if not most, workers would willingly vote for such a tradeoff: a reduction in initial benefits in order to receive some cost-of-living protection during retirement years. In fact, although this question was not specifically asked, results from the 1977 Quality of Employment Survey indicate that workers understand such tradeoffs and specifically would forego a 10 percent wage increase for a variety of fringe benefit increases.

Another approach to this issue would be to introduce such indexation at a time of general changes in wages and benefits such as renewal of a bargaining agreement. It might well be possible that some improvements in wages, levels of retirement benefits, or other fringe benefits could be foregone in order to provide the financing necessary for limited indexation. What is needed now is further discussion of this issue with the hope that a number of employers or employers and unions would initiate this type of action.

Index